THE EDINBURGH INTRODUCTION TO STUDYING ENGLISH LITERATURE

THE EDINBURGH INTRODUCTION TO STUDYING ENGLISH LITERATURE

Edited by Dermot Cavanagh, Alan Gillis, Michelle Keown, James Loxley and Randall Stevenson

EDINBURGH UNIVERSITY PRESS

© in this edition Edinburgh University Press, 2010
© in the individual contributions is retained by the authors

Edinburgh University Press Ltd
22 George Square, Edinburgh

www.euppublishing.com

Typeset in 11/13 pt Monotype Bembo
by Servis Filmsetting Ltd, Stockport, Cheshire, and
printed and bound in Great Britain by
CPI Antony Rowe, Chippenham and Eastbourne

A CIP record for this book is available from the British Library

ISBN 978 0 7486 4026 3 (hardback)
ISBN 978 0 7486 4025 6 (paperback)

The right of Dermot Cavanagh, Alan Gillis,
Michelle Keown, James Loxley and Randall Stevenson
to be identified as editors of this work
has been asserted in accordance with
the Copyright, Designs and Patents Act 1988.

Contents

Section III – Narrative 99

Section IV – Drama 159

Preface

Reading literature offers us diverse and abiding pleasures and can be rewarding in a great variety of ways. Such pleasures, though, can be enhanced, sustained and deepened by the critical study of literature, and such study can be an absorbing, challenging and enriching experience in itself. This book aims to open the door to such experience and to give a glimpse of its rewards. Expert, thorough, up to date and easy to follow, the chapters which follow provide a straightforward and effective pathway towards increasing your enjoyment and broadening your understanding of literature. Anyone wishing to become a more insightful and informed reader will find practical and lasting guidance throughout these pages. If you are studying literature formally as part of a course or for a degree, this book will also impart the skills and knowledge required to begin a more advanced programme of study.

One reason literature matters is its longevity as a practice and an art form. In this book, we have drawn on a wide variety of examples from different periods. This is because the serious study of literature demands historical awareness: literature has changed over the centuries, and will probably change again; unsurprisingly, what is understood or defined as literature has changed as well. All of the literary examples are drawn from easily accessible sources, either standard and familiar editions or widely-available anthologies such as those published by Norton and Longman. You will find a list of all the primary literary works to which our contributors refer in the 'Works Cited' section at the end of the book, along with all the secondary literary and critical material each chapter uses. We have not assumed that you have read these works previously, and the contributors take care to explain the kind of texts they are discussing and their key concerns. The same applies to the secondary material they mention.

The chapters of this book do not need to be read in sequence, and you may find it more useful to read particular chapters or sections in an order that suits your own needs. The book aims to provide you with a comprehensive understanding of the forms and techniques literature uses and the variety of ways in which it can be interpreted. This means that the essays do use specific and specialist terminology to define particular critical approaches and literary techniques. These are explained by each contributor as they arise in discussion; later chapters may refer back to these definitions and indicate where each term first occurs. However, if you find a particular term or idea puzzling, the Index will point you towards the page or pages where it is first explained and to any subsequent uses or elucidation. At the end of each chapter you will find a list of 'Next Steps', indicating critical works that our contributors judge to be good places to continue your own reading and research in a particular area.

All of the contributors to this collection teach or have taught in the University of Edinburgh's English Literature department – an outstanding and long-established department that celebrates its 250th anniversary in 2012. They share extensive experience of introducing students to the joys and demands of studying literature, and this has been crucial both to the way in which the individual chapters have been written and to the overall design of the volume. In this respect, the editors and contributors would especially like to thank successive cohorts of first- and second-year students of English and Scottish literature at Edinburgh whose acute questioning has required us to reflect on the fundamentals of our discipline and to think carefully about how to explain them to an intelligent and enquiring audience. The idea for the collection was first broached by Jackie Jones at Edinburgh University Press, and we are grateful to her for this fruitful suggestion and to her and all at the Press for their subsequent support.

Section I – Introductory

1

What is Literature?

Alex Thomson

Ozymandias

I met a traveller from an antique land,
Who said – 'Two vast and trunkless legs of stone
Stand in the desart . . . . Near them, on the sand,
Half sunk a shattered visage lies, whose frown,
And wrinkled lip, and sneer of cold command,
Tell that its sculptor well those passions read
Which yet survive, stamped on these lifeless things,
The hand that mocked them, and the heart that fed;
And on the pedestal, these words appear:
My name is Ozymandias, King of Kings,
Look on my Works, ye Mighty, and despair!
Nothing beside remains. Round the decay
Of that colossal Wreck, boundless and bare
The lone and level sands stretch far away.'

This striking and dramatic poem was written by Percy Shelley and published in 1818. The overall effect is of the hollow pride of the emperor: nothing could hold back the tides of time, and the drifting sands have covered over every further trace of his achievements. Just as the traveller has come back from a great distance, so the poem bridges wastes of time, bringing to life something like an echo of Ozymandias's imperious tone. To the devastation of the king's political power Shelley opposes the creative power of poetry: against the 'shattered visage' of Ozymandias he lays the dramatic and evocative power of 'Ozymandias', his poem. To write such a poem, Shelley is suggesting, may be to have something in common with the King of Kings. But he also hints that it may have more in common with the sculptor whose genius the poem commemorates, who both defers to and mocks the authority of his ruler.

How do we know that this is a poem? There are few unusual words in it, and if we reproduced it as a piece of prose it would make perfect sense, as the grammar of the sentences seems fairly straightforward. There is a rhyme scheme, and we might say that breaking the sentence up into lines adds to the deliberate patterning of the words: the repetition of consonant sounds between 'stone' and 'stand', for example, is highlighted by placing them on either side of a line break. But these are just technical ways of elaborating something we have already taken for granted: the line breaks offer a further signal that this is a poem, which we expect to differ from prose in the way it looks on the page. This recognition requires prior knowledge. We must already have learned that writing set out this way on a page is what people call a poem, and that when we encounter such an object, we need to frame appropriate expectations about what we are going to read and how we might react to it.

The fact that we recognise the text in front of us as a poem alerts us to the possible significance of its pattern. Without this alertness, we will miss the full force of ways in which the ostensible subject of Shelley's poem is displaced, as we read, by a more profound and ambiguous meditation on the limits of worldly ambition. The conversational tone of the poem's beginning, when replaced by that grandiose inscription – 'My name is Ozymandias . . .' – dramatises the apparent distance between the prosaic world of the poem's composition and the once-imposing but now-departed majesty of Ozymandias's kingdom. Because we are aware that we are reading an artful arrangement of language we know we need to be alert to this kind of effect, and to further hints and suggestions. These include, among others, the contrast between the density of stone which can be made to carry an inscription, and the shifting sands which will not retain the faintest impression; the hint that the fragmentary survival of the sculptor's work surpasses the achievement of Ozymandias himself; the way that a short poem (a mere fourteen lines) can enclose and describe all that remains of the once-proud ruler.

This kind of reading of pattern follows straightforwardly from the simple recognition of 'Ozymandias' as a poem. But there are other recognitions and judgements which follow less straightforwardly. With the appropriate background of knowledge, we might want to move on to judgements about what *kind* of poem this might be. An ode or a ballad? Lyric or dramatic verse? What kinds of metre or rhyme does it use? These are technical issues, and the terminology and expectations each requires may not be available to someone who has not had the opportunity to learn about poetry – or to read introductions offered by Alan Gillis, Lee Spinks and Penny Fielding in Chapters 4, 5, and 6 of this volume. By contrast with these technical issues, the identification of a poem seems instinctive, though this may mean only that we learned it so long ago that we have forgotten that it was something we had to learn. But what about moving on in another direction, and towards another kind of recognition: what does it mean when we identify Shelley's poem not just as a poem but as part of the larger category of *literature*?

This obviously requires a harder kind of identification. We easily recognise 'Ozymandias' as poetry – and respond to its demands on our sense of the pattern of words on the page – simply because it is written in verse. But to see it as 'literary' raises questions about what it might have in common with other works of literature not necessarily written in verse. For example, both novels and plays *may* be in verse, but certainly need not be, and most often are not. So while paying close attention to a single poem leads us to focus on the distinctive and unusual effect of arranging words in lines of verse, to ask 'what is literature?' suggests that there must be some other quality shared by all the forms of writing we perceive as literary.

An answer commonly given to this question is that a work counts as 'literature' when it is *fiction*. In this view, 'literature' is distinguished by a set of conventions according to which readers accept that what they are reading is not literally true. Rather than describing or analysing something in the real world, literature is primarily a work of imagination. As readers, we are happy to accept that the encounter Shelley describes in 'Ozymandias' probably did not take place, that Shelley did not meet a traveller and that no such statue stands in a desert. (Although a little research might tell us that there was an Ozymandias, the pharaoh Ramses II in the thirteenth century BCE, and that at the time of writing there was widespread cultural interest in the ruins found by European travellers in Egypt.)

The idea that literature is fiction can be most clearly seen in the ways we distinguish between literary and non-literary works – for example, when we try to explain how a novel differs from a cookery book. One tells a story, but the other gives us recipes, instructions on how to create a tasty dish. One is drawn from the imagination of the author, but the other is drawn from practical experience of cooking. So when we explain our assumption that the novel is literature but the recipe book is not, we are not saying that there is anything wrong with the recipe book compared with the novel. The term in this use is not evaluative but descriptive, and it signals a difference in the intended function of two types of work. One gives instructions, and while we might be amused or entertained by details of the origin of the recipe or the cook's lifestyle, these are subsidiary to the useful value of the book; the other entertains or engages us through a story which we know not to be true. The difference is significant because it tells us what we can expect the book to be good for: we expect a recipe book to instruct us in the correct methods and ingredients needed for a particular dish, but we do not necessarily expect it to amuse us. Conversely, while a recipe we encountered in a novel might be one that we could safely make, we would not feel deceived if it turned out to be unreliable. The stakes are often higher than this, however. In everyday life we take people at their word, and societies are built on trust. Authors of fiction are given something like a right to lie.

Though an aspect of poetry, fictional relations with the world are clearly particularly important for novels. We expect a novel to be in some sense rooted in the real world: although we allow a degree of licence for unusual things to happen, if a novel were to become too unlikely we might dismiss it. We often draw generic distinctions between novels primarily to indicate their degree of distance from 'everyday' reality (fantasy, science-fiction, horror) and may be suspicious of the literary credentials of novels which rely on overly formulaic plots (detective novels). This rootedness in the world, however, reminds us that while 'fiction' may be the opposite of 'fact' it need not be the opposite of truth. Indeed authors often claim – and readers often accept – that there is a kind of 'truthfulness' about the novel, or about drama. Although a novel or play may not depict a specific event in the world it may rely on a kind of fidelity or truthfulness to the world as we experience it. This points to difficulties in relating literature to the idea of fiction which go all the way back to the ancient Greek philosopher Aristotle in the fourth century BCE and to his approval of writing that offers a general truth, rather than the messy particularity of specific events. In more modern times – and with experience of the novel, rather than the drama and poetry which was Aristotle's main focus – literary historians have gone on to praise authors' ability to present not general truths but accurate versions of specific societies at specific moments in time. For many of these commentators, this accurate representation and 'realism' is the very essence of the modern novel.

Indeed, in a few cases, fiction has been directly influential in drawing a society's attention to real social problems. A good example is offered by the American author Upton Sinclair's novel *The Jungle* (1906), which shed light on the horrific working conditions in Chicago slaughterhouses and led directly to popular calls for legislative action. Historical novels are another interesting borderline case. A historical novel promises to tell us something about how things really were in the past (we expect the author to have done some research) but we allow the novelist sufficient licence that specific details of plot, dialogue or description may be inventions. A historical novel that failed to pay any consideration to appropriate accuracy would either be a bad novel or not a historical one at all. Conventions by which we make this kind of judgement, between truth and fiction, have evolved over recent centuries, and not only since Aristotle's time. For example, although we now think of *Robinson Crusoe* as a novel, on the title page, when it was first published in 1719, it claimed to be autobiographical. Nowadays we would wish to distinguish quite carefully between autobiographies and novels, but the name of the real author, Daniel Defoe, did not appear anywhere on the first edition, encouraging readers to suppose instead it was Crusoe's own story, 'written by himself'.

Literature seems to move freely, in such ways, between real and represented worlds, truths and imaginations, and it is not surprising that playful and provocative writers have written works which tease at the boundaries, taking advantage of literature's licence to deceive. We would not trust a historian or an accountant who made things up, but the possibility that we are being led astray, or our imaginations stretched across boundaries, lies at the heart of literary experience. The Nobel-Prize winning South African writer J. M. Coetzee offered a rewriting of *Robinson Crusoe* called *Foe* (1986) in which a character who had been left out of the novel goes in search of its author, yet she is unable to find him; the book reminds us that the licence we grant to literature detaches its author from his or her responsibility for its contents. When he accepted the Nobel Prize in 2003, Coetzee ignored the convention by which an author gives an acceptance speech and instead read a prose piece written in the third person, describing Crusoe in the act of writing his autobiography. A similar game was being played by the novelist Gertrude Stein when she published *The Autobiography of Alice B. Toklas* in 1933. Since Toklas was Stein's lover, and a fair portion of the book is devoted to her account of their life together, is this a memoir, or a novel? Is it a biography of Toklas or of Stein? One thing we can conclude is that this is not Toklas's autobiography: with Stein named as author, Toklas seems to become a fictional character – rather as Robinson Crusoe does, once the name of Daniel Defoe is added to the title page of the novel alongside his.

These are works which play with the boundaries between fact and fiction. Because this kind of playfulness is exemplary of the allowance we grant to literary works this seems to confirm our original hunch about the relation of literature to fiction. But there is another category of literary works which sits on the same borderline but which troubles the equation of literature with fiction. Some kinds of writing – such as travel writing, autobiography and essays, and more private forms such as diaries and letters – do not seem to belong firmly in either the literary or non-literary camp. They claim to report the factual experience of the author but at the same time they foreground the author's perspective, suggesting that their value lies in recording that which is not simply a matter of verifiable factual report. When we judge that such a work is literary, we are clearly not relying on a distinction between fact and fiction. Indeed, we bring an additional form of judgement to bear upon it. For example, we might distinguish certain forms of travel writing – on the grounds of style or the qualities of the author's reflections – from travel guides: the latter, like recipe books, perhaps offering no more than straightforward instruction about methods and practicalities of travel. We can read for pleasure a piece of travel writing which, while factual rather than fictional, offers us no information or instruction at all.

The most complex example is the essay, a prose form displaying and dependent upon a sense of style and the use of rhetoric – the conscious fashioning of structure, and figures of speech such as metaphor, to persuade an audience or readership. An essay is an experiment – literally, a try at something – and it should be playful and exploratory. For that reason it lends itself to use by literary writers as much as philosophers – indeed Francis Bacon, the early master of the English essay, can be counted as both. Although characterised by a tendency to experimentation, stylistic self-consciousness and speculation, the emphasis of the essay is also on careful argument and not on the imagined but the real world. The essay is therefore considered nowadays as primarily philosophical rather than literary: for the most part it is a form that has become subordinate to its subject matter. The essay, in other words, exists in the service of literary criticism or philosophical debate or historical explanation and is only occasionally treated as a literary form in itself.

We asked, in effect, whether we could explain our idea of literature with reference to our idea of fiction: it turns out that while asking what we mean by fiction is a very useful frame through which to think about literature we cannot simply substitute one for the other. Although we are happy to see much of literature as fiction, there are forms of writing which are clearly literary but not so clearly fictional. The example of those types of writing suggests that there must in fact be various types of judgement involved when we determine whether or not works belong to the category of literature. One such judgement has already emerged, in my comments about travel writing above, when I mentioned 'an additional form of judgement . . . on the grounds of style, or the qualities of the author's reflections' which might allow non-fictional works to be counted as part of literature. This 'additional' form of judgement derives from the equation of 'literature' not with fiction but with 'fine writing'. On this view, literature is writing which is concerned with giving pleasure, through attractive form and expression, as much as with the communication of information. This directs our attention away from the content of the written work ('is it factual or fictional?') and towards its form ('how is it written?').

This is why for many people today poetry is seen as exemplary of literature in general. Poetry is characterised by unusual or at least clearly deliberate use of language, from which we expect not only more striking and memorable phrases than we would from more everyday ways of writing but also something enigmatic or mysterious in quality. Sometimes this can take the form of heightened or awkward language; at other times it will seem to be more natural, while requiring equal care and artifice. Robert Burns's lines in 'To A Mouse' (1785) – 'the best laid schemes o' Mice an' Men, / Gang aft agley' – is conventional enough in sentiment: compare Robert Blair's 'The Grave' (1743): 'The best-concerted schemes men lay for fame / Die fast away'. We find the lines effective not because of the sentiment, but because this has been formed into a memorable and elegant phrase. The use of colloquial and alliterative language – '<u>M</u>ice an' <u>M</u>en', '<u>G</u>ang aft agley' – creates for the poem an aphoristic or concisely proverbial quality, forcibly communicated to readers. The success of Burns's lines is such that they have passed into common usage, just as Shelley's: 'Look on my works' has become an ironic short-hand for a hollow boast. In their passage back into the common phrase-stock of English, these examples remind us that literature is made from and returns to ordinary language. It is the uses to which this language is put, the patterns which it is made to form, which are distinctive.

So by this way of defining the term, 'literature' would mean writing in which something distinctive and striking about the style lends it a quality which goes beyond the communication of information. This attempt to define literature depends, in other words, on something like a distinction between form and content in any act of communication. In daily life, if we have something to say we may think about the way we say it in order to make it clearly understandable or to persuade someone who doesn't want to do something to do it anyway. Our choice of form will be of secondary importance to the intended message, though: designed to enhance the message, but not to draw attention to itself as a way of passing a message. By contrast, literature chooses not to privilege the communication of a message, but instead to allow the relationship between the form and content to be configured in other ways. So whereas the idea of literature as fiction is concerned with the content of works – *what* they communicate, and how this relates to the world – we have now turned instead to consider form: *how* they do what they do. This is an understanding of literature as an *art form*. Considering the formal presentation of any message, separately from its content in part, highlights ways a writer has created a work which may be beautiful, shapely or stylish. Critics who take this line often appeal to the general ideal of a work of art, or to analogies with other art forms: a poem may be imagined on the model of a symphony or a painting, in music or the visual arts respectively.

Defining literature as fine writing – pleasing or effective style in any genre – offers a useful clarification. It seems to explain what happens when we condemn a work as insufficiently literary – when we criticise a novel, for example, which has failed to grip us not because of our personal taste but because of what we take to be technical faults, such as an unbelievable plot, cardboard characters, descriptions riddled with clichés, or clunky and wooden dialogue. Such judgements of technical excellence or inadequacy of style might be made in relation to writing in any mode or form. You might find my second-last sentence unpersuasive because it was itself clunky and wooden, criticising bad writing in terms which have themselves become banal and clichéd. Bad writing can appear anywhere: good writing can likewise be discerned and described as literary even if we find it in what we usually consider a non-literary form. We expect history books to be accurate, and we draw a clear dividing line between the responsibility of the historian to tell the truth and the licence we grant to the novelist to draw on his or her imagination. Yet a well-written history book, as much as a novel, might be described as 'literary': not on the grounds of factual accuracy but because it possesses qualities of clarity, elegance or stylishness in its author's expression.

The emphasis on form, which sharpens our sense of the language used, has allowed something special or different – something other than an idea or piece of information, something hard to paraphrase – to be communicated. But this does not mean that we ignore the content or the work's power to refer. Take Shelley's poem again. Of course it is accepted, as I said earlier, that poems may be fictions. So we are happy to accept that the 'I' of the first line may be a fictional character, and no more Percy Shelley than is the 'I' of another of his poems – 'Song of Apollo', supposedly sung from the point of view of the god. In the case of one of the other poems quoted above, readers and critics often confuse the poet Robert Burns with the ploughman speaking in 'To a Mouse'. Again, though, there is no reason to believe that any particular ploughman ran his plough through any particular mouse's nest; nor should we altogether identify living, breathing poets with the voices speaking in their work. (Not least if, as in the Victorian poet Robert Browning's 'Porphyria's Lover'(1836), the speaker of the poem is confessing to a murder!) Yet when Shelley writes in his 'Song of Apollo' (1824) 'I am the eye with which the Universe / Beholds itself and knows it is divine' he does mean it in at least one sense: the poet is like the sun in shedding light on the universe. Similarly, the ploughman is a conventional figure for the poet, and in imagining the destruction of the mouse's nest, Burns imagines the long struggle of the human over the natural world. In this struggle, poetry is always on the side of the human, and of art and culture's imposition of form, order and 'light' on the natural world – even when it also allows us to sympathise with the downtrodden creatures of the earth.

These are lyric poems (see Chapter 4), and while they may be to some degree fictions they are also drawing attention to the powers of art – including their own. These powers are sometimes thought more in evidence, and more clearly highlighted, in the lyric than in other poetic forms – such as Browning's dramatic monologue in 'Porphyria's Lover', or other stories in verse. This may be because they seem to involve us in authors' reflections and judgements, even if indirectly, through a personification or version of the writer, such as appears in that 'I' in the opening line of 'Ozymandias'. Notice too, though, how many other voices or characters figure in the poem, and how they focus our attention on the functioning of art and language. There are at least three voices at work in 'Ozymandias' – four, if we treat Shelley's own, as author, as separate. At the poem's centre are the words of Ozymandias himself, inscribed in stone by the sculptor; then the voice of the traveller reporting what he has seen in the desert, and finally, what we might take to be the voice of the poet who meets the traveller and relays his story to the reader. The sculptor's use of the king's words is artistic, and not the command originally delivered by Ozymandias himself. Like the poet, the sculptor copies and arranges, rather than commanding or instructing. The rhetoric of the ruler and the creation of literature are each characterised by self-conscious, heightened use of language, but there is a crucial difference. Ozymandias's command requires us to look on his works, but we look on his words at least as much as his works. In the context of the poem, these words do not figure as an order to readers but instead as something for them to contemplate. Looking at works of poetry, or literature more generally, involves the same kind of contemplation. In literature, language is always being transformed from a mere *means* of communication, a window we look through, into something we look at, and that therefore works on us in other ways. But this in turn always leads back to communication, albeit perhaps only as an invitation to critical reflection on the form of communication itself.

We asked whether literature could be defined by the idea of fiction, but found that this could not account for stylish examples of factual writing. Equally, there is a risk of exaggeration, or of applying to all literature ideas probably particularly relevant to the twentieth century, in seeing it primarily as an artistic reflection on form. An account of literature as 'art' does explain some distinctively modern or 'modernist' types of literary work discussed in several later chapters in this volume – by Keith Hughes in Chapter 11, in particular. Authors concerned show a restlessness with established literary styles and some interest instead in pure form, or in the texture and density of language itself, rather than its potentials as a transparent, direct means of communication. But it would be difficult to imagine a literary work which was *purely* form – sheer pattern, and no content – simply because literature's basic constituent is language, the same language we use to communicate every day. So critical discussions emphasising literary form – or literature as 'art' – most usefully suggest an enhancement or alteration of language as communication, not a radical rejection of its communicative function.

This can help us understand one of the oddest aspects of the way we use the idea of literature. Our use of the term seems fairly stable in relation to contemporary writing, following a century or so when it has mostly referred to fictional or imaginative works. We are ready, though, to accept as literary a much wider range of works from further back in the past. This is partly because a greater range of subject matter, even natural science, was once discussed in verse, and because history was much more dependent on storytelling before the evolution of modern standards of evidence. More significantly, works whose communicative function was paramount at the time can nowadays be treated as literary, in two senses. The sheer strangeness of older forms of language may strike us with a fresh intensity, or we may find we no longer need the content of certain works, leaving us freer to think about their form alone. These days, we distinguish quite carefully between history books, which aim to inform us about the past, and perhaps to entertain us, and novels. Yet we are ready to treat some works of history which have survived from earlier ages as 'literature': Edward Gibbon's *The History of the Decline and Fall of the Roman Empire* (1776–89), for example, is no longer read for its views of ancient Rome, but for its style. We read this work, or others like it, not for facts about the past, although these might also become evidence in modern history writing, but for pleasure.

This suggests an intriguing possibility: that the idea or quality of literature is not inherent in works themselves but is related to the ways in which we read them. Indeed, the very idea of literature might be a function of the way that we look at the past. What has been seen as literary in the past has often been treated dismissively by subsequent generations, so it seems perfectly reasonable to say that a book can be literary at one time and not at another. Go back to the cookery book we were thinking about earlier with this in mind and it becomes harder to draw a definite line between it and a novel. If it is written in a particularly pleasing manner, we might call it literature; or if it proves to be particularly historically significant, it might well be seen as literature in times to come. This tells us that the literariness of a text can be independent of the way it would have been viewed at the time of its creation, or of the purposes for which it was originally designed. Certainly, once the original function of a text has faded it can be easier to see other qualities in it. So which books being written now will be defined as literary in years to come is hard to guess at, perhaps impossible. Such definitions might at any time be a matter of deliberate decision: to read the Bible 'as literature' is to suspend our awareness of its religious significance and focus on other aspects, such as the way its stories are told or its use of imagery. This helps to clarify our earlier discussion of fiction and literature. *Robinson Crusoe* also purports to be a religious text – an account of how his survival and life on the island led Crusoe to see God's Providence at work in the world. Read solely for its religious meaning as an account of providential survival it would hardly be literature at all; but when we read it as a novel we choose to treat it as fiction, based on acquired ways of responding to formal hints in the text that all may not be quite as it appears.

In this chapter I have considered three ways of trying to define the term 'literature'. The idea that literature is fiction points us to the ways in which literature is given licence to be less than wholly truthful. But it does not account for those works in which factual material is presented in a stylish way. The idea of style pointed us to the centrality of form in our understanding of literature. This is why we take all poetry to be literature, with little concern as to whether its subject matter is factual or fictional. It also helps account for our use of 'literature' to include all dramatic works in which language is predominant, and all written works in which the emphasis is on style as much as or more than it is on the communication of a particular content. Yet we also saw that our sense of formal significance may vary: that what seems to be striking and literary to us may have been commonplace in an older time. This is also a dilemma for writers: ways of writing that once seemed original and fresh may become stale and worn-out. In response to this our third suggestion was that literature has more to do with ways of reading than to do with any inherent qualities of the works being read.

The approach outlined in the remaining chapters of this book reflects a sense that the second and third answers to the question 'What is literature?' are the most intriguing and important. This is not to say that the question of fiction is not relevant, just that it leads to an unsatisfactorily narrow line of approach. Literature may turn away from the world or it may engage directly with it. But a purely visionary, fantastic or abstract imagination would be unintelligible to any reader other than its author, while a purely instrumental language of command or instruction would be didactic or legislative rather than literary. Literature is always somewhere in between, since going to extremes in either direction might turn it into something else.

The challenge confronting us is therefore how we manage, in our criticism, to bear witness to this mixed condition. As the example of 'Ozymandias' suggested, we immediately recognise poetry because of its presentation on the page, which highlights patterns of stress and sound underwriting its sense and meaning. Formal elements in prose may be less obvious. Some of these may be created, much as in poetry, by elements of pacing, word-choice and sentence-assembly in the language used. The presence of fiction in a work, common to much literature but not essential, also invites us in reading narrative to look at familiar devices of plotting and ordering experience, or the choice of points of view or principal characters around whom these can be focused. We can read not just fictional narratives but *any* prose work – and to an extent dramatic ones – in these literary terms when we direct our attention to formal devices of this kind. We might, for example, look at a historian's use of plotting and point of view just as much as a novelist's, or examine the effectiveness of symbol in religious writing rather than only its religious significance. So perhaps we can say – as a partial and defiantly pragmatic conclusion – that in judging something to be 'literary' we are acknowledging the relevance and importance of its mixture of these qualities, as formal questions intrude upon our awareness and seem essential for appreciating, even for understanding, what we read: questions about language; about kinds of writing; about shaping, plotting and ordering experience; about conventions and their role in communication.

But how essential are such judgements or definitions? Why do we need to talk of a category of 'literature', or the particular qualities of 'the literary', at all? We study specific novels, poems or plays, not literature in the abstract, or in general, and it might be tempting to answer the question 'What is Literature?' simply by pointing at a large pile of books and giving up on the term as a bad lot. But, even if we accept that there can be no absolutely reliable theoretical or logical definition of literature, in practice there is more coherence than this might suggest – sets of overlapping conventions or expectations, even if no rigorous rules. Moreover, because any work of literature exists in relation to these overlapping expectations, its study may benefit from some sense of this larger context. Since this context and its conventions have changed and developed over a long period of time they also help pass on to us a large body of human historical achievement, adding to that feeling of nobility, gravity or importance we sense within the idea of literature as a whole, which may be something other than the sum of its parts. The poet Wallace Stevens saw literature as 'the imagination pressing back against the pressure of reality', although at any point in time different forms of imagination would press against different realities. From this he conceived of literature's nobility in the following way: 'as a wave is a force and not the water of which it is composed, which is never the same, so nobility is a force and not the manifestations of which it is composed' (Stevens 267). Or we might think of Shelley's poem one last time. To limit our gaze to individual works would be to know only the scattered fragments of literature. From our limited perspective it may appear fragmented, but if we do not imagine the whole of the figure to which those 'trunkless legs', that 'shattered visage', belong, we will not be able to gain a sense of its true proportions and appreciate its proper nobility – nor the proper place of the individual works we read.

NEXT STEPS

Genette, Gérard. *Fiction and Diction*. Trans. Catherine Porter. Cornell University Press, 1993.

Lamarque, Peter. *Philosophy of Literature*. Wiley-Blackwell, 2008.

Wellek, René and Austin Warren, *Theory of Literature*. Harmondsworth: Penguin, 1980.

Widdowson, Peter. *Literature* (The New Critical Idiom). London: Routledge, 1998.

2

English Literary Studies: Origins and Nature

Robert Irvine

It is not obvious why novels and plays and poems should be studied in universities under the title of 'English Studies' or 'English Literature'. As English is nowadays a well-established core subject in modern secondary education, it seems natural to us that it should, equally, be a field of study at university. But nobody thought to give university lectures on English authors until the middle of the eighteenth century, and before that nobody, it seems, complained that they were not there. A whole degree in 'English Literature' was not on offer until the twentieth century, so, compared to Philosophy or Theology or Law, ours is a fairly new academic discipline. Literary criticism more generally, it is true, seems to be as old as European literature itself. The ancient Greek philosopher Aristotle wrote the *Poetics* in the fourth century BCE, discussing the purpose and nature of tragic drama, for instance. But until the periods I have mentioned, academic discussion of imaginative writing was of writing in Latin and Greek: classical literature, which enjoyed enormous prestige as part of the foundations of European civilisation. This chapter will run through the story of how writing in English came to have a place on the university curriculum and what was done with it once it was there. It is a useful story to know, but not because our discipline today has necessarily evolved out of these older versions of itself. On the contrary, many of the approaches to literature that this chapter will describe were dead ends from which the subject had to back up and start again down a different route. But thinking about these other approaches can help us define what we want from English Studies today: both how we do it, in our seminars and essays, and what it is for, in relation to society more generally.

English literature first enters the university in the 1760s, in Scotland, but it does so under the (to us) strange-sounding label of 'Rhetoric and Belles Lettres'. This was the title of the series of lectures given by Adam Smith (now most famous as an economist) at Glasgow University and Hugh Blair at Edinburgh. 'Rhetoric' is an ancient subject of study, going back to classical times. It is the study of the art of public speaking, and in particular the persuasive speech-making of political debate and legal process. Most of the (all male) students attending the lectures of Smith and Blair were studying for the law or for the church, so public speech was going to be part of their future professions. But these lectures bracket rhetoric with belles-lettres, a French term taken over into English in the eighteenth century to suggest fine *writing* rather than powerful speech, consumed in private rather than produced in public. For Smith and Blair, developing our taste for literary writers helps us cultivate our personal sympathy with other people more generally. This helps us become sociable in a distinctly modern way, based on shared tastes and feelings rather than on membership of a particular political or religious denomination (the sort of groups rallied by traditional rhetoric).

On the other hand, such tastes and feelings were understood to be those of a particular – high – stratum of society. Most of the students taught by Smith and Blair were from Scots-speaking families who had made some money in commerce or who owned some land. Studying the writing of Jonathan Swift or Joseph Addison, the authors most frequently recommended by Smith and Blair, gave them a standard of English to which they could aspire. A more 'refined' English would make it easier for these middle-class boys to socialise with those in the class above them and with their English peers, with all the career advantages that might follow. Note that this eighteenth-century version of literary study does not distinguish between what we now call 'literature' (poems, plays and novels) and other sorts of writing. Periodical essays in politics or philosophy, or historical or biographical writing, are all part of 'literature' on this view. Blair and Smith recommend the journalism and political satire of Swift and Addison as much as their poetry or drama. Yet reading these texts as belles-lettres seems to involve ignoring the original *political* function of such writing. Addison and Swift were deeply committed to criticising and reforming their society; but for Smith and Blair, fifty years later, all that matters about such writing is its *style*, divorced from the purpose to which it was originally put.

At the same time as the lectures of Smith and Blair, English literary studies was being taught in England, but not at its two universities, Oxford and Cambridge, which remained committed to the classical curriculum. Instead, it was taught at the new academies set up by 'Dissenters': that is, Protestants who rejected the Church of England and who were banned from the English universities because of this. Many of those who taught in the dissenting academies had studied in Scotland instead, sharing its Presbyterian religion as they often did. The literary studies they introduced ran along similar lines to the lectures of Smith and Blair, but the academies' students were mostly destined for commerce rather than the law (where their religion might again cause problems) and studied English alongside natural science (also unknown in Oxford or Cambridge at this time) and practical subjects such as accounting. If the social function of literary study in Scotland was primarily *fitting in* with modern Britain, the concern of the academies was *getting on* despite it.

A combination of English dissenters and Scottish intellectuals also went on to break Oxford and Cambridge's duopoly on higher education in England by founding a new university there. University College London began teaching in 1828 and included on its staff Britain's first 'Professor of English Language and Literature'. The political establishment responded by founding a rival institution, King's College London, the following year; by 1835 it had a professor of English Literature and History too. As the nineteenth century continued, more new universities were founded in other cities across England, Ireland and Wales, and these usually had a professor of English Literature as well. Older universities followed suit: Glasgow in 1862, and Trinity College Dublin in 1867. At last Cambridge University established an examination board in 'Medieval and Modern Languages' which included English as one of its topics in 1878; Oxford established a Professorship in English Language and Literature in 1885 and Cambridge a separate Professorship in English Literature in 1911.

By that point, however, 'English Literature' had changed out of all recognition from the subject taught in Scotland and in the dissenting academies at the end of the eighteenth century. A canon of great writers, from Chaucer through Spenser and Shakespeare to Milton, Dryden and Pope, had been established as an 'English tradition' in literature; 'literature' was now understood much more narrowly as meaning poems and plays (the status of the novel as 'literature' was controversial). In one sense, this was a much more *historical* way of looking at English writing. Each great author was understood in relation to his (you will notice they were all male) predecessors and as building upon their achievements. This new approach also connected literary study very closely to the history of the language, starting with the Old English poems and chronicles of the Anglo-Saxons. English Literature was understood as developing continuously through time just as the language had done. But, in another sense, this was a very *un*historical way of reading poems and plays. The 'English tradition' was imagined as smoothly continuous, even when English society had suffered the sudden dislocations of Reformation, civil war, and economic upheaval. Each literary text was understood in relation to other literary texts which preceded and followed it, not in relation to the political or economic situation in which it was first written or published.

This lack of interest in political contexts was taken over from Smith, Blair and the Dissenters. But where they had seen literary study as a way of becoming *modern*, English Literature in the nineteenth-century universities became instead a way of connecting yourself to the *past*. It allowed students to understand themselves as the inheritors of an English national identity that was embodied in the nation's literature. For the nineteenth-century universities increasingly understood language as a 'racial' characteristic passed down through the generations. The great literature of a language expressed the unchanging spirit of the race that spoke it. This was why its progress could seem untroubled by the various political, religious and economic discontinuities that afflicted the actual society of these islands. And since Great Britain had, by the end of the nineteenth century, become the most powerful and most far-flung empire the world had ever seen, history had demonstrated that the spirit expressed in English Literature was that of a race superior to all the others. For Smith, Blair and the Dissenters, literary study taught you how to *do* something; a century later, by contrast, studying English Literature taught you how to *be* something – that is, more completely English.

This ideology of race was not only (or even primarily) developed in response to Britain's overseas expansion, however. It was also a response to the profound class divisions that had opened up in nineteenth century Britain. Living and working conditions for workers in the expanding industrial cities were terrible. Most middle-class men had been granted the vote by the Reform Act of 1832; but women and those who owned no property, the vast majority of the population, were still excluded from the franchise. In the 1840s, the working-class campaign for the vote (Chartism) caused panic among the property-owning classes. For the rest of the century, they sought to find means of reconciling working men to their subordinate position while leaving Britain's political and social institutions unchanged. One of those means was education. As industrialism became more advanced, it became obvious that Britain required a more technically educated workforce in any case, and a multitude of 'Mechanics' Institutes' were set up to meet this demand. But a man may have an excellent technical education and still resent living in a slum and having no say in the government of his country. Step forward English Literature, which required no classical education to read and offered its students at once an experience of great art to distract and console and a version of national identity which was disconnected from political institutions. Through an appreciation of Shakespeare and Milton, working-class readers could feel themselves to be sharing in a national life more ancient and important than the nation's current political institutions. Literary study might be the means whereby Britain, fractured along class lines, could be reintegrated along the lines of imagined 'race', without having to give working people the vote. And if English Literature was to be taught alongside technical subjects in Mechanics' Institutes and other evening classes, teachers would be needed to teach it. Hence the development of courses in the subject at university level. More directly, English Literature at university could appeal to another group denied both the vote and a classical education: women. Barred from most professions, such as the law and medicine, and from training in the natural sciences, young middle-class women sought out other sources of intellectual fulfilment, and by the end of the century had new career opportunities as teachers and office-workers. They, too, could be accommodated in English classes, the reading of literature fostering what were assumed to be the natural feminine powers of sympathy, and infusing them with the spiritual heritage of their race.

The paragraphs above describe the nineteenth-century origins of English Literature at university as initiated by a ruling class as a means of deflecting threats to its monopoly on power. But, of course, there was no way of ensuring that literary studies would have this effect in the case of any particular student. No learning, once achieved, itself dictates the use to which it is put. Discovering that, however materially poor, you are nevertheless the inheritor of literary riches by virtue of your membership of the English nation, might be an empowering experience. A working man or woman might deduce from *King Lear* (c.1605) or *Paradise Lost* (1667/1674) a version of 'England' quite different from that held by their bosses. He or she would certainly find plenty in Blake or Shelley to lend the authority of the 'English tradition' to their joining a trade union or organising a rent strike. Similarly, if women's work in passing on the tradition in the classroom was so important, it might occur to many women that they could be trusted with the vote.

In any case, British society was changing under the feet (as it were) of the tradition's guardians in the universities. Rapidly increasing rates of literacy among ordinary people, and a general increase in prosperity in the decades before the First World War, meant the development of a mass market for books such as had not existed before. In the first decades of the twentieth century, new technologies such as the cinema and radio also cultivated a mass audience. The last property qualifications for the vote were finally abolished for men in 1918, and for women in 1928: politically, Great Britain became a democracy.

One of the most significant developments in English Studies in the 1920s and 1930s was a response to these changes. Some university teachers, of whom I. A. Richards and F. R. and Q. D. Leavis at Cambridge were the most influential, saw the rise of 'mass civilization' as a threat to what they called 'culture'. In using the latter term, they were drawing on the thinking of the important Victorian intellectual Matthew Arnold. For Richards and the Leavises, as for Arnold before them, reading great literature offered an experience of wholeness and harmony that was otherwise unavailable in the modern world. By doing so, it provided the reader with an ideal standard against which that world could be judged, and to which readers could aspire in the organisation of their own lives. But this experience of great literature depended on the reader being capable of reading it in a particular way. The products of commercial culture (movies and advertising as well as popular fiction) did not cultivate the critical skills required to understand a poem by John Donne or a novel by George Eliot; on the contrary, they tended to deaden the faculties, turning the mind into the passive absorber of lazy sentiment. The higher values embodied in 'culture' had to be inculcated through a rigorous training, and this meant that their preservation in the modern world would be a task for a very few finely tuned individuals, such as I. A. Richards, F. R. and Q. D. Leavis and their students.

This seems like a very anti-democratic version of the social function of English Studies, giving legitimacy to the idea that only the few could really understand literature and implying that everyone else should submit to their judgements. However, once again, the intentions behind these innovations could not determine the use to which they were put. For one thing, the critical training that this approach called for was based on close attention to the particularities of individual literary texts. Identifying the 'wholeness' or 'harmony' that literary texts achieved, and in which their moral lesson lay, required careful analyses of the structure and imagery of a poem, or the characterisation and narrative point of view of a novel (the Leavises were among the first to take the novel seriously as 'literature'). That is, it required the skills of 'close reading' that remain fundamental to English Studies today, and which much of this volume is dedicated to explaining. For another, the Richards/Leavis approach assumed that the job of literary studies was not to *reconcile* students to their society, to help them fit in, get on or knuckle under. On the contrary, the English school in a university was to be a place from which students could learn to *criticise* their society. The literary values which they learned there were to be put to work in opposition to their society's dominant values. Now, for Richards and the Leavises, that opposition was to be a conservative resistance to democracy and 'mass civilization'. But once this critical role for English Studies was established, later teachers could use it to make quite other sorts of criticisms, as we shall see.

Indeed, similar techniques of close reading were developed, and taken much further, in the perhaps more confidently democratic context of the United States. The American universities had adopted the teaching of rhetoric and composition on the Scottish model from their inception; they had also, more surprisingly, taught English Literature as an ethnic tradition, and in relation to the history of the language, in a very similar way to British universities, although American Literature began to be taught in its own right from the late nineteenth century as well. In the late 1930s and 1940s, American teachers developed an approach to studying literature which was immediately christened 'the New Criticism': the best known New Critics being John Crowe Ransom, Cleanth Brooks, William K. Wimsatt and Monroe C. Beardsley. They picked up from I. A. Richards an emphasis on the internal structure and coherence of the literary text, in contrast to the chaos of everyday experience, and the job of criticism as the analysis and explication of that internal complexity. But they also articulated a much more convincing intellectual rationale for this approach, untroubled by the cultural pessimism of Richards and the Leavises. Indeed, the social context of the New Criticism gave it a political purpose quite at odds with those of the Cambridge conservatives. Teachers of English Literature in mid-century American universities were faced with students many of whose parents had arrived in the great waves of immigration from southern and eastern Europe in the late nineteenth and early twentieth centuries. The 'English Tradition' was not something that these students held in common. They shared the language, however, and a short text, usually a lyric poem, could be explained in the classroom with direct reference to the words on the page in front of the students. Referring only to the text in itself made it possible to offer the experience of English Literature to students from widely different backgrounds.

It was in the 1960s that a shift in the nature of literary studies began which remains the context in which English Literature is taught in universities today. To greatly simplify a very complex set of intellectual and institutional developments, one can think of this in terms of the rejection of the two assumptions shared by Richards, Leavis and the various American schools: a comparative lack of interest in historical contexts and an emphasis on the internal coherence of the literary text, of a system of genres (see David Salter's discussion in Chapter 3), or indeed of a national 'tradition' as a whole. On the one hand, historical contexts, the political and economic situations in which texts were produced and to which they were responses, were put back at the centre of the discipline by approaches informed by the thinking of nineteenth-century German philosophers Karl Marx and Friedrich Nietzsche (and the latter's post-war French follower, Michel Foucault). On the other hand, the idea that any text could achieve a self-contained wholeness or coherence has been dismantled by critics drawing on various 'post-structuralist' thinkers, but especially on the work of French philosopher Jacques Derrida. But, although there are serious differences between the intellectual underpinnings of Marxist, 'New Historicist' (Foucauldian) and post-structuralist or 'deconstructive' ways of reading, in practice they often combine and overlap in all sorts of productive ways.

All these approaches make very problematic any talk of the relative *value* of literary texts. For Hugh Blair, for the nineteenth-century professors, for the Cambridge people in the twenties and thirties, and for the New Critics in the 1940s, there was no question about this: some texts, and some types of writing, were just better than others. They knew which they were, and their job was to teach students this; in the twentieth century, at least, they could also give some account of why these texts were better than others. The historicism of the Marxists and the Foucauldians, however, locates the meaning of the text in the political and social *function* it had in its original context and, perhaps, in later contexts too. (This chapter has attempted to do something similar with English Studies in its various historical forms.) Literary writing, understood in this way, is always implicated in the power structures of its society. If it often appears to belong to a higher realm, to reflect timeless ideals or a universal 'human nature', that is precisely how it makes the power of a particular class seem 'natural' and thus inevitable. What counts as a 'good' or 'great' literary text at any point in time may be a measure of its success in pulling off this kind of trick. Deconstructive approaches may be ready to concede the greater ambition towards internal coherence of some texts rather than others. But, because of the instabilities of meaning identified by post-structuralist theory, they are still bound to miss this goal, and the most we can say about a 'great' work of literature is that it is a particularly impressive failure.

The up side of this suspension of the question of value is that what counts as literature has expanded once again to the all-inclusive scope it enjoyed for Hugh Blair and Adam Smith. The narrow canon of the 'English Tradition' as it was taught in the nineteenth century is now revealed as the politically-motivated creation it always was, and English Studies is constantly alert to the ways in which political considerations (of race or gender, for example) may be motivating the inclusion or exclusion of particular texts from those that are taught in universities. The social context for this development includes, on the one hand, the increased consciousness of English as the language not just of the white British and their descendents in former colonies, but also of millions of people of all races all over the world; and, on the other hand, the massive expansion of higher education in the English-speaking world from the 1960s onwards. Universities began to draw in young people from a much wider cross-section of society than previously, and those students were also more ready than earlier generations to question the values embodied in insti-tutions like universities, thanks to the general democratisation of culture in Britain in the 1960s and 1970s and the disillusion produced in America in the same period by the Vietnam War and the Watergate scandal. The revolution in the discipline that I have described in the previous two paragraphs has been enormously controversial , especially in the USA, where the academic 'theory wars' were understood as part of the 'culture wars' over what sort of values US institutions were supposed to promote. But this controversy perhaps rests on a misunderstanding of what education is for. As I hope this chapter has shown, what gets taught, and how it is taught, can never completely determine the use that the student makes of that teaching. That remains as true today as at any point in the development of 'English Studies' as an academic discipline.

NEXT STEPS

Baldick, Chris. *The Social Mission of English Criticism, 1848–1932.* Oxford: Clarendon Press, 1992.

Court, Franklin E. *Institutionalizing English Literature: The Culture and Politics of Literary Study, 1750–1900.* Stanford, CA: Stanford University Press, 1992.

Crawford, Robert. *Devolving English Literature.* Oxford: Clarendon Press, 1992. (See especially, 'The Scottish Invention of English Literature'.)

Williams, Raymond. *Culture and Society 1780–1950.* 1958; Harmondsworth: Penguin, [1958] 1961. (See especially, 'Two Literary Critics: I. A. Richards and F. R. Leavis'. 239–57.)

3

Kinds of Literature

David Salter

GENRE AND 'THE PROMISED END'

Re-enter LEAR, *with* CORDELIA *dead in his arms*; EDGAR, CAPTAIN, *and others following*

LEAR   Howl, howl, howl, howl! O, you are men of stones:
Had I your tongues and eyes, I'd use them so
That heaven's vault should crack. She's gone forever!
I know when one is dead, and when one lives;
She's dead as earth. Lend me a looking glass;
If that her breath will mist or stain the stone,
Why, then she lives.

KENT   Is this the promised end?

EDGAR   Or image of that horror?

(Shakespeare, King Lear V, iii, 257–64)

In the final scene of Shakespeare's *King Lear* (1605), the onstage protagonists contemplate the horrific spectacle of Lear's entrance with his murdered daughter in his arms. The final 'end' to which Kent alludes is Doomsday, the apocalyptic last judgement of all human life. But his wording also poses the question which, in one form or another, all readers of literary texts must ask themselves, either consciously or unconsciously, when they come to the end of a work: is this the conclusion that I expected? What is interesting about Kent's question is that it registers surprise: this is not the ending that he expected, and as we shall see later on, Kent's sense of shock at the death of Cordelia has been shared by many people who have either read the play or seen it performed on stage. What this might suggest is that plays, novels

and other forms of narrative shape our expectations of how they will unfold
and conclude: we make certain assumptions about the kind of story we are
currently reading or viewing by comparing it with similar stories we have
encountered in the past. But, as in the case of *King Lear*, this capacity to
shape expectations can also be used by writers to subvert or undermine them.
Authors can refuse to fulfil the very expectations that they have aroused in
order to surprise or even shock their readers.

Literary critics have drawn on the idea of genre in order to elucidate this
process. The word 'genre' comes from the Latin 'genus' meaning kind or
type, so the study of genre offers a way of dividing and categorising literature
into distinct families or groups. Different genres – that is, different types or
kinds of literature – possess common characteristic features which relate,
among other things, to style, content and plot. Certain generic distinctions
are so widely accepted that their critical deployment is rarely problematic:
so we are able to articulate, without any misunderstanding, the difference
between tragedy and comedy in drama, for example, and are broadly confident that we know what is meant when the generic classification of satire
is invoked. However, the study of genre is not an exact and undisputed
science: there are in fact many different ways of classifying genres which
can both coexist and overlap. A literary work can be categorised according
to its mode of delivery (drama, film, poetry); its effect on the audience (if
it induces laughter it may be characterised as a comedy, whereas tragedy
is traditionally said to inspire fear and pity, as Simon Malpas and Jonathan
Wild explain in Chapters 18 and 19); the time and place of its composition
(the literature of the English Civil War) and so on. And the different criteria by which works are defined can combine in various ways to produce a
host of subgenres or mixed genres, such as tragicomedy, Jacobean tragedy,
Restoration comedy, Victorian poetry and modern American Gothic. (See
Kenneth Millard's further discussion of genre and genre divisions in Chapter
10.)

Since ideas about genre are far from straightforward, this chapter is less
concerned with setting out classifications than with showing how they work
in practice – how authors self-consciously deploy an awareness of genre in
their work. Central to the discussion will be the idea that genres help to
orientate readers in texts. They shape readers' responses to texts by raising
expectations of what those texts will deliver: expectations which authors can
choose either to satisfy or confound. What is worth noting here, moreover,
is that genre is not something that is simply imposed on audiences: authors
are dependent upon the ability and willingness of readers to recognise a
complex assortment of generic cues and signals and actively to respond to
them.

MISDIRECTING THE AUDIENCE: ALFRED HITCHCOCK'S *PSYCHO*

A discussion of Alfred Hitchcock's film *Psycho*, which had its cinematic release in 1960, may not seem like the most obvious place to begin an exploration of genre, but it offers a textbook example of how the deliberate manipulation of an audience's generic expectations can produce spectacular artistic effects. Today *Psycho* is widely regarded as one of the most influential films of the second half of the twentieth century, but what interests me is the contemporary reception of the film, in particular the ways in which the cinema audiences of the time responded to it. What seems remarkable from the vantage point of the early twenty-first century is the highly emotionally-charged – it might even be described as near-frenzied – manner in which contemporary audiences viewed the film. Eyewitness accounts from film-goers suggest that audiences were gripped by a combustible mixture of fear and excitement when viewing *Psycho*, which created an atmosphere almost of mass hysteria within cinema auditoriums. As one contemporary viewer recalled, 'The screaming of the audience and the shrieking of the music sort of combined . . . into this howl which just . . . rose up and bounced off the walls' (Durgnat 17). The emotionally overwrought reactions which greeted the film have usually been understood as quite specific responses to one particular scene: the notorious and still shocking sequence in which the film's heroine, Marion (played by Janet Leigh), is stabbed to death in the shower to the discordant auditory accompaniment of piercing, staccato violins (the famous musical score composed by Bernard Herman). This scene has been widely credited with introducing a new aesthetic to mainstream Hollywood cinema: Hitchcock is said to have pushed back the boundaries of what it was permissible to show on screen with his salacious, voyeuristic and graphic depiction of the murder of the naked Marion.

But rather than simply seeing the hysteria of cinema audiences as a reaction to a hitherto unprecedented level of screen violence, contemporary responses to the film might also be understood as registering a sense of shock at Hitchcock's breach – or violation – of well established generic codes and expectations. For it was not only the violent manner in which Marion died but the fact of her death that cinema audiences found so shocking. To quote another contemporary film-goer: 'we were really in shock from that [the death of Marion] . . . people were in total mourning for the loss' (Durgnat 18). The murder of Marion, who up until that point is the story's central protagonist, occurs less than half way through the film, and the death of the leading lady so early on in the narrative was something that audiences of the time just did not expect. The genre of the Hollywood thriller, whose conventions Hitchcock's audience would have absorbed and internalised, allowed its sympathetic heroines (of whom Marion is certainly one) to be stalked, threatened, menaced and terrorised – but there was a tacit understanding that they would successfully evade serious harm and emerge safe in the end. As I will be arguing throughout this chapter, audiences often tend to confuse generic conventions with immutable natural laws, thinking that because certain things do not happen in particular genres or kinds of narrative they therefore cannot happen in any story that seems to belong to that genre. By playing upon viewers' assumptions about the kind of film they were watching, Hitchcock was able to deliver a completely unexpected and shocking coup de théâtre. As he later reflected in conversation with the French film director François Truffaut, 'I was directing the viewers. You might say I was playing them like an organ' (Truffaut 269).

It might be useful to qualify Hitchcock's comments slightly here. For rather than directing his viewers, it is probably more accurate to think of him as deliberately misdirecting them. Hitchcock led contemporary cinema audiences to believe that they were watching a certain kind of film – a reasonably conventional Hollywood thriller – only to pull the rug from under their feet by killing off the heroine after less than an hour, and then embarking upon a different type of narrative altogether, a type of narrative for which the audience did not have a satisfactory frame of reference. So one of the things that a discussion of *Psycho* can tell us about genres is that they are relatively adaptable, fluid and unstable. Although audiences tend to have very rigid ideas about what certain genres entail, writers and directors are not bound by these audience expectations. Genres are not fixed or set in stone; rather, they evolve, they develop and they change. After *Psycho*, the thriller genre encompassed a broader repertoire of possibilities than it included before the film's release. (For instance, *Psycho* can be seen as one of the antecedents of the so-called Slasher film, which revels in gruesome and macabre displays of violence, particularly violence directed against women. And although it does not use the term, it can also be seen as one of the forerunners of the 'serial killer' subgenre of film, a form which follows *Psycho* in combining graphic violence with pseudo-scientific psychoanalytic explanations of the killer's motivation.)

The simple fact of seeing *Psycho*, then, changed audience expectations not only of the shape and structure of thriller plots but also of the kinds of human experiences that could be represented on screen. And here we can see how developments in genre often reflect broader social and cultural change. *Psycho* was released at the very beginning of the 1960s, and in many ways it can be said to anticipate the concerns and interests of that decade. *Psycho* is frank and explicit in its treatment of the relationship between human sexuality and violence, it is fascinated by extreme psychological states and the pathology of the criminal mind, and it characterises the bourgeois, nuclear family – traditionally seen as the bedrock of Western society – as a sick institution which can lead to severe psychiatric illness. All of these preoccupations chime with certain aspects of the emerging culture of the 1960s, such as a more permissive attitude towards sex, a general relaxation of constraints on personal behaviour as well as literary and artistic expression, greater individualism, a distrust of social norms and a desire to challenge received opinions and conventional ideas.

Genres should therefore not be seen as existing in hermetically sealed bubbles which separate them from the material world of lived existence. Their evolution and development is shaped at least in part by the same social, political and cultural forces that act upon the people who read literature and who see plays and films. Writers and directors can consciously choose to innovate in order to achieve particular artistic effects, but genres also develop in response to the changing beliefs, attitudes and values of their audiences.

A CASE STUDY IN GENRE: MEDIEVAL ROMANCE

Central to the discussion so far has been the idea that particular literary and film genres bring with them certain sets of expectations about the type of narrative that will unfold: its plot, its setting, the kind of characters it will include and so on. One way of thinking about this is that genres are able to evoke both a particular world, and a particular world view, which audiences must recognise and accept if they are to engage meaningfully with the story. It may be a world that is distant from the one that the reader actually inhabits, and a world view that he or she does not share. However, in order to enter sympathetically into the world evoked by a particular story, audiences must consent – at least on the level of the imagination – to its underlying premises and assumptions. And they can only do this if they are able to identify the story's genre from a variety of different conventions, cues and signals that are embedded within its narrative.

The genre of medieval romance nicely illustrates this point because the world it creates is so remote from that of today's readers. Moreover, medieval romance is a highly conventional form: similar plots, settings, characters and incidents frequently recur in romance tales, so that, with a few notable exceptions, they tend to unfold along rather predictable, even formulaic lines. Geoffrey Chaucer's late-fourteenth-century romance, *The Man of Law's Tale* shares many of the characteristic features of the genre, and it is worth discussing not simply because it can be viewed as a reasonably typical example of the form but also because Chaucer can be thought almost to have treated its composition as an exercise in genre writing. It is as though Chaucer – usually so distinctive and innovative – suppressed his own voice, stifled his own personal thematic and stylistic idiosyncrasies, in order to produce a work that more completely conformed to the requirements of the form.

The tale tells of the adventures, or rather the misadventures, of Custance, the beautiful and virtuous daughter of the Roman emperor, who reluctantly has to leave her home in order to marry the Sultan of Syria. However, the Sultan's evil mother – incensed that her son has chosen to marry a Christian – plots the brutal massacre of those attending the wedding, including her own son. Custance alone is spared immediate death, but her unhappy fate is apparently sealed when she is set adrift at sea in a rudderless boat. Powerless to chart her own course, Custance's life is none the less miraculously preserved as her boat floats for years until it washes up on the coast of Northumberland, which at this time is a pagan country. Once she is ashore, supernatural forces again intervene to safeguard Custance's life from mortal danger, and thanks to her great beauty she wins the love of Alla, the Northumbrian king who converts to Christianity under her influence. The two marry, and in due course Custance gives birth to a son, Maurice. But this interlude of domestic happiness does not last long: while Alla is away fighting the Scots, his evil mother treacherously forges a letter which purports to be from her son ordering that Custance and Maurice be set aboard a rudderless boat and cast out to sea. After yet another lengthy voyage in which Custance's life is miraculously preserved, the boat washes ashore in Rome where Custance and Maurice live unrecognised. Meanwhile, in mourning for the loss of his wife and son, King Alla embarks on a religious pilgrimage to Rome, and the tale concludes with two joyful reunions: one between Alla and his wife and son, the other between Custance and her father, the emperor.

In common with many works in the romance genre, *The Man of Law's Tale* is concerned with the separation and eventual reunion of families after a long period of trial and suffering. Like Custance, the typical romance hero or heroine undertakes a hazardous journey that involves a series of perilous tests or ordeals which they must pass before they can return to a state of happiness and wholeness. During this time of wandering they are isolated and deprived not only of their worldly possessions but often of their very identity, their sense of who they are. So the narrative structure of romance can be understood as cyclical: it describes a movement of exile and return, of loss and restoration. Another characteristic that *The Man of Law's Tale* shares more widely with the romance genre is the passivity of its protagonist, which is encapsulated by Chaucer in the image of the rudderless boat. Custance is incapable of forging her own destiny: she cannot steer her ship but is instead entirely at the mercy of elemental forces which determine her course. As is almost always the case in romance, though, these forces are benign. Romance heroes and heroines are guided and defended by higher powers: in the case of Custance we are explicitly told that it is the Christian God who providentially watches over and preserves her, but elsewhere romance heroes are chosen by, and come under the protection of, impersonal superhuman forces which can variously be identified as fate, fortune, chance or destiny. And here we come to another characteristic of medieval romance: the magical, the supernatural and the miraculous are common – one might even say expected – elements. Through a series of rhetorical questions, the narrator of *The Man of Law's Tale* repeatedly draws his readers' attention to the miracles that punctuate the story: how does Custance survive the massacre of wedding guests in Syria? how is her life preserved for years at sea? The answer to these and other similar questions is that God has miraculously intervened to safeguard Custance's life.

One further characteristic – although by no means the last – shared by *The Man of Law's Tale* with other romance narratives is its conception of character. Elsewhere in his works, Chaucer presents highly nuanced interpretations of character: his protagonists have depth and interiority, they are often internally conflicted and their motivations are far from straightforward. This subtlety is entirely absent from *The Man of Law's Tale*, not because it is an artistic failure but because romance tends not to be interested in three-dimensional personalities and complex motivations. Custance is characterised by her constancy, her capacity stoically to endure whatever misfortunes befall her. Custance's two mothers-in-law are wicked, and the narrator associates them both with Satan, but there is no attempt to account for their actions in psychological terms. Romance, then, deals in types: the virtuous heroine, the brave and passionate young hero, the evil crone, the naïve and misguided father, the cruel tyrant and so on. There is therefore something tautological about the representation of character in romance: virtuous young heroines behave virtuously because they are by nature virtuous; in a similar vein, brave young heroes fight courageously because they are brave.

In many ways, the narrative world evoked by medieval romance is highly distinctive and self-contained. Because of the strong degree of structural and thematic coherence between texts within the genre, readers familiar with its conventions are able very quickly to recognise texts as romances and to predict in broad terms how they will unfold. The various elements we have discussed function as cues alerting audiences to the kind of text they are reading. Of course, as we have already seen, generic conventions do not have the status of unbreakable rules. Writers are not bound to observe generic conventions, but these conventions do powerfully shape the expectations and assumptions that readers bring to texts. And what is true for the genre of medieval romance applies equally to other well-established and clearly defined literary forms which similarly create distinct and singular fictional worlds.

SAMUEL JOHNSON AND THE DEATH OF CORDELIA

Like the cyclical structures of the romance genre, this chapter will conclude by returning to its initial point of departure: the death of Cordelia in
Shakespeare's *King Lear*, and the ways in which an awareness of genre can
help to make sense of the responses of readers and play-goers to that event. In
his 1765 edition of Shakespeare's works, Samuel Johnson captures something
of the sadness and powerful sense of disbelief which the play's final scene has
elicited from its readers and viewers over the centuries: 'I was many years ago
so shocked by Cordelia's death', Johnson wrote, 'that I know not whether I
ever endured to read again the last scenes of the play till I undertook to revise
them as an editor' (Johnson, *Samuel Johnson on Shakespeare* 97–8). At first
glance, Johnson's shock at the death of Cordelia may itself seem surprising:
after all, *King Lear* is a tragedy and corpses litter the stage at the end of all of
Shakespeare's tragic plays. Indeed, one of the defining features of the genre is
the inevitably of death (see Chapter 18). So what is different about the case of
Cordelia? Why has her death struck audiences as so distressing when they have
borne the deaths of other no less virtuous and sympathetic characters from
Shakespeare's tragedies – such as Desdemona in *Othello*, for instance – with
much more equanimity?

Our discussion of the narrative structure of romance may offer one way of
approaching this question. In many respects, the development of the narrative
in *King Lear* bears a striking resemblance to romances such as *The Man of Law's
Tale*. Shakespeare's play dramatises the initial separation and eventual reunion
and reconciliation of a father and daughter. Cordelia, like Custance, undertakes a journey of exile and return, and her virtue and constancy are rewarded
when she is finally reunited and reconciled with her father in Act Four Scene
Seven. This narrative pattern, which appears to approximate more closely
to romance than tragedy, is reinforced by the fairy-tale element of the play:
Cordelia is the youngest of three daughters; she is her father's favourite child;
she has two wicked and duplicitous older sisters who meet a violent end. So
at least in terms of family dynamics, Cordelia comes to resemble archetypal
folk- and fairy-tale figures such as Cinderella, and on some level of awareness
this creates an expectation amongst audiences that Cordelia's destiny, like
Cinderella's, will be a happy one.

And this romance pattern is not confined to Cordelia. Lear too undergoes
various forms of exile, both literally, when he is cast out on the heath, and
also metaphorically. Lear's madness can be understood as a form of exile or
estrangement from himself: 'who is it that can tell me who I am?' he at one
point plaintively asks (I, iv, 224). And as with the figure of the romance hero,
Lear's exile appears to be just the first step on a longer, cyclical journey that

will eventually lead to the restoration both of his sanity and of his loving, paternal bond with Cordelia. Indeed, the radical reversal in Lear's fortunes – the seemingly-decisive turning point when descent into madness and isolation becomes a movement towards wholeness and reintegration – is marked by the transformative image of death and rebirth. For when he wakes to find himself back again with Cordelia, Lear imagines that he has died and has been reborn: 'You do me wrong to take me out of the grave' are the first words he speaks when reunited with her (IV, vii, 45).

An awareness of genre, then, can offer some indication of why audiences have reacted so powerfully to the death of Cordelia and Lear at the end of the play. The movement or trajectory of the drama appears to be following a romance pattern in which a series of horribly painful trials are understood as the necessary, preliminary stages on a journey that will eventually lead to happiness. And Shakespeare fulfils these hopes and expectations almost until the very last moment of the play: the narrative logic of the drama appears to be driving it inexorably towards the conventional, romance ending of reunion, reconciliation and restoration. That this is not the conclusion actually delivered is felt all the more powerfully precisely because it is so strongly expected. The apparently random and arbitrary nature of Cordelia's death is caused at least in part by the fact that Shakespeare seems to breach an inviolable generic law. We can be certain that he did this deliberately because in all of the versions of the legend of King Lear that were known to him – Shakespeare did not invent the story; rather he adapted it from a number of earlier sources – Cordelia outlives her father and succeeds him to the throne. And the logic of the narrative's underlying romance structure was so irresistible that the play was rewritten by Nahum Tate in 1681, and given a happy ending: not only does Cordelia avoid death, but she falls in love with and marries Edgar. And in various adapted forms, it was Nahum Tate's version of the play, and not Shakespeare's, that was performed on the stage well into the nineteenth century.

King Lear therefore offers an exemplary demonstration of what we have been discussing throughout this chapter: genres are able powerfully to shape the expectations of audiences, a power which authors can manipulate, exploit and subvert for a variety of different reasons and to achieve a variety of different effects.

NEXT STEPS

Fowler, Alastair. *Kinds of Literature: An Introduction to the Theory of Genres and Modes.* Oxford: Clarendon Press, 1982.

Frye, Northrop. *Anatomy of Criticism: Four Essays.* Princeton: Princeton University Press, 1957.

Frye, Northrop. *The Secular Scripture: A Study of the Structure of Romance*. Cambridge, MA and London: Harvard University Press, 1976.

Snyder, Susan. *The Comic Matrix of Shakespeare's Tragedies Romeo and Juliet, Hamlet, Othello, and King Lear*. Princeton: Princeton University Press, 1979.

Section II – Poetry

4

Poetry: An Introduction

Alan Gillis

In 1595, Sir Philip Sidney argued the end of poetry was to 'teach and delight', echoing the Roman poet Horace from about 1,600 years earlier (Sidney, 'Defence of Poesy', 217; Horace 90). Since then, as before, many different kinds of poem have been written. Indeed, there are so many types of poem, and so many diverging concepts of what poetry is, that we should always take definitions of it with a pinch of salt. Differing poems from differing epochs and cultures amount to a kaleidoscope of contrasting ideas about the nature of language, art, individuality, consciousness, society, politics, history, existence, reality and so on. And yet Horace and Sidney's views still ring true. If poems 'teach and delight', the most pivotal word in the formula is 'and'. The two poles of instruction and felicity work in tandem. What we might learn from a poem, the message or meaning it might impart, is likely to be bound up with its pleasures. And so, the best way to study a poem is to try, in the first instance, to enjoy it.

To be sure, you may feel inclined to treat the concept of poetry's 'delight' with scepticism. The cumbersome terminology of verse criticism tends to make people wary of poems, leading to a misapprehension that poetry is specialised and technical. But truly not liking poetry would seem as strange as not liking music, of any kind, or not liking colour. Just as children respond to the ritualistic sing-song of nursery rhymes, we are all mostly susceptible to advertising slogans: 'One, two, buckle my shoe'; 'A Mars a day helps you work, rest and play'. These are rhythmic jingles which are repeated and somehow bypass our reason to become implanted in our heads. All of us are already responding to poetry from day to day, whether we know it or not. Poetry with a capital 'P' is simply an enhancement of such basic forms.

We might go to a football match, where a striker might shimmy past a defender before scoring with pinpoint accuracy, causing a fan to blurt out, 'Now that is pure poetry!' We might read a review of a film and be informed its cinematography is 'highly poetic'. We might say a bird's flight is 'poetry in motion'. We might hear about a crooked businessman getting his comeuppance and be told 'poetic justice' has been done. But what do these phrases mean? Clearly, they mean something about grace, composure, skill, beauty and a general sense of befittingness. However, pick up some contemporary poetry and it will be clear that a poem can be as dissonant, bizarre, oblique or as downright offensive as it wants to be. So, popular notions of the poetic do not give the whole picture, pleasant though they are.

The one objective link between all the myriad kinds of poem over the ages is merely that poetry is a mode of language-use marked by a high degree of verbal patterning or design. It doesn't really matter what the subject matter is, whether it is tasteful or crude. So long as there is an element of patterning or design, we are in the realm of the poetic. Poetry manipulates language more intensely than any other kind of literature, and poems mostly achieve this through being set in verse. A poet's principal tools of design are the conventions of versification, otherwise known as prosody. These tools bind and arrange language, creating a more charged quality or greater density of meaning than is otherwise possible. This is because verbal patterning emphasises the sound of words.

We might think of language as an inherently twofold medium. Each word has a material-aural dimension (the word as a physical sign) and an abstract-semantic dimension (that which it refers to). In everyday language-use we do not usually worry very much about how words sound: we receive the message being communicated, and that is all. But poetry is concerned with both linguistic dimensions simultaneously: sense and sound. Thus, when John Keats begins a poem with a line such as 'Thou still unravished bride of quietness' ('Ode on a Grecian Urn', 1820), first and foremost, he simply wants to sound good. You might well ask 'what does that mean?' Many have. But you will be unable to convey its sense if you do not account for its musicality. Keats's aural hyper-sensitivity creates deep ambiguity, so that his poem's meaning is inextricable from its 'delight'.

Apparently, our brains are split into two distinct hemispheres. The left side is analytical and functions in a sequential and logical fashion, while the right side is intuitive and bound up with the more irrational elements of our psyche such as emotion, or affect: things excluded from functional language. Poetry is broadly unique as an art form to the extent that it exercises both sides concurrently. When reading a poem, our brain's left side channels the sense, while, in an intertwined but differently modulated operation, the right side channels aesthetic patterning. Information and affect are placed on a level pegging, rectifying the fact that a part of our brain (and thus, a part of ourselves) is left to dangle in normal talk and discourse. And so, poetry is referential: it says things and means things; but it simultaneously approaches the sensuous condition of sound in music, or colour in painting.

A vital aspect of poetry is what we call lexis or diction. These are technical terms for word choice. Language is comprised of an overlapping multitude of idioms. Words have distinct but changeable personalities, always pre-loaded with cultural associations and value. Poetry manipulates both the specific meanings and looser associations of words, is alert to their historical provenance and social domain, while it also plays with their pure sound as a thing-in-itself. But most importantly, words in poems exist, and influence one another, in orchestrated relation, never in isolation.

All the poet's techniques of orchestration are, as we have said, geared towards creating patterned sound. Repetition is at the heart of pattern, and poetry's primal form of repetition is rhythm. All the tools of prosody are essentially aimed at getting a poem's rhythmic pulse beating. Lee Spinks discusses 'Metre and Rhythm' in Chapter 5, following this, so we will not dwell on the topic here. But the crucial thing to remember is that language is already inherently rhythmical, and this is a matter of stresses. Words make up a string of syllables, and when we talk, one syllable tends to be stressed either more or less than the syllable next to it. Poetry merely exploits this natural phenomenon.

Metre arises when stress patterns are regulated into basic, repeating units. Almost always, each unit contains one stressed syllable and one (or, less often, two) unstressed syllables. These units are called feet. Speaking and writing rhythmically is instinctive, but, unfortunately, 'scanning' metric pattern is not. Because metric feet are all about syllables, identifying metre involves cutting across the autonomy of words, which can often seem counter-intuitive. Yet there is no need to become too preoccupied with metre. While metric analysis is our best way of quantifying poetic rhythm, few successful poems ever stick to a strict metre. No one really speaks to the rhythm of 'da dum da dum da dum da dum', and, in poetry, what we actually get are rhythmic variations, borne of natural speech intonation, set to an underlying beat.

The relationship between speech–rhythm and metre is reminiscent of music. Think of a waltz, written in $\frac{3}{4}$ time. The conductor waves his baton: dum-da-da \ dum-da-da \ dum-da-da. But the music does not sound like that. The music swoops and sings, its melody tied to the underlying beat yet seemingly free. In this way, metre measures time, while rhythm is the motion flowing through that measure. The two exist in counterpoint to one another. You might ask if the metre is there at all, if we don't 'speak it'? Yet countless poems do prove that, in a similar vein to the waltz, the ghost of a regulated, underlying pattern is vital to the creation of the free-flowing sounds we hear in a poem.

There is such a thing as a 'prose poem', yet lineation remains central to the Western conception of poetry. Line division is primarily designed for rhythm. Line breaks draw attention to tone and sound: they are not necessary for sense, although the way in which they cut across normal syntax provides another form of counterpoint for poetry. Meanwhile, stanzas – divisions of poems into separate units of several lines – are another element of artifice imposed upon normal language use. The New York poet Kenneth Koch argues stanzas are 'pure poetry language, being essentially nothing more than ways of organizing other forms of poetic music – rhythm and rhyme'. Koch continues

> Stanzas, with their 'rests' that are even more definitive than those at the ends of lines, orchestrate the repetitions and variations of meter and rhyme, and divide what is said into units – as do the different 'movements' of symphonies, or of string quartets. (47)

Clearly, rhyme creates a strong degree of resonance and sonority in a poem. Here is William Wordsworth:

> A Slumber did my spirit seal;
>   I had no human fears:
> She seemed a thing that could not feel
>   The touch of earthly years.
>
> No motion has she now, no force;
>   She neither hears nor sees;
> Rolled round in earth's diurnal course,
>   With rocks, and stones, and trees.
>   (1800)

On one level, it makes no difference to Wordsworth's meaning that 'fears' chimes with 'years', or 'sees' with 'trees'. Yet the acoustic continuity is vital to the aesthetic experience and effect of the poem as a work of art. The crux of rhyme is its duality. Part repetition and part variation: the sound of rhyming words is the same, their sense is different.

Meaning, in language, is basically unfurled in a linear movement, along the sequence of the words. To get the sense of a sentence you read it through to the end. And this, also, is how a poem works. But simultaneously, in a poem, the sound chimes back on itself. So, in Wordsworth's poem, by the time we reach 'earth's diurnal course' in line seven, semantically we have left the words 'no force' from line five long behind; yet the sonic continuity throws the ear backwards, even if subliminally. As such, we might say that meaning is unfolding through time (it is diachronic), but sound is circular and return-ing (it is synchronic). In this way, rhyme and patterned sound can do funny things with our sense of time, and our sense of the interconnections between things. Wordsworth's poem may well be about a death (the linear fate that awaits us all), but the poem's sonic circularity makes palpable an underlying philosophical point that the world and nature (and love and memory) keep turning around.

It should be noted there are various types of rhyme, derived from conso-nants ('C') and vowels ('V'): alliteration ($\underline{C}$ V C: bad/boy); assonance (C $\underline{V}$ C: back/rat); consonance (C V $\underline{C}$: back/neck); reverse rhyme ($\underline{C}$ $\underline{V}$ C: back/bat; pararhyme ($\underline{C}$V$\underline{C}$: back/buck); rich rhyme ($\underline{C}$ $\underline{V}$ $\underline{C}$: bat/bat); as well as 'proper' or normal rhyme (C $\underline{V}$ $\underline{C}$: back/rack). Regarding our Wordsworth poem, notice how the proper rhymes at the end of each line are backed by a multiplicity of other devices. There is alliteration in the first line (slumber/spirit/steal), second line (had/human) and seventh (rolled/round). The con-sonance of that final 's' sound in 'rocks, and stones, and trees' is anticipated by the earlier consonance of 'hears and sees', and line seven's 'course'. We also have the assonance of 'seemed' and 'feel', which briefly returns in line six with 'sees'; while we have further assonance with 'earthly years' and the impressive string of assonantal 'o' noises in the second stanza with 'motion', 'now', 'no', 'force', 'nor', 'rolled', 'round', 'course' and 'rocks'.

Now, before we even consider rhythm, this amount of sonic patterning in the mere forty-eight words of this poem is remarkable. Backing up the strong end-rhymes, all of these minor sonic devices are pivotal to the poem's overall tone and texture. Tricks like these are the nuts and bolts of how a poet makes sound prominent and tickles the right side of our brains. But what needs to be stressed is that poetic form does not really develop from any one device, or mode of patterning, but from several working simultaneously: at the heart of form is the phenomenon of lines, rhythms, rhymes and stanzas all acting in consort with one another, inter-animating to a great variety of effect. By mixing up line length, stanza length, rhyme scheme and rhythm with other devices poets are free to create any kind of form they want. Given the number of possible combinations, there are millions of possible poetic forms. Nevertheless, particular patterns or combinations, over time, have become popular and influential. These are discussed by Penny Fielding in Chapter 6, 'Verse Forms'. Yet it is important to remember that poetic form comes into being when particular combinations of prosodic device are repeated enough to be discerned as a pattern. Well-established verse forms are just the tip of the iceberg, and it is important that we remain alive to the open variety of poetic form.

Prosodic devices, along with syntactic deployment, figuration (see Chapter 7) and rhetoric – described by one critic as the 'art of word arrangements for increased impact or power of affect' (Wolosky 198) – are common to almost all forms of poetry. However, regardless of such continuity, critics frequently attempt to break poetry down into smaller subcategories. At the most general level, they tend to classify verse into three broad categories: epic, dramatic and lyric. According to *The Norton Anthology of Poetry*, an epic is a long narrative poem; a dramatic poem is a monologue or dialogue written in the voice of a character assumed by the poet; and a lyric is a fairly short poem written in the voice of a single speaker (Ferguson 2027–8). The genres of epic and dramatic poetry remind us that poems can communicate extremely directly and have a crystal-clear meaning. Not all poetry is as musical and ambiguous as Keats's. And yet, even the most didactic or plain-sense poem will have a minimum of design intended to enrich the impact of the words. If the word-sequence has been shaped and ordered it will tend to be more memorable (and if it has not been patterned, even a little, then you are not reading a poem). As such, the difference between a lyric, an epic and a dramatic poem is essentially a matter of degree. All are marked by the same basic tendency to manipulate the sound of language. A lyric will merely be marked by such design more intensely.

Nevertheless, linked to the novel's rise since the eighteenth century, poetry is now overwhelmingly associated with the lyric, and most modern poems are, indeed, relatively short. It should be noted, in passing, that many epic and dramatic poems are intensely 'lyrical'. Lyricism, in this sense, refers to a *mode*, or manner, of writing. If we say some poems are more lyrical than others, we refer to the extent to which they are expressly marked by musicality. Often, epic poets (or novelists) might amplify their lyricism intermittently, for local intensifications or effects that will enhance the overall narrative. But in full-blown lyricism, the sense of narrative is diminished and meaning becomes more entirely bound up with the phenomena of patterned structure, sensual affect, tone and imagery. And, although even this level of lyricism pervades in many modern long poems (and in some novels), such aesthetic intensity is most commonly experienced in the short poem.

Most lyric poems are non-utilitarian. Strictly speaking, they are quite useless. Conveying no straightforward intention or direct message, a lyric may seem to simply revel in itself, self-delighted. However, if it is successful, its cadence or rhythm or tone might produce some kind of aftermath or echo in your mind. If this happens, Paul Valéry writes, it has 'acquired a value' and has 'created the need to be heard again' (64). A poem does not want to be finished as soon as it has been read. In the same way that a painting wants to be looked at more than once, more than casually, a poem wants to be read again.

Lyric poetry calls for a specific mode of reading. Because its meaning is bound up with matters of tone, sensuous sound and figurative structure, the inherently open-ended nature of these phenomena entails a degree of investment from the reader, who thus needs a bit of what Keats called 'negative capability': the capability 'of being in uncertainties, Mysteries, doubts, without any irritable reaching after fact & reason' (*Selected Letters* 41–2). Meanwhile, the lyric's inclinations towards brevity and compression, its diminishments of narrative continuity, result in gaps and glitches in the information flow, which the reader is invited to fill in. When we read a poem, the answers to basic questions –Who's speaking? Who are they speaking to? What's the context? – may not be fully answerable. This puts a lot of pressure on each word and nuance; and, once again, it leaves much for the reader to infer. But it also invites our imaginative participation. A lyric poem's pronouns – I, you, he, she, we, they – are ciphers for fictive personae, but also empty spaces waiting to be inhabited by a reader.

The Scottish poet Don Paterson writes of poetry's 'calculated elisions, contractions and discontinuities' and its 'brazen lack of self-explanation'. He argues that

> this often leaves the reader with far more work to do than in a piece of prose . . . and therefore – since each individual will inevitably bring different responses as they meet the poem half-way, in their own way – poetry by its very nature has an inbuilt 'difficulty', or, if you flip it round, a non-fixity of interpretation. Crucially, this interpretative freedom also permits ownership of the poem at a much deeper level through the personalization of its meaning (Paterson, 'The Lyric Principle, Part 1' 61).

The best poems invite a multitude of differing and valid interpretations. A poem demands subjective engagement, even while, as critics, we are obliged to base our interpretative case on the hard evidence of its words.

One of our key methods of making sense of the gaps, leaps and juxtapositions of lyrics is to trace how their discrete parts, or aspects, come together. The first and second stanzas of a poem, let us say, may seem to have little to do with one another. But a convention of poetry reading is that we assume their connection is being implied, and we work to figure out what that connection might be. The idea that a lyric poem should amount to a kind of harmonic unity, or organic totality, has recently been met with some hostility by critics, yet the convention is one we cannot really do without. A lyric may well be fragmented; yet, as Jonathan Culler argues, 'even if we deny the need for a poem to be a harmonious totality we make use of the notion in reading'. He continues, 'poems which succeed as fragments or as instances of incomplete totality depend for their success on the fact that our drive towards totality enables us to recognize their gaps and discontinuities and to give them thematic value' (Culler 171).

Impertinently, a lyric poem will often go to inordinate lengths seemingly to say not very much at all. To be sure, some lyric poems will have conceptually compelling messages to convey. Yet a great many of them also return to the same old things, over and over, repeated through the ages: whether 'I love her', or 'I don't want to die', or 'doesn't the moon look weird?' Yet the recurrent, obsessive tropes and preoccupations of lyric poetry (sex and death, entropy and regeneration, the relationship of mind and body, self and other, fate and freedom) are all fundamental pressure-points of our existence, which, when probed, indicate how little we in fact know about ourselves and reality. Shelley once argued that poetry 'purges from our inward sight the film of familiarity which obscures from us the wonder of our being'. He continued, 'It creates anew the universe after it has been annihilated in our minds by the recurrence of impressions blunted by reiteration' (Shelley, 'A Defence of Poetry' 698).

Lyric poems may well present intellectual propositions, but the great majority of English-language poems have tended to displace their arguments into modulations of tone and figuration. A 'figure', in poetic terms, is a word or arrangement of words that stands for, points to, or represents further senses and meanings. Figures are thus a fundamental tool for 'renewing' our percep-tion. When we use words in their standard functional sense we are using literal language. Figurative language essentially interferes with such common sense. In this manner, figuration is integrally related to the devices of versification. Unlike prosody, figurative language is not unique to poetry, yet poetry is inclined towards figuration to such an extent that it is central to any notion of poetics. This is discussed further by Sarah Dunnigan in Chapter 7, 'Poetic Imagery', but it is worth while dwelling for a moment on some basics.

Shakespeare famously asks, 'Shall I compare thee to a summer's day?' (Sonnet 18, 1609). If he were to make such a comparison, quite obviously, the person in question would become identified with certain qualities or aspects or ideas normally associated with a summer's day. So, we might start thinking of that person as bright and sunshiny. We might associate them with flowers in bloom, or lambs leaping in green fields. The associations would generally be positive and connected with nature. Interestingly, there would be no real reason not to associate the person with hay fever, sunburn or drought. But as we read this first line of Shakespeare's sonnet such negativity does not enter our minds. There is something very immediate about the chains of association the comparison gives rise to. We are automatically guided by conventions, by powerful frameworks of analogy, of which we are not even explicitly aware. The associations seem to be intuitive and are unleashed in a momentary rush. Yet what happens is actually quite complex:

1. The qualities of a summer's day have been *transferred* onto the person.
2. There is something subjective about this transfer: as readers, we each might instinctively associate a summer's day with differing things, and so we will have slightly differing experiences when processing the comparison.
3. Despite this indeterminacy, there is also something immediate and palpable about the image. Therefore, we have something incongruously definite *and* indeterminate.
4. Multilayered chains of association have been manipulated, but in the flash of an instant. We have the surprise of recognition. Something abstract has happened, but with a sensuous result.
5. The comparison creates a paradoxical fusion. Think about the phrase 'the surprise of recognition': surprise indicates something unexpected has happened, while recognition indicates something innate has been revealed. We have strangeness and familiarity, a disturbance *and* deepening of knowledge about this person.
6. Certain qualities have been transferred, while the person and the summer's day remain as distinct phenomena. As with rhyme, identity has been established, while difference has been maintained.
7. The exchange of qualities has arisen out of experience (we associate a summer's day with good things), but has not been circumscribed by the physical limitations of empirical, immediate reality. Differing dimensions of experience and reality have converged.

In such ways, figurative imagery messes about with common sense reality. In tandem with the urge towards sound and musicality, imagery is at the heart of poetry's other great and fundamental reason to exist: indulging our inclination, perhaps our fundamental need, to make things up, to tell lies or, at least, to stretch the truth or speak of a different kind of truth than that we are used to. An empiricist or scientist might say figuration warps reality, but a poetry reader might say it expands the boundaries of reality. At the very least, if we compare a loved one with a season, or an entire aspect of nature, then the parameters of our thoughts about our loved one have been extended, and so, thus, has our love.

Many poems establish a base reality, a kind of literal foundation of imagery, and then animate this level of language with something more figurative so that our sense of reality is deepened or disturbed or enriched. Indeed, many poems make it difficult to distinguish between the figurative and the literal. What *is* real, and what is merely made up? And where is the boundary between the two?

Prosody creates a dichotomy of pattern and variation, rhyme of identity and difference, figuration of reality and imaginative freedom. It should be clear that all poetry is dramatic. Its polarities of instruction and delight call upon us to intuit counterpoints and tensions. Even the most direct poetic statement is made against the pressure of other possible statements. According to Theodor Adorno, 'what crackles in artworks is the sound of the friction of the antagonistic elements that the artworks seek to unify' (177). With such dynamism, poetic form is designed to create an experience: rather than merely saying, at second hand, 'I was anxious' or 'I was content', a poem seeks to recreate those states of mind. Because content and form are inseparable in poetry, verse may be said to absorb and reconstitute its contents. Poetic style is forged as reality and the dreamtime of lyricism constantly pressure one another. Adorno writes,

> The idea of a conservative artwork is inherently absurd. By emphatically separating themselves from the empirical world, their other, they bear witness that that world itself should be other than it is; they are the unconscious schemata of that world's transformation. (177)

NEXT STEPS

Ferguson, Margaret, Mary Jo Salter and Jon Stallworthy, eds. *The Norton Anthology of Poetry*, 5th edn. New York: W. W. Norton & Company, 2005.

Koch, Kenneth. *Making your Own Days: The Pleasures of Reading and Writing Poetry*. New York: Touchstone, 1999.

Preminger, Alex, and T. V. F. Brogan, eds. *The New Princeton Encyclopedia of Poetry and Poetics*. New Jersey: Princeton University Press, 1993.

5

Metre and Rhythm

Lee Spinks

A general introduction to the subject of metre and rhythm might usefully begin by saying that English verse is, in its most basic form, a succession of *syllables*. Some of these syllables will take a strong emphasis (they will be *stressed*, in other words); others will take a much lighter emphasis. What we call *metre* is set up by the way in which the heavily stressed syllables interact with the more lightly stressed syllables. The metrical units in which heavily and more lightly stressed syllables interact are called *feet*. There are many different types of feet that constitute the metrical patterns of the poems that you will read. You will probably know the names of some of them: the iamb (da dum), the trochee (dum da), the anapaest (da da dum), the dactyl (dum da da), the amphibrach (da dum da) and so on.

We should begin right away by making a key distinction between our two terms, *metre* and *rhythm*. By metre, I mean the definitive patterned stress–shape of a poem (the way its beats are organised into a coherent and repeatable form such as iambic pentameter – see below – or trochaic verse), while by rhythm I mean the sound or shapes that this metrical pattern creates as the poem unfolds during the time of our reading. Thus we might identify certain poetic extracts metrically (we will look at the iambic patterning of a Shakespearean sonnet, for example), but in order to gauge the sonnet's rhythm we need to look at the relation between these stresses and pauses and consider how the metre interacts with other elements of the poem's language, such as alliteration and assonance (see Chapter 4).

Derek Attridge helpfully differentiates between metre and rhythm in the following terms: he argues, '*Rhythm is a patterning of energy simultaneously produced and perceived; a series of alternations of build-up and release, movement and counter-movement, tending toward regularity but complicated by constant variations and local inflections.'* By contrast, *'Metre is an organising principle which turns the general tendency toward regularity in rhythm into a strictly-patterned regularity, that can be counted and named'* (Attridge 3, 7; his emphasis).

Now, the rhythm of the English language is fundamentally a matter of *syllables* and *stresses*. In order to speak and understand English, we need to be able to handle both of these, whether we are conscious of this or not. When operating together, syllables and stresses give spoken English the rhythmic drive that keeps it going; they give each linguistic event (each act of speech, mode of narrative or set of phrasal units) their evenness and predictability.

Let me begin to develop these remarks by defining some of the key metrical patterns or types of feet that constitute a good deal of English poetry. We might start by introducing that old classroom favourite: the iamb. The iamb is the most frequently used metrical foot in English and consists of one lightly emphasised syllable followed by a stressed syllable (da dum da dum da dum da dum da dum). We use iambs all the time in everyday speech: think of words like 'again,' 'behind,' 'return,' 'before,' 'aloud' and so on. The iamb is the metrical basis of the Shakespearean sonnet and also of blank verse (the rhetorical form utilised most famously in Shakespearean drama), which consists of five iambic feet in a poetic line. I will look at the sonnet below, but here are a couple of famous examples of different iambic feet in action. The first poem, 'To His Coy Mistress' by Andrew Marvell, affords us a lovely example of iambic tetrameter (a verse form that offers four iambic verse beats to the line):

> Had *we* but *world enough*, and *time,*
> This *coyness, Lady, were* no *crime.*
> We *would* sit *down* and *think* which *way*
> To *walk,* and *pass* our *long* love's *day.*
>   (c.1650)

And then, skipping forward 300 years, we still find this type of iambic rhythm employed in 'The Monument', by the modern American poet Elizabeth Bishop:

> A *sea* of *narrow, hori*zontal *boards*
> Lies *out* be*hind* our *lonely mon*ument
>   (1946)

Bishop's lines are written in the iambic form with which you are probably most familiar: *iambic pentameter*. The term 'iambic pentameter' refers to a line of ten syllables that is sub-divided into five separate metrical feet (the pentameter) of lightly stressed and then heavily stressed units (iambs). We can find a famous example of this form in Shakespeare's Sonnet 12:

When I do count the clock that tells the time,
And see the brave day sunk in hideous night;
When I behold the violet past prime,
And sable curls, all silvered o'er with white;
When lofty trees I see barren of leaves,
Which erst from heat did canopy the herd,
And summer's green all girded up in sheaves,
Borne on the bier with white and bristly beard,
Then of thy beauty do I question make,
That thou among the wastes of time must go,
Since sweets and beauties do themselves forsake
And die as fast as they see others grow;
And nothing 'gainst Time's scythe can make defence
Save breed, to brave him when he takes thee hence.

(1609)

Once you grow used to some of the poem's archaisms, its argument may be paraphrased as follows:

> When I listen to the clock and contemplate the inevitable passage of time, when I see flowers fading, leaves dropping from the trees and the completion of the rich harvest of summer, then my thoughts turn towards the transience of all mortal beauty, yours included, beautiful boy, since every beautiful thing must lose its lustre and die. Only one defence against time's murderous scythe remains: to reproduce the memory of your beauty in your own image by having children and giving your imprint to succeeding generations.

This last point is a regular theme of many of Shakespeare's early sonnets. What is important to our purposes is to consider how the iambic foot contributes to the meaning of the poem. Thus we might note how the heavy iambic stresses in the first line (When *I* do *count* the *clock* that *tells* the *time*) give the impression of what we would today call a speaking clock or metronome. This sense of the remorseless rhythmic progression of time is crucial to the poem's meaning: it is important to note in this regard that the verb 'tells' also plays on 'tolls' (the ringing of church bells that calls the faithful to prayer and marks the passing of the dead gives them a sense of their mortality). Time is remorselessly ticking away, beautiful boy, the speaker reminds him, and you are wasting your beauty in the pursuit of worthless self-gratification (in this sense your casual wasting of time is telling against you) and I am here both to count the passing hours of your youth and to offer you a moral account of your life up to this point.

We might develop this reading by looking at the second line ('And *see* the *brave* day *sunk* in *hide*ous *night*'), where the iambic pattern emphasises the importance of clarity of vision – all of the moral qualities that the speaker can see in the youth but which the young man steadfastly ignores. The iambic pattern also subliminally stresses the bravery or courage that it takes to turn away from a life of idle pleasure, the 'hideous' nature of moral depravity (and we should note the sly play on 'hidden' in 'hideous' that the iambic rhythm permits: much of the point of the poem is that the youth is hiding his virtues and sinking into moral destitution). Stress also falls on the 'night' or moral darkness to which such depravity leads (an image reinforced by the linger-ing undertone in 'night' of the chivalric or knightly virtues the youth may once have laid claim to but has now apparently forgotten). Skipping forward to the sonnet's final line ('Save *breed*, to *brave* him *when* he *takes* thee *hence*'), the iambic metre reaps rich dividends of meaning, permitting a heavy stress both on 'breed' (the youth must start his life again by reproducing himself and bequeathing his lineage to posterity) and 'brave' (the young man is enjoined to brave time by redeeming a moral fall with an act of pure selflessness).

A brief glance at the variety of poetic styles shows us that the iamb is a met-rical unit that can be employed in a number of different verse forms. Thus, although we speak very frequently of iambic pentameter, many poems are written in *iambic tetrameter* (four iambic beats), such as the Marvell poem, or in *iambic trimeter* (three iambic beats). If this sounds a little complicated, bear in mind that you are already very familiar with a metrical form that, instead of being composed either of iambic tetrameter or iambic trimeter, employs *both* of these units at the same time. This form is the ballad. Here is one of the most famous and beautiful examples of the ballad form: Robert Burns's classic 'A Red, Red Rose':

> O my Luve's like a red, red rose
> That's newly sprung in June;
> O my Luve's like the melodie
> That's sweetly played in tune.
>
> As fair art thou, my bonnie lass,
> So deep in luve am I;
> And I will luve thee still, my Dear
> Till a' the seas gang dry.
>
> Till a' the seas gang dry, my Dear
> And the rocks melt wi' the sun:
> I will luve thee still, my Dear,
> While the sands o' life shall run.

And fare thee weel, my only Luve!
And fare thee weel, a while!
And I will come again, my Luve,
Tho' it were ten thousand mile!

(1794)

This is written in four four-line stanzas, or quatrains, consisting of alternating tetrameter and trimeter lines. What this means is that the first and third lines of each stanza have four stressed syllables, or beats, while the second and fourth lines have three stressed syllables. Quatrains written in this manner are called ballad stanzas. The ballad, as you will know, is an old form of verse adapted for singing or recitation, originating in the days when most poetry existed in spoken rather than written form. The typical subject matter of most ballads reflects folk themes important to the ordinary person: love, courage, the authority of the spiritual and supernatural world and so on. Now, we can see the regular and emphatic effect that the dependence of many traditional ballads upon the iambic measure produces when we compare the first two lines of the Burns poem: 'As *fair* art *thou,* my *bonnie* lass / So *deep* in *luve* am *I.*' It is worth noting, though, if only to sharpen the picture a little bit, that the disposition of stresses for effect is not unvarying; sometimes the poet varies his metrical measure for local matters of emphasis. Look at the opening couplet of the poem again. Certainly we are confronted with a tetrameter followed by a trimeter, but is the rhythmic effect produced here consistently iambic? I would be inclined to read the couplet like this:

O my *Luve's* like a *red, red rose*
That's *newly sprung* in *June.*

In other words, the first line is a tetrameter – it has 4 stresses – but the doubled adjectives 'red' and 'red' and the main noun 'rose' each receive a stress, which violates iambic orthodoxy. But the poem is more powerful for its simultaneous invocation of a conventional metrical expectation in its audience and its refashioning of this metrical model for local effect (who, once she has heard it, can forget the vivacity and splendour of that 'red, red rose'?). Exactly the same refashioning of a conventional metrical model for local emphatic effect occurs in the poem's powerful last line. This line has three stresses, it is true, but where are they to be located? We *could* read it as follows: 'Tho' it *were* ten *thou*sand *mile!*' Indeed, this may well be the accepted way to read the line in tune with common iambic expectation. Yet it seems that the conjoined senses of distance and expansiveness that the poet appeals to (I will return to you, My Love, even if it meant travelling fully ten thousand miles) asks us to read the line in the following way: 'Tho' it were *ten thou*sand *mile!*' Once again a conventional metrical expectation is invoked but also gently subtilised. In such ways do great poets work.

Following this brief look at the iamb and iambic pentameter, we might glance at another metrical unit: the *trochee*. The *trochee* is the iamb reversed. It consists of one stressed and one unstressed syllable: the term comes from the Greek name for a unit of *long plus short*. You can hear examples of the trochee in everyday words like '*for*ward', '*back*ward', '*la*ter' and so on. Trochaic verse is much less common than iambic verse; indeed, it is rarely found in five-beat verse (such as the pentameter that we considered earlier). Trochaic verse is a metre that usually begins on a *beat* and usually ends on an *offbeat*. Here is an example drawn from 'Lines on the Mermaid Tavern' by John Keats:

> *Souls* of *Poets Dead* and *Gone,*
> *What* Ely*sium have* ye *known,*
> *Happy field* or *mossy ca*vern,
> *Choicer than* the *Mermaid Tavern?*
> *Have* ye *tippled drink* more *fine*
> *Than* mine *host's Ca*nary *wine?*
>   (1820)

This example, like almost all trochaic verse, is composed in trochaic tetrameter. It has, that is, four trochees in each line (which makes it a tetrameter); and each line begins with a stressed followed by an unstressed syllable: '*Souls* of *Poets dead* and *gone*'. We should note, by the way, the rhythmic effect that trochaic tetrameter produces: it has an insistent, indeed almost chant-like quality. This emphatic rhythmic effect, of course, has its limitations – it is not necessarily the subtlest metrical form you will ever encounter – which means that trochaic rhythm is seldom used.

I have so far been discussing some relatively clear and uncomplicated metrical models. But as you know, poetic life is rarely as simple as that. So let me offer you the following two poetic extracts to consider, both of which you will know well (and one of which we have already encountered in this chapter). The first is from Andrew Marvell's 'To His Coy Mistress':

> But at my back I always hear
> Time's winged chariot hurrying near;
> And yonder all before us lie
> Deserts of vast eternity.

What is the metrical pattern of those lines? The first line could be read as regularly iambic, although there is more than a hint of the trochaic in 'But at' (does 'but', in other words, take a rather strong stress?). But what happens in line 2? This line might look suspiciously trochaic to some, at least at the beginning, before metrical order is restored. The possessive 'Time's' certainly takes a heavy stress: the poem is, after all, an entreaty to the poet's beloved to seize the day, to sleep with the speaker *now,* while youth is lovely and life is vital. In fact, what we have here at the beginning of line 2, is a nice example of a *spondee*. A spondee is a duple or double foot with two stressed syllables (dum dum). Although it is rare for any two adjacent syllables to receive exactly the same stress, in spondees there is no obvious stress on one syllable rather than the other. Some examples from everyday parlance are 'pen-knife', 'ad hoc' and 'heartburn'.

We might also pause at line 2 to note a sudden deviation of rhythm: 'chariot hurrying' is not iambic but dactylic. A dactyl is composed of a stressed syllable followed by two unstressed (dum da da): *'cha/ri/ot hurr/y/ing/'*. Why, we should ask, does Marvell suddenly adopt the dactyl at this point in his poem? Because its pattering, accelerated rhythm skilfully emphasises the main ideas of the line: the sense of a chariot hurrying ever nearer while the lady continues to vacillate.

A metrical unit we have yet to encounter is the anapaest. This is a foot composed of two lightly stressed syllables followed by one strong syllable (da da dum). An excellent example of anapaestic verse can be found in Byron's 'The Destruction of Sennacherib'. Here is its opening stanza:

> The Assyrian came *down* like the *wolf* on the *fold,*
> And his *co*horts were *gleam*ing in *pur*ple and *gold;*
> And the *sheen* of their *spears* was like *stars* on the *sea,*
> When the *blue* wave rolls *nightly* on *deep* Galilee.
>
> (1815)

Here Byron's metric is attuned to his subject matter because the anapaests' momentum is redolent of action, the movement of men, the flashing of bright spears. But while the anapaests are intermittently sprightly they are also, over the long haul, somewhat mechanical: creating a trooping quality that evokes, if only subliminally, the sense of an inexorable march towards doom (the destruction of the poem's title).

To return now to the spondee: rather like the trochee, this is mostly used as a kind of metrical exception or substitution within a broadly iambic line. A powerful example of the kinds of effect that the use of spondees may engender appears in Gerard Manley Hopkins's short poem written in 1877 about the wonder and mystery of God entitled 'Pied Beauty':

> Glory be to God for dappled things –
>   For skies of couple-colour as a brinded cow;
>   For rose-moles all in stipple upon trout that swim;

> Fresh-firecoal chestnut-falls; finches' wings;
>   Landscape plotted and pieced – fold, fallow, and plough;
>   And all trades, their gear and tackle and trim.
> All things counter, original, spare, strange;
>   Whatever is fickle, freckled (who knows how?)
>   With swift, slow; sweet, sour; adazzle, dim;
> He fathers-forth whose beauty is past change:
>   Praise him.
>   (1918)

We could say a great deal about this extraordinary poem, but let me just note two things in passing. Line 6 suddenly interjects a spondee ('all trades'). Why? Because Hopkins's semantic stress (the argument of the poem) is upon the universal benevolence and inclusiveness of God's love. His potentially redemptive presence is apparent in every walk of life, and so Hopkins uses a spondee to slow down the poetic rhythm and hold our attention at the wonderful thought of the possibility of universal redemption in the locution 'all trades'. All trades: that phrase potentially includes you and me too. But such redemption is only possible if we accept God into our lives. And so the poem ends with another spondee artfully isolated in its own individual line in order to underscore this need for religious obedience: *praise him.*

Now that we are looking at examples of metrical innovation and complexity, let us consider a famous piece of blank verse:

> Now is the winter of our discontent
> Made glorious summer by this sun of York;
> And all the clouds that lour'd upon our house
> In the deep bosom of the ocean buried.
> Now are our brows bound with victorious wreaths;
> Our bruised arms hung up for monuments;
> Our stern alarums chang'd to merry meetings,
> Our dreadful marches to delightful measures.
>   (Shakespeare, *Richard III* I, i, 1–8)

The broader plot of Shakespeare's *Richard III* (1591) introduced by this soliloquy is well known: after a long civil war between the royal families of York and Lancaster, England enjoys a period of peace under King Edward IV and the victorious Yorkist faction. But Edward's younger brother Richard resents Edward's power and the happiness of those around him. Malicious, power-hungry and bitter about his physical deformity, Richard begins to aspire secretly to the throne and decides to kill anyone who stands in the way of his ambition to crown himself king. But more important to our purposes is the metrical form this soliloquy takes. We are taught in the schoolroom to read blank verse predominantly as iambic pentameter – indeed, this is our default Shakespearean setting – and we can certainly scan this soliloquy in this way after a fashion. But look again at that opening line. Where should the first stress fall? You could argue for 'is' ('Now *is* the winter of our discontent'), which would stress that this state of affairs *is* really happening. But I would argue that this opening is actually a trochee, because this soliloquy is given its energy and its drama by Richard's sense that he must *now* begin to seize the day and begin his Machiavellian manoeuvrings: '*Now* is the winter of our discontent'. As the line progresses, Shakespeare then regularises his metrics (if we were to try and read the whole line as trochaic we would have to emphasise 'the' rather than 'winter', and plainly that will not do) so that the familiar tread of the Shakespearean line resurfaces. But there has been a disturbance in time because Richard potentially *embodies* a disturbance in time. After all, he wants to redirect the narrative of English history.

We might extend our consideration here of the relationship between metre and rhythm by pausing momentarily at line 2 of Richard's soliloquy ('Made glorious summer by this sun of York'). What, we might ask, is the metrical pattern of this line? Well, it would appear at first glance to be a line of unexceptional iambic pentameter. Yet if we read the line slowly we discover that it has, in fact, eleven syllables ('glorious' takes three syllables in common parlance). However, to read the adjective in this way seriously disturbs the iambic pattern (it would mean, among other things that the first strong syllable of 'summer' would go unstressed while the important pun on 'son/sun' would be lost beneath a weak emphasis). How does Shakespeare resolve the problem of keeping the adjective without losing the metrical pattern? He *contracts* the three syllables of 'glorious' into two syllables, so that the line now reads 'Made *glor*ious *sum*mer *by* this *son* of *York*'. The underlying strength (and familiarity) of the iambic pattern regularises this disruption, but the sharp-eared among us will be aware that a small metrical trick has been played.

Let me conclude by switching registers from Shakesperean tragic drama to the language of modern popular culture. Although it may seem surprising to many of us, some of the most famous popular songs depend for their effects upon subtle modifications in the relationship between metre and rhythm. For example, the Beatles' psychedelic 1967 track 'Lucy in the Sky with Diamonds' has a strongly dactylic structure. Here is the opening stanza:

*Pic*ture your*self* in a *boat* on a *riv*er,
With *tan*gerine *trees* and *mar*malade *skies*.
*Some*body *calls* you, you *an*swer quite *slow*ly,
A *girl* with kaleidoscope *eyes*.

Cellophane flowers of *yellow* and *green,*
Towering over your *head.*
Look for the *girl* with the *sun* in her *eyes,*
And she's *gone.*

This verse example should interest us for a number of reasons. To begin with, it is pleasingly regular in its dactylic emphasis. Yet this does not mean it is metrically uncomplicated or unsubtle. By line 2 of the song we are already confronted by the kind of question that makes reading verse a profoundly individual experience: which word do we stress at which particular point? Clearly 'trees' and 'skies' have to be stressed; these nouns are crucial to the imaginary, indeed psychotropic, landscape that John Lennon is trying to evoke. But if the song is to preserve its regular dactylic structure, this would surely mean that the dactylic stress must fall on the second syllable of 'marma- lade'. Now, anyone who has heard the song sung – probably most of us – will know that Lennon's voice stresses the first syllable to give him the languorous effect produced by the long 'a' vowel. So here we learn an important lesson: the sound of a poem or song – by which I mean the range of sonic effects it is capable of producing – may create a rather different impression in our minds than the one given by the visual stressing of words on the page. This play between the ear and the eye, and between metre and rhythm, is something we should always keep in mind when attempting to determine the type of effects that a particular poem is capable of generating and the kinds of interpretative decisions in which it might involve us as readers and critics.

NEXT STEPS

Adams, Stephen. *Poetic Designs: An Introduction to Meters, Verse Forms and Figures of Speech.* Peterborough, ON: Broadview Press, 1997.

Carper, Thomas and Derek Attridge. *Meter and Meaning: An Introduction to Rhythm in Poetry.* Oxford: Routledge, 2003.

Hobsbaum, Philip. *Metre, Rhythm and Verse Form.* Oxford: Routledge, 1995.

6

Verse Forms

Penny Fielding

If rhythm and metre are the building blocks of poetry then verse forms are its architectural structure. Using some of the terms introduced in the previous two chapters by Alan Gillis and Lee Spinks, we will see how the effects and usages of metre and rhyme grow into larger shapes. 'Verse form' is quite a general category. It includes the technical combination of the length of the poem, its divisions into sections, its rhyme scheme and its metre. A sonnet, for example, has fourteen lines and it rhymes in one of a number of patterns. Some verse forms have regular patterns of lines, rhymes and stanzas but do not have special names. Some poems do not rhyme and do not have regular patterns of lines, but they still have form.

In some cases verse forms are identified not only with their metrical form or shape, but also with their subject matter, which contributes to how poems are understood to belong to certain genres. Poems in the genre of elegy, for example, commemorate a death, and pastoral poetry is usually concerned with the idyllic life of shepherds, nature or rural pursuits. Other forms are likewise identifiable by elements both of structure and of subject matter. An epic, like John Milton's *Paradise Lost* (1667/1674), has to be long, and about an important subject or event. An ode was originally a Greek classical form of celebratory performed poetry with three sections and irregular line patterns. The English ode does not always maintain these sections but is generally an elevated address to a person or thing (its subject matter) and written in an expansive, varied verse form.

Some verse forms are basically simple but very flexible and adaptable. 'Blank verse', unrhymed lines of iambic pentameter, is a good choice for a very long poem as it flows freely, the writer can include long paragraph-like sections or insert short pauses or vary the metre slightly without drawing too much attention to the rhythm. Milton's *Paradise Lost* and William Wordsworth's *The Prelude* (1799/1805/1850) are written in blank verse, and it is probably the most popular of all verse forms in the history of poetry in English. Other verse forms are very precise, involving complex combinations of lines and rhymes, and we will encounter some of them throughout this chapter.

Why should we care about describing the verse form of a poem? One reason is that form conveys the meaning of the poem, and another is that verse forms can tell us about literary history – the way poetry changes because of historical attitudes to what poetry is and does. We will consider both these aspects in this chapter.

Let us start with a very short poem from *Academic Graffiti* (1971) by W. H. Auden:

William Blake	A
Found Newton hard to take,	A
And was not enormously taken	B
With Francis Bacon.	B

This is a verse form with a name (it is a 'clerihew', named after its inventor, Edmund Clerihew Bentley) and its 'rules' are that it is a four-line single-stanza biographical poem, rhyming AABB, with the first line taken up by the name of the its subject. Like all verse forms, this one draws attention to the way the form itself delivers up the poem's meaning. The joke is that a whole biography could be carried in such short lines and in a miniaturized poem, an aspect equally important as the poem's content (which is the fact that the poet William Blake didn't think much of scientists). Clerihews work by making fun of form itself (Auden sticks in the wayward third line, which has too many syllables for comfort or ease of reading), but it is nevertheless *through* the form that we understand the poem.

Although Auden's poem is comic, the short verse form has been used for more serious purposes. Another example is the Japanese *haiku*. In Japanese, the *haiku* is measured rather differently, but when used in English it generally consists of three lines, each a separate phrase, and has a limited number of syllables. Here is a *haiku*-like poem, called 'Ts'ai Chi'h', by Ezra Pound:

> The petals fall in the fountain,
> The orange-colored rose leaves,
> Their ochre clings to the stone.
>   (1914)

The poem uses its bare, stripped-down form to be evocative rather than explanatory. Because there are no linking words ('so', 'because', 'like') the relations between the lines must form in the mind of the reader; the poem does not have an argument, but it invites us to consider ideas about nature, transience and memory. We are not told how to measure our own experiences against the image; the sparse form encourages associations rather than metaphors.

Poems can be long and short at the same time. Tennyson's *In Memoriam* (1850) is a very long poem written in very short stanzas. The poem is about Tennyson's grief for the death of a close friend and his difficulty in resolving questions about death, God, nature and science. The overarching form of *In Memoriam* follows the ebb and flow of the speaker's feelings, circling round a series of three family meetings at Christmas and moving away from the death towards the more hopeful marriage of the dead man's sister at the end of the poem. The individual stanzas, meanwhile, are short and often quite terse, as if showing how difficult it is to mourn. The ABBA rhyme scheme turns the stanzas in on themselves, almost as if the poet is hugging his grief to him:

He is not here; but far away	A
The noise of life begins again	B
And ghastly through the drizzling rain	B
On the bald street breaks the blank day.	A

The poem uses its verse form to enact two different time schemes which also evoke thought processes or states of mind: the stanzaic form enacts the difficulty of grief, and the form of the poem as a whole provides a larger perspective against which the immediate emotions that arise in the individual stanzas can be set.

Poets can also use verse form for the purposes of argument. Alexander Pope's 'Windsor Forest' (1713) is written in rhyming couplets of iambic pentameter with verse paragraphs rather than regular stanzas. Verse paragraphs are sections of a poem with irregular numbers of lines. They are determined by units of sense, like prose paragraphs, so are good for making an argument in poetry. This form gives Pope both flexibility and a fine control over the reader's attention. Particularly, it allows him to focus simultaneously on small details and large arguments. In the following extract Pope is describing the landscape of an aristocratic estate. It is a strongly political poem and Pope wants to show how the hierarchal social order is reflected in the natural world to produce a general harmony. Although the world is a highly complex structure, it is also patterned:

Here hills and vales, the woodland and the plain,
Here earth and water, seem to strive again;
Not *Chaos* like together crush'd and bruis'd,
But as the world, harmoniously confus'd:

> Where order in variety we see
> And where, tho' all things differ, all agree.
> Here waving groves a checquer'd scene display,
> And part admit, and part exclude the day;
> As some coy nymph her lover's warm address
> Nor quite indulges, nor can quite repress.

Just as the natural and social worlds are in equilibrium, so the lines of the poem are balanced to demonstrate these harmonious relations. Pope uses the devices of antithesis, where a contrast is pointed out, and parallelism, where similarities are juxtaposed, to illustrate this state of affairs. The trees form a perfect aesthetic picture poised between darkness and light, mirroring a human relationship where sexual desire and social decorum balance each other. The small pauses in the middle of each line perform this equilibrium, like a pivot, and the rhyme scheme points up the pattern. The form of the poem is rather like the regular architecture of an eighteenth-century country house, and, just as those houses were held to reflect their owners' high status and good taste, so the poem celebrates an elegant, knowledgeable, aristocratic perspective. To the common eye, the world might seem merely various and 'confused', but the educated reader can see the patterns in this variety.

Another eighteenth-century poet who made particularly good use of line length and rhyme scheme was Robert Burns. Burns uses a stanzaic form that was very popular in eighteenth-century Scottish poetry. Here are two stanzas from 'Holy Willie's Prayer' (c.1789). The speaker is a hypocritical minister of the church, puffed up with self-importance. He glories in the belief that he is one of God's chosen, elected before birth to be admitted to Heaven, so that although most other men are condemned by Adam's original crime of disobeying God, he is not:

What was I, or my generation,	A
That I should get sic exaltation?	A
I wha deserv'd most just damnation	A
For broken laws,	B
Six thousand years 'ere my creation,	A
Thro' Adam's cause.	B

So confident is Holy Willie that he will escape damnation that he goes on to confess to a series of social sins (mainly drunkenness and illicit sex), clearly rather enjoying the memory:

O Lord! yestreen, Thou kens, wi' Meg	A
Thy pardon I sincerely beg;	A
O may't ne'er be a livin' plague	A

To my dishonour,	B
An' I'll ne'er lift a lawless leg	A
Again upon her.	B

The first thing we notice is that this verse form is quite a complicated arrangement. It rhymes AAABAB, so the poet has to think of a lot of rhymes without
the poem seeming forced or laboured, and it has four lines of iambic tetrameter interspersed with two short ones of dimeter. But this highly stylised form
feels quite chatty and free-flowing. We do not, after all, speak in symmetrical
lines of iambic pentameter, but in a mixture of short and long phrases. Burns
carefully uses variations within the form to condemn Holy Willie out of his
own mouth. The first of these two stanzas uses grand, four-syllable rhymes
as Willie shows off his exalted status, but soon these are replaced in the next
quoted stanza with short end-stopped lines (that is, ones with the final stress
on the last syllable of the line). The Latinate words 'generation' and its rhymes
are replaced with common English words and a colloquial Scots name: 'leg'
rhymes with 'Meg'. Willie is being mocked by the verse form itself, as Burns
introduces the comic rhyme of 'dishonour' and 'upon her'. It is through the
structure and rhyme pattern that Burns satirises his target.

How do verse forms come into circulation? There is no single answer to
this as they serve more than one purpose. Take, for example, the quatrain (a
stanza of four lines). Many songs and poems that have an oral circulation fall
into 'ballad quatrains'. They are usually narrative poems, with 4-line stanzas
rhyming ABAB. Lines can be any length but are often tetrameters. Here are
the first two stanzas of the ballad of Sir Patrick Spens, a traditional oral poem
first recorded in 1765:

> The king sits in Dunfermline town
> Drinking the blude-reid wine:
> 'O whar will I get a guid sailor
> To sail this ship of mine?'

> Up and spak an eldern knicht,
> Sat at the king's richt knee:
> 'Sir Patrick Spens is the best sailor
> That sails upon the sea.'

The ballad form has no particular rules, but seems to have evolved through
usage, particularly through the need for people to remember it so that they can
sing or recite a version of it themselves. Ballads do not have one set version;
they can change each time they are told or printed. The form uses a basically
regular rhythm which can be interrupted to fit the words in (the seventh line
does not scan particularly well but that is not the point); it dispenses with

anything that might disrupt the forward movement of the ballad (there is no 'he said' to denote the two speakers quoted above). The ballad moves on quickly to tell its story, and it is as if any extraneous detail has been whittled away by the passage of the poem from one telling to the next.

We can contrast this with another quatrain:

> The boast of heraldry, the pomp of pow'r,
>   And all that beauty, all that wealth e'er gave,
> Awaits alike th' inevitable hour:
>   The paths of glory lead but to the grave.

This is from Thomas Gray's 'Elegy Written in a Country Churchyard' (1751), once one of the most famous and influential poems in the English language. This quatrain works not because it is a link in a moving narrative chain, but because it wants the reader to stop and think. It has one more foot in each line than the ballad. Gray slows up the rhythm in a series of graduated pauses culminating in the long break at the end of the third line emphasising the sententious last line, which we are clearly supposed to take to heart before moving on with the rest of the poem. Ballads rarely pause to tell us their abstract meaning. Gray's poem has a very different function, and assumes a different audience from that of 'Patrick Spens', and he has selected this quatrain form of ten-syllable lines (which was sometimes known as the 'heroic stanza') because of its past use by poets such as John Dryden for sonorous or stately poetry.

Of course, not all poetry is written in a verse form with a name. How can we use the idea of verse forms to talk about verse that doesn't appear to have a fixed form? This sort of poetry is sometimes called 'free verse' (originally this was a term used by some specific poets of the early twentieth century, but it is now used more generally). This sort of poetry does not have a form that pre-exists the individual poem, but many of the aspects of poetry we have seen in this chapter still apply. Here is an example:

> No wind;
> the trees merge, green with green;
> a car whirs by;
> footsteps and voices take their pitch
> in the key of dusk,
> far-off and near, subdued.
>
> Solid and square to the world
> the houses stand,
> their windows blocked with venetian blinds.
>
> Nothing will move them.

This is the second half of the poem 'Houses' by F S Flint, published in 1915 in a very influential anthology of modernist poetry called *Some Imagist Poets*. Although there are no rhymes, the poem is not divided into regular stanzas, and the line lengths vary, it is nevertheless very carefully structured. This is a poem that offers its readers an impression rather than speculation upon its subject matter in an intellectual or abstract way. Flint uses the verse form to convey a city at night: the separate lines let us hear the sounds or visualise the images coming at us from different directions. The experience is not just sensory, however, but evocative of how we apprehend city life in time and space. The description of the houses (you might spot a *haiku* embedded in here) enacts the sense of their permanence and immobility. The last line stands on its own, as if the houses are occupying the poem itself: they are just there and nothing further can be said about it.

An understanding of verse forms can help us read any specific poem, and it can also teach us about the history of poetry in general. Nowadays, many people have the idea that poetry comes from a moment of inspiration and flows spontaneously from the poet's imagination, although he or she may then consciously craft the verse. But until the late eighteenth century this would have been quite a strange notion. Poetry was a social form that preceded the inspiration of any specific poet. Rather than shaping the poem around an initial creative impulse, poets would choose a verse form. Originality was not especially a virtue, and imitation was seen as a mark of sophistication, respect for the past and a shared cultural understanding. Poetry was primarily a public form, not a private meditation. We should remember that these were highly stratified societies. Not everyone could read, and among those who could, only a very few could afford to buy books of poetry. Such people would most likely have had a Classical education and would know what to expect: forms such as the elegy or the ode were often deliberate imitations of Classical models. A poem was judged on the way it employed a pre-existing form.

Verse forms come into use not only through the social expectations of readers but also for more nakedly economic reasons. In a very simple sense, this may dictate whether a poem is long or short. The later eighteenth century saw the rise of poetry published in magazines and anthologies as well as collections by a single author. These were cheaper forms aimed at an expanding literary market. A bookseller would be unlikely to sell more than one edition of a very long poem like Milton's *Paradise Lost* to a single customer, but that customer might well be persuaded to buy a short poem first in an anthology and then in a collection by the author. Today there is a very small market for poetry, and hardly any for very long poems, apart from translations of older poems by very famous (and thus marketable) poets – an example of this is Seamus Heaney's translation into modern English of the Anglo-Saxon poem *Beowulf*.

Let us see how some of these ideas come together in what is perhaps the best known and most persistent of all short poetic forms in English, (although it was originally borrowed from Italian in the sixteenth century): the sonnet. A sonnet, as we saw earlier, is a poem of fourteen lines, traditionally of iambic pentameter. The first eight lines are called the 'octave' and the second three the 'sestet'. There is generally (though not always) a change of tone or meaning between the octave and the sestet, and this is sometimes called by its original Italian name, the 'volta' (meaning 'jump'). Within these boundaries the sonnet has been an exceptionally flexible form. Different units can form within the sonnet (the octave might be made up of two quatrains) that invite the reader to make comparisons, see how ideas are extended or emotions qualified. Reading a sonnet is like listening to music as we recognise how ideas, motifs and variations combine, echo and change within the work. Shakespeare introduced a variant to the sonnet's rhyme scheme, by changing the last two lines to a rhyming couplet, so that the Shakespearean sonnet rhymes ABABCDCD EFEFGG. That last rhyming couplet gives Shakespeare the chance to make a comment on the rest of the poem or change the line of argument one more time. Sonnet 73, for example, spends the first twelve lines on a series of variations of related metaphors that describe the speaker's sense of his own impending death: the poet is like a tree in winter or a fire going out. The last lines are

> This thou perceivs't, which makes thy love more strong,
> To love that well, which though must leave ere long.
> (1609)

Suddenly the poem is not about the speaker's frailty, but about his confidence that the closeness of death will strengthen his lover's affections for him. The rhymed line endings 'more strong' and 'ere long' emphasise the contrast between the warmth of their love and its shortness.

The history of the sonnet also tells us about how poetry is shaped and formed by social expectations and practices. Because the sonnet is quite difficult to get right, it flourished in sixteenth-century court culture as it was an urbane, stylish form that could easily be circulated in manuscript among a coterie of friends. Its highly sophisticated use of rhythm and metre suited an area where courtly poets wanted to show off both their ingenuity in writing poetry and the sophisticated nature of their relationships. The sonnet is both a public form, with an easily recognisable structure, and one which became associated with the expression of intense feelings and emotions. It fell out of favour in the late seventeenth century, but started to come back into popularity at the end of the eighteenth century, when it was taken up by women writers. Poets such as Anna Seward and Charlotte Smith chose to write sonnets because of the form's history of intellectual ingenuity and personal expression. For women writers the sonnet was an ideal form: it was short, so could be included in the new vogue for anthologies and collections, it allowed them to exploit the 'feminine' poetic virtues of feeling and sensibility, but it was also hard to write and allowed women to show the intellectual dexterity and linguistic skill that was thought to be a male specialisation.

I will end with a poem that shows how the sonnet works as a verse form, but also one that emphasises how no particular verse form need constrain or limit poetry. This is a sonnet by Wordsworth:

Surprised by joy – impatient as the Wind	A
I turned to share the transport – Oh! with whom	B
But Thee, deep buried in the silent tomb,	B
That spot which no vicissitude can find?	A
Love, faithful love, recalled thee to my mind –	A
But how could I forget thee? Through what power,	C
Even for the least division of an hour,	C
Have I been so beguiled as to be blind	A
To my most grievous loss! – That thought's return	D
Was the worst pang that sorrow ever bore,	E
Save one, one only, when I stood forlorn,	D
Knowing my heart's best treasure was no more;	E
That neither present time, nor years unborn	D
Could to my sight that heavenly face restore.	E

(1815)

The speaker is mourning the loss of someone he loves (Wordsworth later identified his daughter who died as a child). But more than this, the poem takes place at a time where he momentarily forgets that she is dead and he is torn between his grief at her loss and self-recrimination at his forgetfulness. So the poem not only describes a relationship and a state of mind but also looks at the way time and memory work. Wordsworth is trapped in a kind of tortured present, which he recognises at the end of the poem: the past reminds him of what he has lost and the future promises no consolation. The sonnet moves towards this recognition by enacting this sense of the pain of living in the present. It is a sonnet, and uses repetition and variation, but it also conveys a state of mind by breaking up the verse form. Instead of a clear volta between the octave and sestet, the poem keeps breaking in mid-line as another thought comes to the speaker, as if he is trapped in recurring grief. Just when it seems to be as bad as it can get ('That thought's return'), it gets worse. Despite its regular verse form, the poem breaks away from symmetry. Although the poem rhymes ABBA ACCA DEDEDE 'return' doesn't really rhyme with the other D endings, marking out the way Wordsworth feels he cannot accommodate himself to living in the present, accepting his past grief, or contemplating the future – his thoughts return to jar him out of the possibility of resolution through mourning. Although it is generally written in iambic pentameter, the metre too is affected by the Wordsworth's evocation of the relation of time and grief. In line 9, following the break, 'that thought's' is a spondee, further slowed up by the repeated 't' that ends one word and begins the next. It is physically tricky to say, emphasising the way the speaker castigates himself, dwelling on his failure to remember. 'Surprised by Joy' shows us how it is sometimes the way a poet *mis*uses a verse form that makes verse forms most useful.

NEXT STEPS

Furniss, Tom and Michael Bath. *Reading Poetry: An Introduction*, 2nd edn. Harlow: Pearson, 2007.

Fussell, Paul. *Poetic Meter and Poetic Form*, rev. edn. New York: McGraw-Hill, 1979.

Strand, Mark and Eavan Boland. *The Making of a Poem: A Norton Anthology of Poetic Forms*, New York: W. W. Norton & Company, 2000.

7

Poetic Imagery

Sarah M. Dunnigan

A wayle whit as whalles bon,	*beautiful woman / whale's*
A grein in golde that goodly shon,	*rosary bead / beautifully*
A tortle that min herte is on,	*turtle-dove*
In tounes, trewe . . .	*in the world / alive*

Why might female beauty be likened to a whale bone? This is the extraordinary image presented in the opening of this anonymous lyric poem from the fifteenth century. It seems strange to measure human beauty by a thing no longer living, and of gigantic proportion. The image stands out oddly in a poem in which the speaker is clearly flattering his beloved; after all, she is then compared to the perfection of a brightly inset rosary bead and to a turtle dove, a bird which symbolises love. In fact, the whale bone image was not uncommon in medieval love poetry: suggestive of rarity, whiteness and sharp clarity it could be used to mirror ideas about the ideal beauty of a woman's skin. Though we, as contemporary readers, might puzzle at its incongruity, we can still recognise its effectiveness as it forces two different images into unlikely juxtaposition. An arresting opening image pulls us into the poem's world, making us more keenly alive to further worlds of possible meanings which even the smallest of lyric poems contains.

Poetry is in part an act of perception, and a renewal, or heightening, of our ordinary perceptual powers at that. Reading, or hearing, a poem engages our responsiveness on many different levels because a poem itself is created out of different aspects – structural, grammatical, rhythmic, metrical, verbal, visual – which together make a composite whole. To focus on imagery, therefore, is to concentrate on just one aspect of poetry's multidimensional power. In Robert

Burns's poem, 'To a Louse, on Seeing one on a Lady's Bonnet at Church'
(1785), the image of the 'ugly, creepan, blastet wonner' as it 'sprawl[s]' and
'sprattle[s]' its way to the 'very tapmost, towrin height / O' Miss's bonnet'
is vital to the poem's visceral comic edge. Yet it is not the sole source of its
ironic wit, which comes from Burns's use of voice and perspective as well as
the sound textures and patterning that evoke the creature's alarming ascent.
Poetry need not be imagistic, or contain any images, still to be poetic; nor
is imagery, of course, confined to the poetic genres. Yet perhaps because
of poetry's distinctive formal and structural composition, imagery is more
intensely heightened and highlighted, its sensory impact more acute.

In a famous essay of 1917, the Russian formalist critic, Victor Shklovsky,
argued that the key to poetic language was its power of 'defamiliarisation'. He
wrote,

> Art exists that one may recover the sensation of life, to make the stone
> *stony* . . . The technique of art is to make objects 'unfamiliar', to make
> forms difficult, to increase the difficulty and length of perception because
> the process of perception is an aesthetic end in itself (Shklovsky 18–19).

'Rain Towards Morning' (1955) by Elizabeth Bishop can be said to use
'defamiliarising' imagery in Shklovsky's sense, challenging our conventional
perceptual understanding of rain:

> The great light cage has broken up in the air,
> freeing, I think, about a million birds
> whose wild ascending shadows will not be back,
> and all the wires come falling down.

Bishop's poem uses imagery in the first and basic sense that the term can be
understood: as a pictorial or visual representation in words of an external phenomenon. But it is worth noting how the perception of images, or of 'seeing
things', in poetry is different from seeing images in the medium of visual art.
When we look at a painting, for example, we experience its image almost
instantaneously. Even though we might return to it, noticing qualities which
were not at first observed, the experience of viewing that piece of art is different to how we experience the imagistic elements of poetry. A single image
might be immediately striking, but the power of a particular image unfolds
'across' the space of the text and the duration of our reading of it, accruing
meaning from the poem's other aspects (whether auditory or grammatical, for
example).

Still, 'seeing art' and 'seeing poetry' are not wholly different processes:
a painting and a poem both have an effect upon their viewer and reader.
The dynamic interaction between poem and reader in part springs from the

evocative powers of imagery: the possibility of the poem's emotional, intellectual and imaginative associations. For the Irish poet W. B. Yeats, this was exactly the strength of Burns's image from 'Open the Door to Me, Oh' (1793):

> The wan moon sets behind the white wave,
>> And time is setting with me, Oh . . .

Yeats argued that

> these lines are perfectly symbolical. Take from them the whiteness of the moon and of the wave, whose relation to the setting Time is too subtle for the intellect, and you take from them their beauty. But, when all are together, moon and wave and whiteness and setting Time and the last melancholy cry, they evoke an emotion which cannot be evoked by any other arrangement of colours and sounds and forms. (155–6).

It is worth remembering that while we tend to think of imagery as an almost essential component of poetry, it has not always been considered in this way. At least in terms of critical or theoretical approaches to imagery, views have been divided across the centuries regarding its importance or necessity. This is because imagery is not simply visual representation but is also part of figurative language, able to sustain or comprise figures of speech such as the following:

> My heart opens like a cactus flower

In this simile from Stevie Smith's 'Le Désert de l'Amour' (1938), the grounds of the comparison are overt, introduced through the word 'like' (similes also use the word 'as', as in 'cold as snow'). Metaphor, however, is perhaps poetry's central figure of comparison (and comparison is implicitly at the heart of all figurative language). In metaphor, the ground of likeness or association between two, often disparate, things is compressed but suggestive enough to allow a process of transference, or the mapping across of ideas and associations, to occur, as in this example from Emily Dickinson:

> 'Hope' is the thing with feathers –
> That perches in the soul –
>> (1891)

Smith's simile and Dickinson's metaphor imbue their respective poems with extra layers of conceptual as well as visual weight. In the Renaissance period, such figures of speech were viewed as important ornamentation, rhetorical devices which embellished the work of a poet, who was conceived as an artificer or a maker, in pursuit of the ideal poetic goal of imitation. George Puttenham, for example, was full of praise, in 1589, for figures and figuratiue speeches, which be the flowers, as it were, and coulours that a Poet setteth vpon his language of arte, as the embroderer doth his stone and perle or passements of gold vpon the stuffe of a Princely garment. (175)

A century later, when aesthetic ideals of clarity and plainness were desired more, figurative language came under intellectual and artistic attack.

Imagery, as a branch of figurative language, has therefore fallen in, out of, and then back into poetic fashion again. As well as this historic variance, might there also be a generic one? We might also ask whether certain genres or literary modes have shaped particular kinds of imagery. Is one literary mode more imagistic than another by the particularity of its subject matter? Are certain subjects necessarily more imagistic than others? In the Renaissance, the subject of erotic love, for example, generated its own body of poetic images, creating a systematic way of codifying, categorising or speaking about love in externalised and concrete ways. The tangibility of this imagery acted as a means of counteracting the intangibility of love as an abstraction or experience; yet this made it ripe for subversion. Shakespeare's sonnet sequence, for example, seeks to discover new ways of imagining love. As we saw in the medieval lyric fragment, one way of achieving that is to represent the beloved's beauty imagistically: to figure that beauty by means of an external comparison, no matter how strange (as if only by means of something else, rather than the beauty as it *is*, can it properly be captured).

One of Shakespeare's most famous sonnets describes the lady's beauty, but so skilfully and playfully that every image of beauty it sets up is immediately refuted:

> My mistress' eyes are nothing like the sun;
> Coral is far more red than her lips' red;
> If snow be white, why then her breasts are dun;
> If hairs be wires, black wires grow on her head.
> I have seen roses damasked, red and white,
> But no such roses see I in her cheeks;
> And in some perfumes is there more delight
> Than in the breath that from my mistress reeks.
> I love to hear her speak, yet well I know
> That music hath a far more pleasing sound;
> I grant I never saw a goddess go,
> My mistress, when she walks, treads on the ground;
> And yet, by heaven, I think my love as rare
> As any she belied with false compare.
>
> (Sonnet 130, 1609)

Addressed to a dark-haired beloved, the sonnet mocks conventional Renaissance ideas of female beauty; it demythologises the mythology of beauty through casting an entire literary convention of poetic imagery in ironic light. This convention had sprung from the medieval Italian poet Petrarch and his sequence of 366 poems, the *Rime sparse*, written to his beloved Laura. This fourteenth-century collection offered subsequent generations of love poets across Europe a rhetorical and conceptual model of love: a means of imagining desire, not just as an emotional or psychological experience, but of the beloved herself as a verbal and imagistic concept: 'Her head was fine gold, her face warm snow, ebony her eyebrows, and her eyes two stars whence Love never bent his bow in vain' (Sonnet 157).

This imagistic externalisation of beauty became a staple feature of Renaissance love poetry, as in this example from Sidney's *Astrophil and Stella* (1591) where a visual metaphor is extended:

> Queen Virtue's court, which some call Stella's face,
>> Prepared by Nature's chiefest furniture,
>> Hath his front built of alabaster pure;
> Gold is the covering of that stately place.
> The door, by which sometimes comes forth her grace,
>> Red porphyr is, which lock of pearl makes sure;
>> Whose porches rich (which name of 'cheeks' endure)
> Marble, mixed red and white, do interlace.
>> The windows now, through which this heavenly guest
> Looks o'er the world, and can find nothing such
> Which dare claim from those lights the name of 'best',
> Of touch they are that without touch doth touch,
>> Which Cupid's self, from Beauty's mine did draw:
>> Of touch they are, and, poor I am their straw.

Most of Stella's facial features are not named, but the extended visual metaphor acquires a currency of its own: an alabaster and gold palace (white skin and fair hair); red porphyry doors (her lips); red and white porches (cheeks); windows (eyes). An elaborate process of substitution occurs, and the chief metaphor being used of a building or edifice is apt: each constituent image belongs to the same imagistic domain but the sonnet's overall visual power is derived from the imagery's cumulative, accretive strength.

Sidney's sustained multiple images comprise a conceit; in other words, an elaborate figurative device. Petrarchan imagery may seem oddly contrived to us, but it enabled poets to display their own ingenuity in crafting and shaping such conceits and extended metaphors; these are poems about art as well as love and beauty. Sidney's poem derives images from established Renaissance ideas about female beauty and builds them in striking permutation; it results in the creation of one startling new conceit. Shakespeare's sonnet is even more audacious, suggesting how standards of beauty are based on arbitrary judgements and fashionability (his dark-haired lady is as beautiful as any golden-haired Laura). It heightens the Petrarchan idea of love's transformative power: it alters vision so that nothing (even a forehead) is what it seems. As much as being about the variability of beauty, the sonnet is about the variability of perception: if we see each beauty differently then this suggests the subjective nature by which we view the world. And this implication that imagery might differently impinge on different individuals raises interesting questions for our role as readers of, or respondents to, poetic images.

If each of us is subject to elements of individuality or singularity in our perceptions, can we agree on the meaning of an image? It might be helpful to distinguish an image from a symbol. The former (as in Dickinson's 'feathered hope') might be highly specific to a particular poem or poet (in that sense unique) while the latter may be an image or figure which has gathered meaning through repeated use. This meaning becomes fixed, universal or archetypal: for example, we readily interpret a white dove as a symbol of peace. There are even dictionaries to sum up such established meanings such as Michael Ferber's *Dictionary of Literary Symbols*, which offers illustrations and explications of such diverse things as swans, roses, serpents, stars and dogs. He lists the possible significations of a nightingale, for example, as springtime, mourning, song, the soul and love but also comments:

> This is not to say that whenever a nightingale appears in a poem it must mean all the things it ever meant, or that it must allude to all the previous appearances of nightingales. What Freud said about cigars is sometimes true of literary symbols: sometimes a nightingale is just a nightingale. (Ferber 5)

Perhaps it is safest to say that the 'meaningfulness' of poetic imagery cannot be fully determined. The possible tension between the 'fixity' of symbolism and the 'openness' of imagery is illustrated by this well-known lyric by William Blake, 'A Poison Tree' (1794):

> I was angry with my friend;
> I told my wrath, my wrath did end.
> I was angry with my foe:
> I told it not, my wrath did grow.
>
> And I waterd it in fears,
> Night & morning with my tears:

And I sunned it with my smiles,
And with soft deceitful wiles.

And it grew both day and night,
Till it bore an apple bright.
And my foe beheld it shine,
And he knew that it was mine.

And into my garden stole
When the night had veild the pole;
In the morning glad I see;
My foe outstretchd beneath the tree.

The tree and apple imagery might readily evoke in our minds the tree of knowledge and the fruit of temptation in the biblical garden of Eden, suggesting that it draws on Christian religious symbolism, and may therefore be about sin and guilt. Yet Blake's poem remains cryptic, suggesting that the correspondence between the symbols and their recognisably universal or archetypal meaning may not be absolute. Why, for example, is the apple the fruit of both the speaker's 'smiles' and 'wiles'? Clarity of meaning is also complicated by the deceptively riddle-like, lilting, rhythmic nature of the poem. In addition, the use of the first-person lyric voice suggests a 'privileged' perspective: a tantalising assumption of knowledge (echoed in the unexplained knowledge of the speaker's enemy in line 12) that makes readers question their own perceptions about the strange events unfolded in the poem.

Since Blake's lyric suggests that even what we might regard as the 'straightforwardly' archetypal meaning of an image (the apple standing for the biblical fruit of the forbidden tree) may be challenged by strategies of poetic strangeness, perhaps all that we can agree is that every image has a number of associative or connotative powers which we can come readily to identify and recognise. We can also observe that certain images recur in the work of particular poets (so that we can speak about a symbolic language, for example, peculiar to W. B. Yeats) and in particular poetic genres or modes. An interesting example of such imagistic recurrence is found in traditional ballads. A ballad can be defined as an oral verse narrative, usually sung, which, in many ways, resembles other 'symbolic stories' such as fairy tales, myth and fable. In Scottish balladry, the particular frequency or clustering of certain visual images defined by colour can be observed: green, gold, red, 'milk-white'. For example: 'Now she has kilted her robes of green'; 'But quickly run to the milk-white steed'; 'An' she washed the reed blude frae his wounds'; 'Wi ae lock o his gowden hair' (Lyle 1994). Each colour has its own associative and connotative meaning within the ballad world: green readily signifies nature, sexuality, or the fairy world, for example. The meaning of certain ballad images derives from their repeated patterning (mnemonic, or memorable, devices aid the storyteller or singer). Their associative meanings are anticipated or understood but there is also scope for what Robert Frost calls 'a meaning . . . unfolded by surprise' (133). We can see an example of this in the otherworldly ballad 'Thomas the Rhymer' (late medieval in origin, first published in 1802), in which the fateful journey on which Thomas is taken to Elfland is described in arrestingly visual terms:

> O they rade on, and farthar on,
>   And they waded thro rivers aboon the knee,
> And they saw neither sun nor moon,
>   But they heard the roaring of the sea.
>
> It was mirk mirk night, and there was nae stern light,
>   And they waded thro red blude to the knee;
> For a' the blude that's shed on earth
>   Rins thro the springs o that countrie.

The image of their crossing through rivers of red blood is startling, 'surprising' the readers (or, more appropriately in the ballad context, its listeners) into discovering other meanings for the significance of Thomas's otherworldly journey: might the blood even have a Christian meaning (evoking Christ's sacrifice)? Might 'that countrie' (Fairyland?) be here portrayed as a kind of Purgatory (a place of temporary suffering where dying souls expiate, or make amends for, their sins)? Such meanings are possible because the ballad interweaves language and images which are both recognisably pagan and Christian.

We have been exploring images which are predominantly visual in nature. Earlier, one of Blake's lyrics was discussed as an example of a sharply focussed but nonetheless ambivalent use of symbol. Blake himself was an engraver, and the poetry of his *Songs of Innocence and Experience* was accompanied by his etchings, making it a dually layered text. The obviously visual nature of imagery has been pursued in other ways by poets, even to the point at which the poem itself becomes a visual sign or emblem: Renaissance poets were especially keen on this visual conceit (see, for example, George Herbert's poem, 'Easter Wings', first published in1633); and modern 'concrete poetry' makes the form and shape of the poem an image in itself, as in 'Siesta of a Hungarian Snake' (1968) by Edwin Morgan:

s sz sz SZ sz SZ sz ZS zs ZS zs zs z

Such poetry elicits a different kind of perceptual response in the reader. But in other ways visual imagery can appeal to our other senses. The 'sensoriness' of poetry – the fact that imagery might be *experienced* – is richly illustrated by Gerard Manley Hopkins's poetry, as in this extract from 'The Starlight Night' (1877, published 1918):

> Look at the stars! look, look up at the skies!
>   O look at all the fire-folk sitting in the air!
>   The bright boroughs, the circle-citadels there!
> Down in dim woods the diamond delves! the elves'-eyes!
> The grey lawns cold where gold, where quickgold lies!
>   Wind-beat whitebeam! airy abeles set on a flare!   *white poplar trees*
> Flake-doves sent floating forth at a farmyard scare! –
> Ah well! It is all a purchase, all is a prize.

This is an urgent, ecstatic vision, expanding the reader's perceptual eye so as to involve a challenge to the idea of space (assembled pinpoints of stars look like 'citadels'). These are capacious and spacious worlds which are both recognisably familiar, and yet made strange by Hopkins's word-coinages: 'elves'-eyes' and 'quickgold' (like quicksilver) evoke the sky's alchemical beauty. Whiteness binds together the closing visual emblems. Imagistic and auditory richness here creates synaesthesia, or a fusion of different sense impressions so that a single image – a starlit night – burgeons into other things through Hopkins's associative, expansive vision.

In 1918, Ezra Pound famously articulated his vision of the contemporary poetic movement known as 'Imagism' of which he, and other writers such as Amy Lowell, 'H. D.' and others, were part. He wrote,

> An 'Image' is that which presents an intellectual and emotional complex in an instant of time . . . It is the presentation of such a 'complex' instantaneously which gives that sense of sudden liberation; that sense of freedom from time limits and space limits; that sense of sudden growth (Pound 4).

We will look briefly at two poems which might seem to have little in common: 'Oread' by H. D. (Hilda Doolittle), from 1914, and 'Now goth sonne under wod', so that we end with an anonymous medieval lyric just as we began with one. But both are short, strangely elliptical poems which exemplify the imagery's evocative powers at their sharpest and most condensed. First, here is H. D.'s poem:

> Whirl up, sea –
> Whirl your pointed pines,
> Splash your great pines
> On our rocks,

> Hurl your green over us,
> Cover us with your pools of fir.

This is an order, a series of incantatory imperatives spoken, we infer by the lyric's title, in the voice of one of the Oreads, or mountain nymphs, of classical Greek myth. Speaking to the sea, we visualise her at the shore or mountain's edge, though all borders or boundaries are unclear. But what else do we visualise? Through the nymph's 'eye', or consciousness, we see not a sea which looks like a forest but one which is a stormy sea-forest (is it a forest made out of the sea, or a sea of forests?). A single image is forced upon us, like the 'pointed pines', through the fusion of two images; a kind of metamorphosis has taken place. It is difficult, and perhaps not even necessary, to know fully what H. D.'s image *means*: meaning, here, may be as fluid as her watery image. Imagists strived for 'precision' but the beauty of their images often lies in their imprecise meaningfulness. However, some kind of transaction does occur between image and reader, for we might wonder why she desires the sea/forest to 'cover' (drown?) 'us'. Her shared vision evokes her creative powers: whether she sees a literal, or imagined, sea/forest is unknown, but it suggests a creativity of vision, a creating consciousness, which shapes an illusion that may or may not be real. And poetry, especially when it has imagery, is an illusionistic art where 'seeing things' is possible.

We can see Pound's 'sense of sudden growth' from an image in this final example:

> Now goth sonne under wod: *woods*
> Me reweth, Marye, thy faire rode.   *I pity / face*
> Now goth sonne under tree:
> Me reweth, Marye, thy sone and thee.   *I pity*

This is a religious lyric from the thirteenth century and is known as a Passion poem (it addresses the subject of Christ's suffering in his final days). The poet (who is unknown) reaches for images by which to express what might be considered 'ineffable': something beyond visual and verbal representation. In line 1, we have the images of sun and wood, and in line 3 we have the images of sun and tree (in line 2, there is an act of perception as the speaker looks at the face of Mary, Christ's mother). These images are natural, simple, organic; we watch the sun slip behind the trees. But the image contains a further layer of meaning, or a verbal pun: 'wod' might refer not simply to the wood or a single 'tree' but to the wooden structure of Christ's cross; 'sonne' may be a pun on the word' son' – meaning Christ, the Son of God and son of Mary – so that the image of the setting sun encompasses the dying Christ as well. The poem, like H. D.'s, presents these possible meanings subtly and indirectly, through the delicate interplay of visual and verbal associations. A contemporary critic of H. D.'s poetry called it 'a kind of "accurate mystery"'; this could be said of the medieval 'image poem' too where the 'ultimate effect . . . is mysterious and only to be comprehended by the imagination' (Hughes 119–20).

In conclusion, we have seen how imagery was vital to the popularity and then subversion of an entire poetic style and movement; how it might involve figurative devices such as metaphor; how it might influence and interact with other 'sensory' aspects of poetry; and how its 'exteriority' (as in objects, trees, landscapes and so on) can act as a bridge to the 'interior' emotional and intellectual worlds of the poems which we have explored. Imagery, of course, remains only one dimension of a poem, and of a poem that constitutes only one dimension of a writer's work which itself has many dimensions – cultural, political and social in scope as well. Hopefully, though, the chapter has suggested ways in which imagery is a powerful poetic device, and why it prompted Mina Loy to call poetry 'prose bewitched' – 'a music made of visual thoughts' (157).

NEXT STEPS

Cook, Jon, ed. *Poetry in Theory: An Anthology 1900–2000,* Oxford: Blackwell, 2004.
Hawkes, Terence. *Metaphor,* London: Methuen & Co Ltd, 1972.
Lewis, C. Day. *The Poetic Image,* London: Jonathan Cape, 1947.

8

Poetry and History

Greg Walker

The historical contexts of literary works have regularly interested critics and readers, though the extent and nature of their interest has varied over the years. Some ways of understanding a text's relationship to its own times are long-established: contributing to a 'traditional' historicism which studies an author's life, career and intellectual milieu; the nature of contemporary language use; or the ways in which writing and publishing were organised in a particular period. More recently, criticism has moved on to consider other factors too, concentrating further on matters of race, gender and class, drawing into the debate the kind of understanding offered by postcolonial criticism, feminism and Queer Theory (see Chapters 9 and 21). This more recent criticism, often termed 'New Historicism', has insisted that a text's relations with the period of its creation are reciprocal. The history is not just a 'background' to the text, but is in dialogue with it. Literary texts are informed by, but can also contribute to or amend, dominant forces or hierarchies structuring a culture and shaping all its expressive modes. In particular, in this way of thinking, 'history' is no longer an altogether neutral or stable context. It is instead a kind of 'text' in itself. History is partly written or understood for us through the literary texts we read, but is also, reciprocally, a shaping force within the writing of those texts themselves – often inscribed subtly and inconspicuously within them, and recoverable only from close analysis of the language and rhetoric they use.

This chapter will illustrate analysis of this kind, as well as some of the more traditional forms of historicist criticism, in relation particularly to a period not necessarily widely familiar to readers or students – the 'early modern' period of the sixteenth and seventeenth centuries. It is worth beginning, though, by recognising that recent re-emphases on historical reading have made 'always historicise' a kind of general rallying cry heard in all sorts of ways across the field of literary study. It has led to some powerful re-readings of canonical texts, and to the realization that texts and genres once dismissed by scholars as unimportant were actually extraordinarily powerful at the time they were created. Historicist critics have, for example, been increasingly sensitive not only to what texts say, but also to what they are conspicuously *not* saying, to those topics on which a poem is conspicuously, perhaps sus-piciously, silent. How is it, for example, that Geoffrey Chaucer could write thousands of lines of verse on social issues in his *House of Fame* (1378–80) or *The Canterbury Tales* (1388–1400) and not reflect upon the series of pro-found political crises that shook England in the wake of the Peasant's Revolt of 1381, in which several of his friends and associates lost their lives? Does his apparent avoidance of these events (save for a brief, flippant allusion to the peasants' rising in his *Nuns' Priest's Tale*), while fellow poets John Gower and William Langland seemed obsessed with them, suggest that he was indif-ferent to the issues they raised? Or was he too cowed by fear or ambition to voice his views?

Recent criticism has re-examined the poet's canon with such questions in mind, and discovered it to be shot through with sophisticated discussions of popular social forms, tyrannical government and religious and political self-determination. Chaucer, it seems, was an intensely political poet after all, but expressed his political concerns in unexpected ways, exploring issues prompted by the crises of national government more often through discus-sions of personal relationships, sexual difference or marital dysfunction than through more direct means. So, for example, he could examine the dangers of tyrannical government by discussing relationships between husbands and wives in his *Clerk's Tale* and *Tale of Melibee*. But to see this, we need first to be aware of the political and social environment in which he wrote. To notice a poet's apparent silence on an issue, to feel its absence in a work which seems to invite its discussion, we need to know that the issue was there in the first place, clamouring for attention at the edge of vision, and this requires a sense of historical context.

Historicist criticism has also been invaluable in revealing why certain seem-ingly conventional genres proved popular at particular moments in history. Panegyric, for example, the praise poetry addressed to political leaders, seems at first glance to be a trite exercise in formulaic sycophancy, and yet it was hugely popular in the late-medieval and Renaissance periods (roughly 1350–1650). Why? Looking only at the verses themselves offers little clue, as they all seem remarkably similar. But re-reading them in the light of the classical models from which these authors borrowed (such as the works of

the Roman satirist Horace, in the first century BCE) suggests they were one
of the few effective means by which early-modern writers could advise and
even criticise their rulers without risking punishment. By showing a prince
a seemingly flattering representation of himself as a truly virtuous sovereign,
an author implicitly reminded him of how far short of that ideal he might be,
and so tacitly encouraged him to reform. Thus, as the most influential humanist scholar of the early sixteenth century, the Dutchman Desiderius Erasmus,
wrote, 'no other way of correcting a prince is as efficacious as offering the
pattern of a truly good prince under the guise of flattery to them' (vol 2: 81).
Once again, by looking at texts in the light of the culture which produced
them, we see them afresh, and can sense something of the power and urgency
they contained for those who wrote and first read them.

The value of 'always historicising' differs from poem to poem, of course.
Not every historical event is a useful 'context' for every contemporary text.
An indication of how recourse to history might actually obscure a text is provided by the poet and critic Tom Paulin's surely mischievous assertion that
reading Keats's ode 'To Autumn' (1820) with a careful eye for contemporary
events might reveal a revolutionary subtext – a set of meanings implied, but
not directly stated – to its opening lines.

> Season of mists and mellow fruitfulness,
> Close bosom-friend of the maturing sun,
> Conspiring with him how to load and bless
> With fruit the vines that round thatch-eves run;
> To bend with apples the moss'd cottage trees,
> And fill all fruit with ripeness to the core . . .

Although Keats himself cited viewing a field of autumnal stubble as his inspiration, Paulin suggests that what the poem is really about, when looked at
historically, is not seasonal change but the 'Peterloo Massacre', the violent
suppression of a working class rally in Manchester in 1819, the year in which
Keats wrote the poem. In the light of Peterloo, he suggests, there is surely
a 'subtle anxiety and discomfort behind' the poem's 'apparently attractive
images'. Does not 'mists' hint at political subterfuge, and 'conspiring' echo
'the Manchester *Conspiracy*', as the right-wing press dubbed the rally? By the
time we reach the claim that 'The *sun run* combination brings *gun* almost to
mind, and those loaded apple trees make me uneasy', we might suspect a
playful glint in the critic's eye, suggesting that his real point is that historicism can be taken too far. Chapter 7 suggested that 'sometimes a nightingale
is just a nightingale': sometimes a line about fruit really is just about fruit, too
(Paulin, *The Secret Life of Poems* 80–1).

Literary criticism and history are not, of course, always natural bedfellows.

Indeed they can pull in contrary directions. Social and economic historians, for example, tend to study human activity on a scale significantly broader than the individual, whereas literary criticism of most kinds focuses not on the mass or the typical example but the rare and striking individual utterance. Hence the suspicions of some historians for what they see as the subjective, atypical, 'misleading' evidence that literature has to offer, and the objections of literary critics that historians handle literary texts crudely, extracting passages as 'evidence' without regard for genre, conventions or nuances of tone. More generally, of course, history tends to look outward, extrapolating from single documents to wider truths, seeing more value in an idea frequently encountered than one rarely seen. History claims to be objective, detached from the subject of study, while literary criticism insists rather that the emphasis be placed inward, on the particularities of *this* text *here*, *now*, and on language *as* language in all its particularities of vocabulary, syntax and rhetorical tropes. Moreover, this is a process in which the reader is always already implicated: part of the equation to be acknowledged, bringing his or her own feelings, experiences and values to bear on the texts as they read them, whether they acknowledge the fact or not.

To read a text historically is in my view essential, but this should not mean reading it for its content alone – nor only as a narrative in which certain cultural values or assumptions might be uncovered (often the same assumptions about race, class, gender and sexuality that one finds in other texts from most other periods). Reading historically should also involve reading a text as a sequence of words and rhythms, sounds and silences, and rhetorical strategies aimed at the evocation of certain imaginative effects and emotional, sometimes even physical, affects.

Texts can never stand wholly alone – even if we wanted them to. We need to appreciate their social, cultural and political contexts if we are to understand their evolution, the rhetoric they used and the cultural work they performed in their own time. This was never truer than during the Renaissance, a period when many of the great poets (Thomas Wyatt, Sir Philip Sidney, Edmund Spenser), were diplomats and politicians, and many of the great politicians were also writers (Henry VIII and Elizabeth I composed prose works, poems and songs, Sir Walter Raleigh was a poet and historian). This was an age in which rhetoric, or persuasive speech, was the foundation of both political life and poetic activity, and so the realms of literary production and politics often intersected and overlapped, sharing traits and conventions, discursive tropes and practices designed not simply to explain something to a reader or listener, but also to move them – to address not just the mind, but also the heart, seat of the passions.

The Spanish humanist, Juan Luis Vives argued that justice and language were the twin links that held civil society together, but of the two, language was the stronger. He argued in his *De ratione dicendi* (*Concerning the Methods of Speaking*, 1532) that 'justice, being peaceful and mild, is only felt as obligation in the conscience . . . language, however, does not just win minds, but above all rules the affects, whose dominion over men is uncontrollable and onerous' (Vives 8).[1] And it was this affective power of poetry to move people – especially when it was read or sung before an audience – that made it so dangerous, especially in the eyes of those who championed the dispassionate principles of reason and faith. This distrust stands behind both the classical Greek philosopher Plato's banishment of the poets from his ideal state (described in his seminal political treatise *The Republic* (c.360 BCE)) and the condemnations of literary and theatrical representation made by St Augustine and the earliest theologians of the Catholic Church in the first five centuries after the death of Christ. And this conflict between principles of morality and of art echoes down through the thought – and the poetry – of the following centuries. Only in the later fifteenth century was there a turn from the medieval scholastic insistence on reasoned argument back to an interest in rhetorical *persuasion*. Behind the declaration of the Roman rhetorician Cicero (106–43 BCE), much loved of the humanists, that the ideal orator should demonstrate, delight and *move* his hearers, was the acceptance that rhetoric – and thus poetry – could be allied to reason and used beneficially to prompt action in the world. The humanist ideal was thus the 'good man skilled in speech' – the moral thinker who could use the tools of rhetoric and poetry to inspire his fellow citizens. This was the model that his contemporaries celebrated in Sir Philip Sidney, and which the Earl of Surrey represented in his 1542 elegy on Sir Thomas Wyatt ('Wyatt resteth here that quick [living] could never rest'), which describes each part of Wyatt's corpse as a testament to aspects of his virtue, anatomising a stoic hero who combined poetic excellence, moral rectitude and personal integrity.

The ideal form of historical reading, then, would combine both history and literary criticism in a way that Cicero or Surrey would probably have understood. It would read a literary text not only for content – for its rational, demonstrative elements, but also for its form, for its affective, emotive elements. If we consider a practical example of how literary criticism and historical analysis might be brought fruitfully together, what sorts of historical knowledge might we need to read a poem such as the following short lyric?

---

[1] This translation of the Spanish is from Jose Maria Perez Fernandez's forthcoming 'Translation, Trade and Common Sense: The Englishing of La Celestina'. I am grateful to Professor Fernandez for the chance to cite his, as yet unpublished, book.

Lux, my fair falcon, and your fellows all,
How well pleasant it were your liberty!   *would be*
Ye not forsake me that fair might ye befall.[2]
But they that sometime liked my company
Like lice away from dead bodies they crawl:
Lo, what proof in light adversity!
But ye, my birds, I swear by all your bells,
Ye be my friends, and so be but few else.

We need textual scholarship to tell us that this is a poem ascribed to Thomas Wyatt in one of the earliest printed anthologies of Tudor poetry, Tottel's *Miscellany* (1557), where the editor gave it the title 'Of such that had forsaken him'. We need linguistic knowledge to reveal that 'Lux' plays on both 'light' and 'luck', and was a common name for a falcon, and that 'light', when it is punningly picked up again in line 6, means 'trivial'. Some familiarity with cultural history would remind us that falcons were a common aristocratic accessory in this period, and often stood symbolically for aristocrats themselves (in literary representations such as Chaucer's *Parliament of Fowls* (1380–2) or Sir David Lyndsay's *Testament of the Papyngo* (c.1530)), as they were thought to embody naturally the virtues of courage, loyalty, truth and stoic disregard of adversity, which were part of the idealised repertoire of the nobleman.

More prosaically, we might draw on social history to suggest that lice were a common infestation, even for courtiers, and on political history to suggest that the poem probably arises from the anxious, fiercely competitive system of courtly patronage, in which every aspirant courtier sought the favour of those above them in the social hierarchy, aiming ultimately for the employment and rewards that came from a place in the intimate circles around the king and his noble advisors. The 'they' who once liked the speaker's company but have now deserted him were thus plausibly lesser courtiers and 'hangers on' who used him as a means of improving their own fortune while he was in favour, but have abandoned him now that he seems no longer to be influential.

A knowledge of Wyatt's other poems would reveal that he wrote elsewhere on similar themes – for example, in 'They flee from me that sometime did me seek' (first printed in Tottel's *Miscellany*), where the desertion of former friends and lovers is, as we shall see, again lamented. More specific knowledge of Wyatt's biography might suggest that he could have written the poem on one of those occasions when he was in prison, as when he was sent to the Tower of London in 1536 on suspicion of adultery with Henry VIII's second queen, Anne Boleyn. Thus the situation that the poem imagines, with the

---

[2] (Yet) you do not forsake me to seek better fortune.

speaker abandoned and desperate, might well have been a real one – and one with potentially mortal consequences.

This would be to read the poem for content: for its meaning as a narrative related to the poet's own life. But if we go a little beyond traditional historicism and approach the poem instead as a linguistic field, a series of rhythmic sounds and silences creating aural and emotional effects, what else might we learn? We might note the powerful alliteration in the opening line, how the liquid 'l' and labial 'f' sounds in 'Lux, my fair falcon, and your fellows all' are brought up sharp by the plosive 'p's and 'b's in line 2. We might see how the same movement returns in more concentrated form in line 5, as the ease with which former friends drift away is hinted at in 'like lice away', and the stark implications of their desertion embodied in the dead stop represented by the double buffer of 'dead bodies'. We might note how the rhyme-scheme of the first six lines charts parallel descending movements in the lexicon, first physically, in 'all' 'befall' and 'crawl', and then sociopolitically in 'liberty', 'company', 'adversity', leaving the speaker, metaphorically at least, abject, alone and on his knees. We could also notice how the word 'all' is a frequent refrain in the poem: suggesting the extremity of the poet's predicament. It is there in line 1 as an indication of the universal integrity of Lux and his kind, and returns in line 7, again associated with the birds, in contradistinction to the 'few' (by implication none) who can be relied upon from the human world. It is there covertly too in 'befall' and 'crawl', and gestured towards in the half rhymes of 'bells' and 'else', suggesting, if only to the reader's subconscious, that life at court is indeed a zero-sum game, a matter of 'all' or nothing, in which the consequences for the losers are devastating.

Rhythmically, the prevalence of end-stopped lines gives the lyric a straightforward, affirmative quality, save for the single case of lines 4–5. Here the falcons' reliability is contrasted with the elusive sliding away of the unfaithful companions – a move enacted linguistically by the sliding over of one line to the next (enjambment): the sibilant, liquid lightness of 'sometime liked' slipping easily into the bitter pay-off of 'like lice away'. Structurally, the first three lines affirming the raptors' noble nature form a natural sense unit. The falcons' instinctive capacity to act against their material self-interest by staying with the poet is then contrasted with the fickleness of the former companions (who, unlike Lux, remain unnamed), and whose desertion, because no reason is given for it beyond 'light adversity', seems merely capricious and contemptible.

Thus far the lyric seems straightforwardly to exemplify the popular proverb, 'a friend in need is a friend indeed'. And yet, there is an affective subtext here that suggests a richness to the text not evident on the surface, a subtext that runs counter to the drift of the speaker's angry assertions. While the poem praises the natural, unforced loyalty of the noble birds, and by implication, demonstrates the speaker's own stoic affinity with their virtues, there is, in his choice of allusions, a suggestion of another, less heroic reading of events, not least in the apparently very un-stoic petulance of the last line. By choosing to swear by the falcons' bells, and by *all* of them – thereby implying just how many there are – the speaker, perhaps unwittingly, draws into the poem's discursive field a striking image of the birds' captive status. These falcons are not really choosing to stay with the poet through noble, self-denying loyalty. Secured to their perches with leather jesses, and probably belled and hooded, they could not claim their liberty if they wanted to, even if their training from birth had not already accustomed them to a life of captivity. Indeed, the very bells lauded by the poet are designed to betray their whereabouts and prevent them hunting for themselves in the wild. Wyatt had applied a very similar image to himself in the satire 'Mine Own John Poins' (first printed in Tottel's *Miscellany*), where he describes the way that the pleasant freedom he enjoys on his estates in Kent is sullied by the fact that he knows that he is actually confined there, banished into internal exile by the king: a confinement symbolized by a metaphorical 'clog' – a block used to restrict the movements of animals – tied to his heel.

> In lusty leas at liberty I walk . . .   *pleasant fields*
> Save that a clog doth hang yet at my heel.

The sense of captivity felt so keenly by the speaker of this poem is conspicuously absent on the surface of 'Lux my Fair Falcon', albeit it returns unbidden to its subtext in the mention of those bells, themselves as much a talisman of captivity as the clog that so disturbs the 'Wyatt' of 'Mine Own John Poins'.

Similarly the image of crawling vermin, portraying the loathsome betrayal of his companions, also carries with it a subtext suggestive of the complexity of the political situation the poem describes. The comparison speaks both to the mortally high stakes for which Tudor politics was played at court, and also to the plausible motivation of the companions. The poem is an affective construction, it bespeaks and evokes emotions as well as conveys information, so where the speaker asserts the fickle, verminous treachery of his former companions, seeking to focus readerly contempt upon their behaviour, the text simultaneously speaks of his own bitterness and vulnerability, and hints at the desperate nature of his situation. If the former companions are like lice, then the speaker himself is like a dead body – an image that gains in resonance if the poem really was written from prison.

In his other great lyric of frustration with courtly life, 'They Flee from me', Wyatt again reached for natural comparisons to describe his speaker's sense of abandonment by ungrateful former suitors. The first stanza presents a queasily

ambivalent conflation of human and animal images, in which at one moment
the treacherous suitors seem to be human lovers, creeping, whether predato-
rily or fearfully, towards his bed on 'naked foot', and the next they seem to be
timid birds or small animals, lured to him by offers of bread.

> They flee from me that sometime did me seek
> With naked foot stalking in my chamber.
> I have seen them gentle, tame and meek
> That now are wild and do not remember
> That sometime they put themself in danger
> To take bread at my hand; and now they range
> Busily seeking with a continual change.

The focus sharpens in the second stanza, when the speaker dwells on one
'special' moment, when a woman let her loose gown fall from her shoulders,
and, kissing him, 'softly said, "Dear, how like you this?"' But, as the third
stanza reveals, the power relation between the two has since reversed. Now
she is seemingly in the ascendancy at court, and he has been casually dismissed
from her company, leaving him to ask angrily, 'since that I am so kindly
served / I would fain know what she hath deserved.' (ll.20–1).

Again, here is a poem that invites our sympathetic identification with
a speaker who has been betrayed by an ungrateful suitor. But the scenario
described to prompt that sympathy again offers both too little and too much
information to make identification with him unproblematic. The first stanza's
conflation of the stalking lovers with timid wild creatures implies that the
speaker was not simply the victim of others' guile but himself a player in the
game of courtly seduction. While he had the upper hand, it was they who
had to 'put themself in danger' to approach him, drawn by the lure which,
by his own admission, he held out to tempt them in. And the insistent plurals
of the first nine lines themselves undermine the speaker's claim to outraged
innocence. If the woman of stanzas 2 and 3 was 'special', she was hardly
unique; and her desertion of the speaker once she has got from him what
she desires, was hardly unprecedented. He had lured others before her, and
seemingly more since: the anonymous 'they' who once stalked his chamber
but now roam elsewhere are part of a fluid, self-interested courtly sexual
economy in which the speaker has played his own willing role. So there is an
implicit irony to his final, indignant question, suggestive of the kind of self-
exposing comments to be found in Robert Browning's dramatic monologues
written three centuries later. When the speaker says 'since that I so kindly am
served', he intends the irony of 'kindly' – meaning both 'generously' and also
'appropriately to one's nature or "kind"' – to cut only the treacherous 'she'
who has offended him. He claims that he has been nothing but generous to

her, and thus deserves to be treated accordingly; she, though, being naturally cruel, has behaved according to her 'kind'. However, thinking back to those opening lines, what might such a promiscuous player of the game of courtly conquest really expect and merit? Might it not be that the man who lured so many women to his chamber, in being rejected by a more successful female courtier, has got exactly what he deserves after all? Reading the poem 'against the grain' of its apparent sympathy for the male speaker thus suggests a second, alternative meaning that opens up its courtly and sexual politics for critical scrutiny.

Poems like these suggest the value of combining literary and historical approaches to enrich an understanding of the scenarios represented. But to think merely in terms of texts and contexts is probably too limited a model of what such readings offer. Historical criticism adds richness to our understanding of the contexts *of* a poem, but those contexts in turn create new meanings *in* the poem. Literary close reading in turn implies subtexts which further enrich the context: both suggesting how a poem might *move* its readers as well as inform them, while also revealing the poet's own degree of emotional investment (potentially conflicted), born of his or her own attitudes and anxieties. In such ways, poetry enriches our knowledge of history every bit as much as the other way around.

NEXT STEPS

Armstrong, Isobel. *Victorian Poetry: Poetry, Poetics, Politics*. Oxford: Routledge, 1993.
Eagleton, Terry. *How to Read a Poem*. Oxford: Blackwell, 2006.
Norbrook, David. *Poetry and Politics in the English Renaissance*, rev. edn. Oxford: Oxford University Press, 2002.

9

Vernacular Poetry

Colin Nicholson

'Words strain,' T. S. Eliot tells us in 'Burnt Norton' (1936); they 'will not stay in place, / Will not stay still'. He could well be describing the effect of the vernacular on language at large. With different meanings accumulated over time, the term 'vernacular' stems from the Latin *vern[a]cul-us*, meaning 'domestic, native, indigenous'. This in turn derives from *verna*, the term for a slave born on his master's estate, who is thus classed as a native but not a citizen of the place. So we might say a relationship of power and subordination is inscribed in the word 'vernacular' from the beginning, and that uses of it have been developing and redefining that relationship ever since. One definition given by the *Oxford English Dictionary* is 'the informal, colloquial, or distinctive speech of a people or a group'. As such, 'vernacular' moves from country or national-territorial application to social class and regional locality, and includes the transforming extension of speech (orality) into writing (literacy). This chapter briefly surveys the evolution of the vernacular, in relation to the historical development of English literature, and culture more generally, before looking more closely at forms of vernacular writing appearing in recent works.

We have no way of knowing how long spoken languages were operational before the advent of written forms; but several human eras is a safe guess. The vital point to note, for our purposes, is that the evolution of scripted language (which, unlike face-to-face talk, is transmissible across time and space) entailed a marked expansion of control over information and representation for people who were educated into new sign-systems – and a corresponding disempowerment of those who were not. Tandem and related developments include the adaptation of 'rhetoric' from its original Greek application of rules for effective, persuasive speaking into the codification of writing tech-niques, and of 'eloquence' from polished and effective utterance into the arts and attractions of persuasive script. We can begin to think about how these shifts and changes play out in English contexts by recalling that between 1380 and 1384, Yorkshire-born John Wycliffe persuaded colleagues to write out by hand a literal translation of the Latin Bible. This version preserved Latin constructions and word order that patently conflicted with English usage. The decisive break with imported syntax came when a revised manuscript version, circulated after Wycliffe's death, used English idiom in the ordering of its sentences. Around the same time, Geoffrey Chaucer began working on *The Canterbury Tales* (1388–1400), and had already broken with long-dominant forms of written language – either Latin, or Anglo-Norman (a form of French) – which had been the medium of England's rulers ever since the Norman Conquest in 1066. Chaucer, instead, produced recognisably English verse, and is thought of as a founding father of English poetry. Wycliffe, by opening Bible-reading to the individual judgement of people who had no Latin, challenged the authority of the Catholic priesthood and ultimately the Pope, and was called the morning star of the Reformation as a result. His was the first English example of what became known as vernacular bibles, a bid for intellectual and spiritual freedom that would lead to him being condemned as a heretic, his remains disinterred and burnt, and all his writings banned.

But following the introduction of moveable type, the sixteenth-century's transformation into the 'early modern' period Greg Walker discusses in Chapter 8 got under way largely through the instrumentality of this most thoroughly disseminated of texts. The subsequent publication (in 1611) of the King James Bible established an Authorised Version of vernacular literacy that now had state approval. The printing press made book selling a marketable proposition, stimulating production on a hitherto unimaginable scale, so that for the first time in history communities of believers could read their foun-dational scriptures without the mediation of traditional priest-craft. In several European countries, including England and Scotland, this almighty empower-ment fuelled a seventeenth-century democratisation of access to vocabularies and ideas that changed our world.

Vernacular print was here to stay, but its first impact was on those who could read. Multitudes of people could not; moreover, of those who could read, even fewer could write. They could listen and talk, though, and despite the standardisation of spelling and syntax which printing foreshadows, they continued to do so in a range of local accents and regional dialects. We still do, despite repeated attempts to discipline our unruly variety. One of these appeared in the elevated register of 'poetic diction' and formal rules for the composition of 'polite' writing that were successfully established across mainstream British culture in the eighteenth century, with accompanying emphases on orderliness, reason and improvement that were shaping the Enlightenment movement at the time. Preferred styles fashionably polished and energetically dispersed for middle-class consumption make it seem that vernacular energies in the world of print had been consigned to cheap and popular publishing known by contemporaries as 'Grub Street' productions.

It would be difficult, then, to overestimate the culture shock delivered by Robert Burns when his *Poems, chiefly in the Scottish dialect* first appeared in 1786. Scotland was in the eighteenth-century vanguard as far as English-language developments of 'polite' learning and acceptable Enlightenment discourse were concerned: now, at a stroke, Scottish difference in terms of speech-world and cadence – the sound patterning of language – was indelibly imprinted in the minds and memories of a growing readership. Through his confident handling of a West of Scotland rural register, Burns made the use of vernacular language a form of cultural self-definition, and the 'ploughman poet' was consequently hailed as a national bard. William Wordsworth – often considered the leading English poet of the time – thought Burns 'a man of extraordinary genius' (Wordsworth, *The Prose Works* vol. 3: 121). Together with Samuel Taylor Coleridge, he adapted Burns's example to English contexts with the experimental publication of *Lyrical Ballads* (1798). In his 'Preface' to the 1802 edition Wordsworth emphasised his intention to use 'as far as was possible' a 'selection of language really used by men'. 'Selection' becomes the crucial determinant in a book of poems that signals the emergence of English Romanticism. Burns's experiential life-world becomes Wordsworth's chosen preference for 'low and rustic life' because, he claimed: 'in that condition . . . our elementary feelings coexist in a state of greater simplicity, and, consequently, may be more accurately contemplated, and more forcibly communicated'. But for this to happen, he made clear, 'selection' must be made: everyday speech must first be 'purified indeed from what appear to be its real defects, from all lasting and rational causes of dislike or disgust' (Wordsworth, 'Preface' 650).

That cleansing operation becomes the testing ground for subsequent efforts to move verse beyond English proprieties and into the democratic American inclusiveness of Walt Whitman, whose *Leaves of Grass* first appeared in 1855, sustaining eight expanded and revised editions between then and his death. Whitman updates Wordsworth's imaginative alliance with rural speech and ways of feeling and transforms its context when his 'Preface' asserts that 'the genius of the United States is . . . always most in the common people' (Whitman 741). Seeking genius among the common people, Whitman turns his back on what the American philosopher Ralph Waldo Emerson called 'the courtly muses of Europe' and becomes, in turn, a founding figure in the development of United States verse (Emerson 105). In 1881 he renamed his most famous poem as 'Song of Myself', and proclaimed in one of his additions, 'I too am not a bit tamed, I too am untranslatable / I sound my barbaric yawp over the roofs of the world.' Although he tamed his work somewhat to protect his sexual identity, Whitman's yawp offers moral and political as well as linguistic democracy: poetry 'conquers' benignly and by example, so that 'no man thenceforward shall be degraded for ignorance or weakness or sin' (Whitman 745–6).

Since America's vernacular tonalities have come to such prominence in the anglophone world and beyond, it is useful to remind ourselves that prose fiction was always readier than poetry to accommodate and incorporate everyday conversational speech rhythms (see also Chapter 11). Admiration for inventiveness in bringing spoken idioms alive on the page encouraged Ernest Hemingway to conclude that 'all modern American literature comes from one book by Mark Twain called *Huckleberry Finn*' (Hemingway 22). Hemingway warmed to the linguistic experiment promised in Twain's preliminary note to *Huckleberry Finn* (1884):

> In this book a number of dialects are used, to wit: the Missouri negro dialect; the extremest form of the backwoods Southwestern dialect; the ordinary 'Pike County' dialect; and four modified varieties of this last. The shadings have not been done in a haphazard fashion, or by guesswork; but painstakingly, and with the trustworthy guidance and support of personal familiarity with these several forms of speech. (Twain 48)

While Huck was crossing frontiers into a new world of expressiveness, in the more oppressively class-conscious and deferential culture of the imperial British state the regulation of spoken English remained a cornerstone of both educational and social policy. In 1917 Daniel Jones produced an *English Pronouncing Dictionary* that became the twentieth-century's most influential textbook of its kind, with phonetic models based on the 'everyday speech in the families of Southern English people who have been educated at the public schools':

> If a boy in such a school has a marked local peculiarity in his pronunciation, it generally disappears or is modified during his school career under the influence of the different mode of speaking he hears continually around him; he consequently emerges from school with a pronunciation similar to that of the other boys. Similar considerations apply to modern boarding schools for girls. (Jones xv)

Jones was confident that standards of pronunciation thus conceived would be readily understood across the English-speaking world, but he knew that in the homeland they were *used* by only 'a rather small minority': 'There exist countless other ways of pronouncing English, some of them being used by large communities.' He also wonders about the potential effect of a communications revolution that was in its infancy when his book began its long shelf-life: 'Whether broadcasting will in the long run alter this state of things remains to be seen' (xv–xvi).

The promotion and nationwide delivery of 'Standard English' or 'Received Pronunciation' through the state education system was immeasurably advanced by the founding of the BBC in 1922, initially as the 'British Broadcasting Company' (it became a publicly funded corporation five years later). 'BBC English' set benchmarks of good practice that were a major reinforcement for the relatively small minority already familiar with its codes and conventions, as well as being aspirational for those who thought of themselves as upwardly mobile, and a daily reminder of social separation for the large communities who spoke differently.

In Scotland's several speech-communities, for example, people who aspired to alternative modes of self-definition were stimulated by the synthetic Scots invented in the 1920s by Hugh MacDiarmid, deployed in poems such as 'Farewell to Dostoevski' from *A Drunk Man Looks at the Thistle* (1926)

> The stars are larochs o' auld cottages,   *foundations*
> And a' Time's glen is fu' o' blinnin stew,   *blinding / storm*
> Nae freen'ly lozen skimmers: and the wund   *window / gleams / wind*
> Rises and separates even me and you.

His extraordinary skill in displaying the discursive, lyrical and meditative richness of Scots as a self-renewing resource set an influential example for what became known as the 'Scottish Renaissance', conceived as part of a campaign for the recovery of the country's independence. The movement's engagement with the history of Scots language also related it to the wider linguistic and formal innovations marking 'Modernist' writing in the early twentieth century. The kind of transformations Burns achieved at the end of the eighteenth century MacDiarmid sought to recreate in the early decades of the twentieth.

The BBC continued to supervise its audience's morals and police the nation's speech habits, most markedly where a particular form of the vernacular – expletives – were concerned. When the writer and theatre critic Kenneth Tynan said 'fuck' for the first time on television in 1965, the governors issued a formal apology, and four separate House of Commons motions were signed by 133 Labour and Tory backbenchers: the tabloids went into a fit of simulated outrage. By then Allen Ginsberg was entertaining large audiences with performance poetry that scandalised 1950s conservative America; adapting

Whitman's long-line free-flowing verse to a liberated sense of selfhood that in 1956 invited his country, in the poem 'America', to 'Go fuck yourself with your atom bomb'. By the beginning of the 1960s, though, attitudes were showing some signs of change. In 1960 a British jury threw out a government attempt to stop Penguin's publication of *Lady Chatterley's Lover*, completed in 1928 by D. H. Lawrence, and Philip Larkin recalled a relaxation of his own occurring between the *Chatterley* case and the release of the Beatles' first long-playing record in 1963. He went on himself to use iambic tetrameters and an alternating rhyme scheme to parody English lyric practice in 'This be the Verse' (1971), flippant and colloquial in its tone, but touching on serious issues:

> They fuck you up, your mum and dad.
> They may not mean to, but they do.
> They fill you with the faults they had
> And add some extra, just for you.

Larkin was politically right-wing and a jazz-lover. Tony Harrison is a left-wing aficionado of opera whose film-poems, newspaper verse and extensive theatre work widened poetry's audience and broadened its popular appeal. The 1987 Channel Four television film of the poet reading *V.* projected the whole British nation as invited (late-night) audience for its pungently aggressive elegy in a city graveyard. The narrative reflects on the devastating implications of the 1984 miners' strike during which the poem was written, and the performance created a political storm in right-wing newspapers with their parliamentary associates, who claimed to be upset by its use of expletives but were equally offended by its radical sympathies: *V.* also won a Royal Television Society Award. 'Vernacular poetry' signifies a willingness to incorporate colloquial or demotic elements from everyday speech: Harrison stretches literary tolerances of these elements to the limit. In his handling, 'vernacular' is both returned to its etymological roots and developed into a powerful critique of England's class-based cultural hierarchies. The *Oxford English Dictionary* advises that the term is 'usually applied to the native speech of a populace, in contrast to another or others acquired for commercial, social, or educative purposes,' and is 'now frequently employed with reference to that of the working classes'. This becomes something of a manifesto for Harrison's well-schooled eloquence.

Vivid, urgent 'native speech' and working class idioms in *V.* contrast demotic language with the soothing and accommodating rhythms and contexts borrowed from Thomas Gray's 'Elegy Written in a Country Churchyard' (1751), still one of the best-known English poems (see also Chapter 6). *V.* uses these counterpointed linguistic and poetic idioms to explore damaging tensions within a broken society. Harrison's autobiographically-based sequence of sixteen-line sonnets, *The School of Eloquence* (1978), had already used tactics of this kind to examine England's historically-refined and ruthlessly effective class-divided systems of cultural dominance and social subordination. Many of these sonnets include italicised fragments of a parent's uneducated speech, thus placing working-class vernacular at the heart of their concerns. Harrison's sensitivity to a father 'England made to feel like some dull oaf', as he puts it in 'Marked with D.', gives him direct access to usually silent elements in society, and hones a razor-sharp sense that received pronunciation is itself a class-marked accent wielding significant social power. The twinned sonnets 'Them & *[uz]*' introduce and demonstrate, even in their title – reflecting phonetically a northern working-class pronunciation of 'us' – a dialogue between differ-ent dialects and speech forms. This dialogue continues within the sonnets; not only in tensions between the characters of father and son, but in marked contrasts between the language forms they and others use. Remembering the humiliation he suffered for his working-class accent as a scholarship boy at an independent grammar school in the late 1940s and early 1950s, the first son-net's voice is crushed by the classroom sarcasm of a 'nicely spoken' teacher of English. The combative adult of the second sonnet announces an intention that Harrison the poet had already fulfilled:

> So right, yer buggers, then! We'll occupy
> your lousy leasehold Poetry.
>
> I chewed up Litterachewer and spat the bones
> into the lap of dozing Daniel Jones,
> dropped the initials I'd been harried as
> and used my *name* and own voice: [uz] [uz] [uz],
> ended sentences with by, with, from,
> and spoke the language that I spoke at home.

Vernacular usage had claimed its place and showed itself a powerful tool in English verse.

Poetry in Scotland engages differently: 'vernacular' might not be strictly applicable generally to writing in Scots, which has the status of a language in itself, but can certainly include the several ways of speaking the country's borders contain. Edwin Morgan, for example, explores a wide range of ver-nacular territories, and, like Harrison, also directly addresses issues of language-use and the systems of power that reside within certain terms and locutions. In one of Morgan's *Sonnets from Scotland* (1984), written in response to the failed devolution referendum of 1979, three unemployed workers stagger out of a pub looking to take on any Standard English user who might employ the kind of language used to rationalise their redundancy:

Naw naw, there's nae big wurds here, there ye go.
Christ man ye're in a bad wey, kin ye staun?
See here noo, wance we know jist where we're gaun,
we'll jump thon auld – stoap that, will ye – *Quango.*
Thaim that squealt *Lower Inflation,* aye, thaim,
plus thae *YY Zero Wage Increase* wans,
they'll no know what hit thim.

For the speaker in 'Gangs' Morgan uses formal rhyme and structure to organise a self-identifying resilience: 'Ah'm oan ma tod. But they'll no take a len / a me. Ah'm no deid yet, or deif, or dumb!' (Morgan, *Collected Poems* 449)

Knowing where we're 'gaun', or going, between vernacular and established forms of language is hardly an issue confined to Glasgow. The development of English into a world language has helped to generate a cornucopia of vernacular possibilities. Carol Ann Duffy realises one such in her monologue 'Translating the English, 1989', representing the colloquial voice of a streetwise Indo-Pakistani. His truncated speech-patterns also illustrate how quickly and sharply the vernacular can absorb patterns in contemporary culture – in this case, a general collapse of values ten years into Margaret Thatcher's Prime Ministership (from 1979 to 1990), as well as details including pricey performances of the musical *Les Miserables* and Health Minister Edwina Currie's warning about salmonella in eggs:

Welcome to my country! We have here Edwina Currie
and the *Sun* newspaper. Much excitement.
Also the weather has been improving
even in February. Daffodils. (Wordsworth. Up North.) If you like
Shakespeare or even Opera we have too the Black Market.
For two hundred quids we are talking *Les Miserables,*
nods being as good as winks. Don't eat the eggs.

(Duffy 68)

An epigraph superiorly suggests that 'much of the poetry, alas, is lost in translation . . .'. The poem, though, illustrates the power of the vernacular to 'translate' its readers into highly specific outlooks whose positioning outside mainstream culture allow particularly sharp satiric scrutiny of its values.

We can trace a Caribbean genealogy for vernacular usage as regional self-definition in what hindsight allows us to call the 'rap' verse of Louise Bennett (1919–2006). Known as 'Auntie Lou', her work was first designed for oral transmission on Jamaican radio, and so enjoyed large local audiences. But beyond a shared concern with orality, diversity rules in this region too:

(Edward) Kamau Brathwaite (born in1930 in Barbados) has developed an effective Afro-Caribbean poetics out of what he terms 'nation language': an oral culture which lives 'not in a dictionary but in the tradition of the spoken word.' Since this culture is based 'as much on sound as it is on song . . . the noise that it makes is part of the meaning': lose 'the sound or the noise,' Brathwaite suggests, and 'you lose part of the meaning' (Brathwaite 17). Incorporating free-forming riffs associated with jazz, as well as adapting calypso and reggae, Brathwaite's historical imagination commands a range of registers to complex effects, including combinations of local anglophone speech-patterns with phrasing that opens the mind to radically alternative senses of identity and relationship. 'Wings of a Dove' (1967) turns traditional pieties into a protest against traditional submission, leaving a ganja-smoking protagonist ('I / Rastafar-I / in Babylon's boom / town') to rehearse insurrection:

> So beat dem burn
> dem, learn
>
> dem that dem
> got dem nothin'
>
> but dem
> bright bright baubles
>
> that will burst dem
> when the flame dem
>
> from on high dem
> raze an' roar dem
>
> an' de poor dem
> rise an' rage dem
>
> in de glory of the Lord.

Brathwaite often focuses on Afro-Caribbean derivations and relationships; from a different ethnic group, but with related themes, David Dabydeen, born and raised on a sugar plantation in Guyana, immigrated to England as a thirteen-year-old and is now Professor of Literature at Warwick University. His first poetry collection, *Slave Song* (1984), shifted paradigms by making a broken music out of the degraded lives and language of plantation field-workers, many of them shipped from India into the virtual slavery of inden-tured labour. With a chorus responsive to its complaint at unremitting toil, 'Song of the Creole Gang Women' jerks and grunts its restricted lexis into a fragment of tragic opera:

Wuk, nuttin bu wuk
Marn noon an night nuttin bu wuk
Booker own me patacake   *cunt*
Booker own me pickni.   *children*

Conventional notions of vernacular efficacy shifted several gears when Bob Marley gave his words and music to the world. Black British writers brought their own experience to the beat, as when Linton Kwesi Johnson – born in rural Jamaica in 1952 but moving to London in 1963 – took performance poetry into the blend of music and verse known as 'dub', which he is generally credited with inventing. Mostly written in street language, Johnson's performances activate challenging perceptions of immigrant experience against a background of the reggae music he also writes. 'Di Great Insohreckshan' (1984) uses these rhythms to document the riots that broke out in Brixton in the early 1980s. Grace Nichols grew up in a coastal Guyana village and has lived in Britain since 1977. Her first collection, *I Is A Long Memoried Woman* (1983), closes with an 'Epilogue' that speaks to migration and renewal across the world, and so reaches beyond this chapter and further into the intertextual domains of anglophone poetry:

I have crossed an ocean
I have lost my tongue
from the root of the old one
a new one has sprung

With the proliferation of English as a world language, especially in the wake of empire, postcolonial criticism has focused increasing interest on the various ways in which language is used to resist or subvert the authority of Standard English as the dialect of colonial education (as in Samoan Sia Figiel's riposte to Wordsworth in 'The Daffodils – from a native's perspective' (1998)), or alternatively to explore the liberating creative possibilities associated with the blending of 'Western' and 'non-Western' linguistic and cultural traditions (as in the allusions to Homer and Dante in the work of St Lucian poet Derek Walcott). Many postcolonial poets (from Linton Kwesi Johnson to Ghanaian poet Kofi Anyidoho) have favoured performance poetry as a means by which to signal the importance of oral traditions, and the unique aural and rhythmic inflections of postcolonial vernaculars, within and alongside traditions of written verse.

Alan Gillis began this section by suggesting (in Chapter 4), that poetry can both delight and teach. Vernacular poetry – even when it is less explicit about the relationship between language and power than Tony Harrison's tends to be – has much to teach us, particularly in a period when global migration, as well as class, has so reshaped the particularities of spoken English. The choice of vocabulary, and the differences of register we can hear even within individual poems, reveal a great deal about the power, class or other hierarchies which prevail both between countries (including the constituent nations of the United Kingdom) but also within them, generating, transforming and differentiating speech and writing in all their forms. Patterns of speech, vocabulary and language use, even in individual poems, offer a kind of fingerprint, identifying lines of force running through the whole society that produced them (see also Chapters 11 and 14 on Mikhail Bakhtin, dialogism and social and linguistic hierarchies and frictions).

In the restless ingenuity and promiscuity of the literary imagination, vernacular poetry also offers much delight, finding quirky, idiosyncratic new verbal possibilities in the irrepressible inventiveness of colloquial and vernacular utterance. The Northern Irish poet Tom Paulin shares this sense of rekindling freshness in poetry that seems detached or distant from, or otherwise at odds with, orthodox canons. At the end of the Introduction to his *Faber Book of Vernacular Verse* (1990) Paulin acknowledges that the disaffected and powerless

> know that out in the public world a polished speech issues orders and receives deference. It seeks to flatten out and obliterate all the varieties of spoken English and to substitute one accent for all the others. It may be the ruin of us yet. (xxii)

But Paulin also celebrates vernacular writing's 'intoxication of speech, its variety and crack and hilarity'. This in itself is a mode of resistance.

NEXT STEPS

Paulin, Tom, ed. *The Faber Book of Vernacular Verse*. London: Faber and Faber, 1990.

Markham, E. A., ed. *Hinterland: Caribbean Poetry from the West Indies and Britain*. Northumberland: Bloodaxe, 1989.

Patke, Rajeev. *Postcolonial Poetry in English*. Oxford: Oxford University Press, 2006.

Talib, Ismail. *The Language of Postcolonial Literatures: an Introduction*. London: Routledge, 2002.

Wordsworth, William. 'Preface' to *Lyrical Ballads* (1802). In *Norton Anthology of Theory and Criticism*. 648–68.

Section III – Narrative

10

Genre and Form: The Short Story

Kenneth Millard

Sections II and IV (Chapters 4 and 16) begin with introductions to their respective areas, poetry and drama, each of which may still be fairly new to students beginning advanced study of literature. Narrative needs less introduction, as it is encountered so regularly in everyday life: not only in novels and stories, but in magazines and films, as well as in newspapers and all sorts of other factual reporting. Non-fictional narrative is considered by Laura Marcus in Chapter 15, and briefly by Randall Stevenson in Chapter 12. For the most part, this section concentrates on fictional and imaginative narrative, with much of its material equally relevant to the novel and the short story. This chapter, however, introduces the specific generic properties of the short story, using two examples by well-known modernist writers: 'The Horse Dealer's Daughter' (1922) by D. H. Lawrence and 'Araby' (1914) by James Joyce. The chapter begins with an overview of the history of the short story as a genre, before going on to some more detailed close readings of these two twentieth-century examples of the form.

At school, we might have tried to understand Lawrence's and Joyce's stories in terms of their characters and themes, and we might have asked, what human predicaments do these stories dramatise? There is nothing wrong with that approach, and my interpretations will still ask important questions about what the stories mean to us, as readers, by employing similar skills of literary interpretation. But the challenge at first-year university level is more specialised, particularly in terms of the questions that we ask of these texts. In the context of this chapter, for example, we might ask in what ways are these stories informed, influenced, or even determined, by having been written in the specific genre of the short story? How is the story different, or even unique, by virtue of the fact that it is specifically a short story, rather than a novel, or a play, or an epic poem, each of which is capable of telling the same story? This is a question about understanding the value of a text's proper genre, and in order to address it properly we need to investigate the specific genre of the short story before we return to Lawrence and Joyce in the latter half of this chapter.

The first important point to be made about this, and one that has crucial bearing on how we understand short stories, is that recognising and identifying any individual work's relation to its specific genre is often fundamentally important to the act of interpretation. This recognition of genre is a way to approach a text that enables us to establish vital aspects of its meaning. In fact, very often our understanding of what a text might mean is heavily dependent upon our implicit sense of its particular generic category, or on its use of generic conventions. Further, it is even possible that there are some aspects of a text's meaning that are entirely attributable to the presence of specific generic conventions, and the reader's failure to recognise those generic conventions in operation will result in an incomplete interpretation, or even a wrong interpretation. This is true not only for the broad categories of tragedy and comedy (see Chapters 18 and 19) but for much more specific prose genres such as detective fiction, the coming-of-age novel, an obituary in a newspaper or a tabloid headline.

To conclude provisionally, then, we might think of generic conventions as a form of vocabulary or grammar by which we situate texts within a specific interpretative paradigm. Identifying a text's rightful genre is a fundamental component of our interpretative competence: it is a specific form of knowledge that makes certain forms of interpretation and meaning possible in the first place. Knowledge of a text's genre enables us to bring to literature an understanding and a critical repertoire that tells us what to look for to help establish what a text means. The critic Jonathan Culler expressed this succinctly when he wrote that 'the function of genre conventions is essentially to establish a contract between writer and reader so as to make certain relevant expectations operative, and thus to permit both compliance with and deviation from accepted modes of intelligibility' (147).

It is important to add here that the study of genre is not simply a way to approach literature, but can be used to interpret any other art form, such as painting, music, film and television. Consider dance, for example: ballet, disco, robotics and Irish country dancing. Each of these genres within dance has specific forms of generic convention that regulate or govern what kinds of physical movement can take place, and therefore how emotion can be expressed within that specific genre. This is one of the things that gives genre study its particular value: it can be employed to examine a wide range of artistic forms. All art forms function within broader genres that have a crucial impact upon how any individual text operates.

Further, it is not only the reader who needs to recognise generic affiliations, because often a literary text will comment directly on its own textual antecedents in order to give the reader specific guidance on how to interpret and how to attribute meaning. For example, the first twenty lines of Milton's *Paradise Lost* (1667/1674) are exactly such a statement of generic affiliation, specifically to the genre of the epic. Jane Austen's first novel, *Northanger Abbey*, completed in 1803, makes explicit references to *The Mysteries of Udolpho* (1794), by Ann Radcliffe, in order to establish its gothic credentials, and Henry James' story 'The Turn of the Screw' (1898) refers self-consciously to both *The Mysteries of Udolpho* and to Charlotte Brontë's novel *Jane Eyre* (1847) to make it clear to the reader how to understand important elements of its narrative. The deployment of generic convention is a way for a text to say to the reader 'I belong to this group', and to encourage us to recognise the rules of how that group functions in order to understand properly the individual text within it. Part of our literary education consists of recognising generic affiliations and conventions, of showing a thorough historical knowledge of them, and of understanding what specific impact they have on any individual text that we study. Often a text's individuality is established precisely by its deviation from our understanding of the established conventions of the genre within which that text is operating. (See Chapter 3 for further discussion of this and other aspects of genre.)

How, then, do we begin to define the short story as a distinct genre? One easy argument to address at the outset is worth stating facetiously: a central characteristic of the short story is that it is a story which is short. Thus it can be distinguished from a novel, which is a story that is long. This argument is worth expressing in this way because a surprising amount of critical attention has been devoted to the question of how short is short? Such questions of length (or, 'does size matter?') are ultimately fruitless because a genre does not define itself by size but by particular aesthetic characteristics. By 'aesthetic' we mean creative or artistic: what specific formal or stylistic characteristics does the genre of the short story possess? Does the short story have a tendency to depict forms of experience that are different from those of its big brother, the novel? What is a short story, as a unique art form, if it is *not* simply defined by word length? The best way to address these questions is to return briefly to the historical origins of the genre.

It might surprise some readers to discover that the short story did not always exist. Although one could argue that Geoffrey Chaucer's *The Canterbury Tales* – dating from the late fourteenth century – consists of a collection of stories that are indeed short, it is generally agreed that the genre of the modern short story as we recognise it was in fact invented in the nineteenth century, and specifically in the United States. As critic Martin Schofield observes,

> the reason was primarily economic: American writers stood little chance of competing against English novelists, whose works were cheaply and readily available in America because of lack of copyright control. The American periodical magazine form, the perfect vehicle for short fiction, thus arose in part to provide a means for American writers to publish their work. (Schofield 6)

We might not conventionally make a connection between art forms and economics, but actually the genre of the short story came into being for practical as much as for artistic reasons. The first recognised short story writer, credited with 'creating' the modern genre, is the American author Washington Irving. Irving wrote two classics of the short story genre, 'The Legend of Sleepy Hollow' and 'Rip Van Winkle', which are still widely studied today. These stories were published in 1820, and they are important to understanding the genre because they helped to define American literature at its very beginning (by depicting uniquely American subjects) and because they evolved from a kind of prose composition known as the travel sketch. The travel sketch was a short depiction of the wonders of foreign parts and of the awe they inspired in the narrator, and it was a genre that already had some commercial currency. Irving was a master of this genre, and he began to use it to write stories that were not principally devoted to foreign travel – and this is how the short story came about. Indeed, the two stories by Irving I have mentioned were published in a collection called *The Sketch-book of Geoffrey Crayon, Gent.*

This sense of the origins of the short story genre being specifically American is underscored by the fact that the pioneer theorist of the new genre was also American: Edgar Allan Poe. Poe wrote a famous critical article about the unique qualities of short stories in the 1830s. One critic has argued that 'Poe's critical comments on the form in the 1830s are largely responsible for the birth of the short story as a unique genre' (May 108). Poe defined three characteristics of the genre, to which most subsequent discussion of the genre of the short story has been indebted:

1. Unity of impression: for Poe, the short story writer 'first conceived with deliberate care a certain unique or single effect to be wrought out' (Poe 94). This emphasis on singleness of effect and economy of means suggests that the short story is unique as a genre because of the way that it presents a single experience to the exclusion of all else.
2. Moment of crisis: most short stories tend to focus on a single character in

a single episode, and to reveal that character at a moment when he or she undergoes some decisive change in attitude or understanding.

3. Symmetry of design: Poe argued that the good short story must have a plot in which there is initial conflict or disharmony, some sequential action deriving from that initial predicament, and then some form of narrative resolution.

For Poe, then, examining the profusion of short stories in the United States in the 1820s and 1830s, there are specific characteristics that define what formal structure the genre has, and what forms of experience it is best suited to dramatising. Poe's argument is important for elucidating how the short story is a new art form with unique characteristics; it is especially suited to depicting certain kinds of experience in a particular way. Since Poe's definition of the short story genre the form has proliferated enormously, but most short stories still tend to share particular aesthetic characteristics.

We might now paraphrase Poe in our contemporary context and argue that the modern short story, which has evolved internationally since the 1820s, generally tends to conform to three particular characteristics: it makes a single impression on the reader; it tends to focus on a moment of crisis; it makes that crisis pivotal in a tightly controlled plot. These features are not generally characteristic of the novel, a literary form which has a completely different historical origin and radically different aesthetic qualities. It is not the case, therefore, that the short story is simply a prose narrative that happens to be much shorter than that of a novel. The short story has its own distinct aesthetic characteristics that distinguish it from the novel.

The two short stories to be examined now are both from the early twentieth century (200 years on from Washington Irving), and neither is by an American writer, but they both demonstrate aesthetic qualities that conform reasonably well to Poe's pioneering definition of the genre. In D. H. Lawrence's story, the horse dealer of the title has died and left his family – three sons and Mabel, a daughter of twenty-seven – hopelessly in debt and on the verge of eviction. Mabel has lost her mother, who died when she was fourteen, and was estranged from her father when he remarried; she has endured a long period of dire poverty through which she tried desperately to retain some sense of pride and self-determination. Mabel now tends her mother's grave and feels a strong emotional attachment there: 'For the life she followed here in the world was far less real than the world of death she inherited from her mother' (Lawrence, 'The Horse Dealer's Daughter' 2263). Despite these inauspicious and unromantic circumstances, the local doctor, Jack Ferguson, is nevertheless mesmerised by Mabel. There is something mystical in her appeal to him, 'a heavy power in her eyes which laid hold of his whole being, as if he had drunk some powerful drug' (2263). Jack follows Mabel to a local pond, where he is astonished to see her wading slowly out into the deep cold water in a clear attempt at suicide. Even though he cannot swim, the doctor wades into the water, pulls Mabel out unconscious and carries her home. Here Mabel revives and almost immediately professes her love, in passionate terms, for the man who has saved her life. The doctor is initially appalled at this new intimacy between them, perhaps because it is contrary to his professional training; yet despite this he finds himself powerless to deny Mabel's appeal and he begins to respond to her passionate intimacy. The doctor kisses Mabel and tells her that he loves her because at this point 'he never intended to love her. But now it was over. He had crossed over the gulf to her, and all that he had left behind had shrivelled and become void' (2268).

The story ends with the doctor's declaration of love and marriage and with Mabel's expression of self-loathing:

> 'I want you, I want to marry you, we're going to be married, quickly, quickly – tomorrow if I can. '
> But she only sobbed terribly, and cried:
> 'I feel awful. I feel awful. I feel I'm horrible to you.'
> 'No, I want you, I want you', was all he answered, blindly, with that terrible intonation which frightened her almost more than her horror lest he should *not* want her. (2269)

Lawrence's story dramatises an extraordinary focus on a single crucial moment of experience, an incident that is revelatory and transformative; the characters show a sudden and remarkable commitment to one another; the doctor rescues Mabel and in doing so he overcomes feelings of professional reserve; a relationship is suddenly forged out of the intensity, and especially the remarkable physicality, of the life-saving incident. Mabel's desperate circumstances are to be remedied by the doctor's offer of security, while simultaneously his previously unspoken interest in her is powerfully overcome by the physical experiences of both the water and Mabel's body. It is a form of redemption for them both.

As regards genre, we might argue that it is characteristic of the short story to focus with great intensity on a single episode that is hugely dramatic and significant. The story's ending in particular leaves the reader with unresolved issues of interpretation. The language of the last lines seems deliberately ambivalent or contradictory: it suggests that there is something more fearful about the doctor's commitment to Mabel than there would have been about his rejection of her. This enigmatic form of expression at the story's end leads us back to the story's details, to try to ascertain and establish the nature of the doctor's desire for Mabel: is it authentic, or is it a tragic mistake in the heat of the moment? Lawrence's story is reasonably clear here: the doctor in particular has experienced a transformative moment and his life has been changed utterly by it.

A useful word for this sudden and dramatic revelation is 'epiphany', a word that is crucial to the short story as a genre. An epiphany has been defined as 'a fleeting moment of mythic perception when the mystery of life breaks through our mundane perception of reality' (Lohafer and Clarey 22). The word 'epiphany' is religious in origin (it meant divine manifestation) and there is a vestige of this religious sense in some of the language of Lawrence's story, where, for example, 'She looked at him again, with the same supplication of powerful love, and that same transcendent, frightening light of triumph' (2267). Mabel's suicide attempt brings about an epiphany for her and the doctor: it is a moment of extraordinary realisation that will change their lives forever.

James Joyce's short story 'Araby' is a first-person narrative in which the young male narrator has a schoolboy's crush on the unnamed girl known only as Mangan's sister: 'I had never spoken to her, except for a few casual words, and yet her name was like a summons to all my foolish blood. Her image accompanied me even in places the most hostile to romance' (2169). The boy's romantic infatuation is something of a fantasy, because he is so distant and removed from the girl he is infatuated with. This unnamed girl tells the boy that she would love to go to the Dublin bazaar known as 'Araby', but she is unable to. So the boy commits himself to bring something for her, a love token that is an expression of his desire for her and which the exoticism of the bazaar seems to symbolise: 'The syllables of the word *Araby* were called to me through the silence in which my soul luxuriated and cast an Eastern enchantment over me' (2170). But the boy is delayed, and when he finally arrives at the bazaar it is about to close, and the opportunity to buy something for Mangan's sister slips away in awkwardness and embarrassment. The story ends with the expression of the boy's disappointment: 'Gazing up into the darkness I saw myself as a creature driven and derided by vanity; and my eyes burned with anguish and anger' (2172). The boy's foolishness suddenly and dramatically comes home to him with remarkable emotional force; he feels how ridiculous he has been to invest in this quest to make a romantic gesture for Mangan's sister, the girl who, even at the story's end, is still not named.

The use of the specific genre of the short story gives enormous power to this crucial final moment of self-recognition: it is a moment of significant self-consciousness, a sudden new awareness of himself that comes to the boy independently of any relationship. The use of the first-person narrative perspective also adds weight to the intensity by which the boy's anguish and anger are directed at himself. The short story genre is ideally suited to dramatising such a fragile but powerful moment of self-recognition: the economical narrative contributes strongly to the force of the story's final moment of revelation. The total effect of the story is dedicated to producing the impact of the final moment of the last lines: it has the intensity of a lyric poem in the care of its particular word-choice, yet it requires a short narrative to bring about that vital sense of the young boy's sudden self-realisation. All of his previous infatuation falls away in that description of himself as a 'creature driven and derived by vanity'. It is a coming-of-age moment, an epiphany of remarkable power that dramatises the boy relinquishing a particular kind of romantic sentimentality that he has foolishly attached to Mangan's sister. Unlike the novel, it is not the story's purpose to dramatise the longer-term development of the boy's consciousness, simply to reveal that single moment of self-awareness in all its poignant force.

The two stories therefore have important aspects in common: both of them conjure moments of powerful romantic transformation from working-class environments that appear on the surface to be inhospitable to conventional ideas of romance. Both stories leave the reader wondering what will happen next, and that sense of contingency or suspense makes a strong formal contribution to the final moments' impact; that is to say, the economy of the specific genre of the short story is largely responsible for the emotional power of the narrative's lasting effects. The ending of each story is characterised by a foreboding sense of a radically different future: they lead us to wonder strongly what will happen next, and novels tend not to do this. The short story is the perfect genre for such feelings, partly because of its economy: it can depict a free-standing moment of epiphany which is the sole focus and purpose of the story.

Further, both stories depict moments of epiphany that specifically concern the subject of desire. The boy in 'Araby' suddenly realises that his form of desire for Mangan's sister is immature and without real substance except in his fantasies, and in that moment of recognition he outgrows that particular form of attachment and moves towards another, more mature, conception of romance. In 'The Horse Dealer's Daughter', the two lovers express a suddenly-discovered desire for each other, but again in ways that might lead us to question the nature of desire: is it authentic, is it fulfilling, will this desire result in a happy future, or is it misplaced, founded on a precarious moment of connection that will prove, like the boy's in 'Araby', immature or inappropriate? In this way it might be argued that both short stories examine the real nature of desire: what is it exactly? how is it known or experienced authentically? and what is its life-changing potential? It is therefore appropriate that both stories should depict moments of epiphany to do with desire, because it might be argued that desire, too, is precarious and elusive, but potentially intense and transformative.

It is worth noting, finally, that such moments of dramatic personal transformation are absolutely central to the experiences of the characters in Washington Irving's short stories from the 1820s. This suggests that despite centuries of experiment and innovation in the genre, there is still a great deal of formal continuity in terms of what the short story does best.

NEXT STEPS

Bayley, John. *The Short Story: Henry James to Elizabeth Bowen*. Brighton: Harvester, 1988.

Levy, Andrew. *The Culture and Commerce of the American Short Story*. Cambridge: Cambridge University Press, 1993.

Reid, Ian. *The Short Story*, London: Methuen, 1977.

Shaw, Valerie. *The Short Story: A Critical Introduction*. London: Longman, 1983.

11

Narrative Language

Keith Hughes

This chapter is concerned with the ways in which prose fictions deploy language. We might begin by asking how does 'narrative language' differ from other types of language?

One useful point of entry into the topic of narrative language is to define what we mean by 'narrative' in the first place. 'Narrative' is often used quite loosely to refer to a story, any story, being related by a variety of means. So, a film or television drama will have a narrative, many songs have narratives, a newspaper report with photographs will have a narrative. However, for the purposes of discussion here, what we mean by narrative is specifically literary narrative; even more specifically, prose narratives. Literary narrative is a telling. Put simply, it is delivered through words alone. Where a playwright can rely on *showing* the story, on actors – as well as props, lighting, sound and so on – physically expressing the drama's meanings, a novelist can only *tell*. The ways in which this telling might affect the reader, the sensations it might invoke in the reader, depend to some extent on the forms in which the narrative is delivered: length of the text, length and layout of individual chapters, and other formal elements. Above all, though, it is a narrative's language, and its use of language, which shapes our response to a text. When we engage in literary study we will want to pay particular attention to the sometimes peculiar ways in which language is deployed in order to create particular effects. The aim of this chapter is to introduce some of the main *types* of narrative language, as well as some of its most important generic conventions.

In particular, this chapter will concentrate on the ways in which the narrative form of the novel may use language in very specific ways – although, as with all generalisations, we need to remember that other genres can and will deploy such linguistic usages. A distinctive linguistic feature of narrative prose as it has developed since the publication of the earliest English novels – Daniel Defoe's *Robinson Crusoe* (1719) and Samuel Richardson's *Pamela* (1740) are two well-known examples – is its attempts to invoke a sense of *reality*. The rise of the novel is generally seen as a cultural expression of the rise of an increasingly affluent – and time-rich – middle-class, and as an instrument for and reflection of growing literacy. Narrative prose, seeking to convince its readers that what it has to say is believable and relevant to them, has developed ways of reflecting and representing, linguistically, thought and emotion, as well as experience of the external world. Importantly, as narrative prose is pure telling, writers have developed various methods by which the written word can seem to be the embodiment of the spoken word, and of unspoken thoughts. The overwhelming push for what became known as 'realism' in prose narrative may well be the most crucial development in narrative language over the past few centuries. By realism we do not mean that what is on the page is a 'real' representation of actual thoughts or actual people, but that it is a convincingly real 'representation' of these and other things. And it is through the medium of language that this realism is produced.

One useful approach to the ways language is used in prose narrative is to think more in terms of languages, rather than a single language. A literary prose narrative contains many different kinds of language, a diversity of different registers and 'voices'. By seeing narrative as an interaction between different voices, we can move as critics from considering language as a stable object to considering it as always a matter of process and friction. One obvious means of delivering these diverse languages is through the speech of different characters within the narrative; again, this is part of the realism effect: having characters speak, or appear to speak, as they would in real life, according to their class, gender, nationality, regional affiliation and so on.

Charles Dickens is a good example of a writer for whom the voice is a crucial aspect of characterisation. The first words spoken by Josiah Bounderby in *Hard Times* (1854), for example, are an index to his self-pitying, falsely modest character:

> I hadn't a shoe to my foot. As to a stocking, I didn't know such a thing by name. I passed the day in a ditch, and the night in a pigsty. That's the way I spent my tenth birthday. Not that a ditch was new to me, for I was born in a ditch. (59)

So in terms of characterisation (see also Chapter 13), the spoken language of each character is important. Yet this is not distinctive to narrative prose: it is also the case, of course, in drama. How does the audience *know* that Shakespeare's Othello is a noble hero? Well, one indicator is the way he speaks, the language he uses. What is distinctive to narrative prose is the voice of the narrator, the guiding voice which leads us through the narrative – or at times *mis*leads us, becoming what Wayne Booth (in his 1961 study *The Rhetoric of Fiction*) would call an 'unreliable narrator'. The diverse voices which may be introduced as an aspect of characterisation are further complicated and extended by the presence of a non-character voice, in the case of third-person narration, and, in other ways, first-person narrative, too. Because narrative prose is not, usually, pure dialogue, the reader is given access to a linguistic world beyond those of the characters. This diversity of voices, of languages within the novel form, marks it out as a distinctive literary genre.

NARRATIVE MULTIPLICITY

A novel's capacity to represent a plurality of voices, or languages, and to show them interacting, while allowing the reader to navigate this complex arrangement, is, of course, dependent upon the skills of the individual author. We also need to bear in mind, though, the idea that language and languages are partly beyond the control of the author, just as they are beyond the control of the reader. As language is intent on communicating something, there are necessarily at least two participants in a language act: the one doing the telling and the one doing the listening/reading. Does the teller/author control the ways in which the language works? To a degree, of course. Yet authors are themselves listeners or readers: this is how they know language in the first place. And the meanings of language are heavily influenced by, or indeed formed by, the social contexts in which the words have been acquired and are being used. Not only are a novel's characters invested with personality through the language they speak, but the text as a whole is a collection of different languages, registers, idioms, and the author may well be unaware of the existence of some of these linguistic layers within the text. There is, therefore, no such thing as a 'monological' narrative that speaks with a single voice or mode of enunciation; rather, all narratives are dialogical, in dialogue with themselves (not just through the interaction of characters, but also through the narrator's use of different forms of language), and with the external world (including the reader).

There are two useful terms to which we can turn when seeking to describe the collation of languages *within* a single text: polyphony (meaning many voices) and heteroglossia (more specifically about diversities and differences between voices in a text). For the hugely influential Russian linguistic and literary theorist Mikhail Bakhtin, this heteroglossia 'is the indispensable prerequisite for the novel as a genre' (Morris 114). So whether we are reading characters' dialogue, or a narrator's description or interjection, we are reading a range of different languages, all in a process of friction and competition for their place in the world of the novel – just as they compete in the real world. This is why the novel may appear to be the most realistic of literary forms.

In the following passage from Vladimir Nabokov's novel *Lolita* (1955), a first-person narrative, the attentive reader may notice that although the narrator is a single character, Humbert Humbert, his narration is infused with different languages and registers:

> We had rows, minor and major. The biggest ones we had took place: at Lacework Cabins, Virginia; on Park Avenue, Little Rock, near a school; on Milner Pass, 10,759 feet high, in Colorado; at the corner of Seventh Street and Central Avenue in Phoenix, Arizona; on Third Street, Los Angeles because the tickets to some studio or other were sold out; at a motel called Poplar Shade in Utah, where six pubescent trees were scarcely taller than my Lolita, and where she asked, *à propos de rien*, how long did I think we were going to live in stuffy cabins, doing filthy things together and never behaving like ordinary people? (158)

Lolita has attracted controversy since publication because the narrator is a paedophile who attempts both to describe and to explain his sexual activities with young girls. The fact that it is the paedophile himself telling the story naturally heightens the reader's unease and wariness in approaching the narrative. Humbert is a pederast and a liar: he needs to be in order to carry out sexual acts on a young girl. The passage above aptly conveys his distorted perspective on sexual relationships, and it is the polyphonic nature of his narration that helps us to read Humbert critically.

Take the lines 'at a motel called Poplar Shade in Utah, where six pubescent trees were scarcely taller than my Lolita, and where she asked, *à propos de rien*, how long did I think we were going to live in stuffy cabins, doing filthy things together and never behaving like ordinary people?' Now, Humbert loathes 'ordinary people' and the values of the society he inhabits, and the mocking phrase '*à propos de rien*' is typical of his own self-regarding, aloof personality. Humbert's ironic position, however, looking down on others, is undermined here by words – 'doing filthy things together' – he invokes from 'my Lolita', or 'Dolly' as he sometimes calls her (both names being diminutives of Dolores, her legal name) and by his revealing personification of the trees as 'pubescent'. The childish simplicity of Dolly's words, and the way in which she parallels the 'stuffy' places with the 'filthy' acts, reminds the reader simultaneously of her youthful innocence and of the sordid reality which the narrative ultimately reveals. Humbert's obfuscations cannot conceal this forever, and it is the clash between languages and registers which continuously exposes it.

If, as readers, we recognise this aspect of his 'character' then we may be able to gain an ironic distance from Humbert Humbert, with the help of the author, Nabokov. *Lolita* clearly marks out the difference between author and narrator: so, although Humbert Humbert repeatedly attempts to justify his abuse of Dolly, the reader is compelled to judge his pronouncements from a critical distance. The multiplicity and diversity of registers – not only Dolly's, but also the banality of place-names and heights – prevents Humbert's view from being all-dominant, giving the reader the space to engage with the text and its narrative without feeling the need to reject the story outright. Constant, complex intermingling of registers also ensures that in a sense the novel is *about* language; about Humbert's attempts to control it and exert control through it.

As mentioned earlier, in seeking to evoke a realistic world, the novel as a genre makes great efforts to represent speech: it tries to sound as if it is talking. However, whether the novel is written in the first person, like *Lolita*, or the third person, as with our next example, Virginia Woolf's *Mrs Dalloway* (1925), the narrative voice is never a unitary voice, but always multiple. The language of the novel is not monological, but dialogical: the language of a fictional text is formed by competing discourses, not by a singular voice. As Jacob Mey puts it, dialogical discourse is 'the basis of the construction of the literary universe with its population of voices, among these the author's and the reader's' (235).

FREE INDIRECT DISCOURSE

A distinctive feature of the novel genre, particularly since the beginning of the nineteenth century, is the development of a literary method which looks to cross the divide between the observing narrator and the observed character. The relationship between narrator and character in a novel is key to our interpretation of the novel's events, character motivations and so forth; and specifically, the ways in which characters' thoughts and speech are delivered to the reader help determine our relationship with character, narrator and text as a whole. Consider the following short extract from Woolf's *Mrs Dalloway*: '"The English are so silent," Rezia said. She liked it, she said' (77). The first sentence – '"The English are so silent," Rezia said' – is an example of what is termed *direct discourse*: we are given Rezia's exact words, from her own mouth, without the narrator even adding an adjective to describe Rezia's tone. The second sentence – 'She liked it, she said' – is an example of *indirect discourse*: we get Rezia's words, but mediated by another voice, that of the narrator. If the second phrase were to be direct discourse it would read '"I like it," she said.' Both of these methods of reporting speech are common in narrative prose, and of course we need to bear in mind that even direct discourse is itself being communicated to us by another voice telling us what 'Rezia said', deciding which of Rezia's many words to tell us about. Despite this added complication, the categories of direct discourse and indirect discourse are a useful and necessary starting point if we wish to understand the specific methods of representation in narrative prose.

Within the critical history of the development of the novel as a genre, however, it is a third method which is commonly held to be the most interesting and important, because the most particular to the novel. This method is known as free indirect discourse, or free indirect style (see also Chapters 12 and 13). Free indirect discourse is a property of many of the great novels of the nineteenth and twentieth centuries, and we will look at a selection of passages from Woolf's modernist novel *Mrs Dalloway* to exemplify what it is and how it works.

As the title suggests, *Mrs Dalloway* is largely concerned with telling the story of a woman, Clarissa Dalloway, whose thoughts, feelings, conversations and so on over the course of one day are the focal point of the narrative. Crucially, however, through its use of free indirect style, the story is told in the third person, not in the first person. As the name implies, free indirect discourse is related to indirect discourse: to such phrases as 'she liked it, she said', cited above. The key difference is that in *free* indirect discourse, the second clause is often dropped: we would have simply 'she liked it'. This method opens up the text, and the reader's interpretation of the text, to ambiguity and multiple interpretations. Put simply, in the example just offered, we are not told that Reiza *said* she liked it, just that she did like it. So it may be a thought, but not spoken. Moreover, free indirect discourse challenges the barrier between narrator and character as the narrator not only reports the character's thoughts, feelings and words, but does so in the idiom of the character herself. This is done to differing degrees, and therefore with differing effects, but as a generalisation it holds true.

In the following two passages from Woolf's novel, instances of free indirect discourse can be identified, along with other means of representing thoughts, and their effects summarised:

> She was wearing pink gauze – was that possible? She *seemed*, anyhow, all light, glowing, like some bird or air ball that has flown in, attached itself for a moment to a bramble. But nothing is so strange when one is in love (and what was this except being in love?) as the complete indifference of other people. Aunt Helena just wandered off after dinner; Papa read the paper. Peter Walsh might have been there, and old Miss Cummings; Joseph Breitkopf certainly was, for he came every summer, poor old man, for weeks and weeks, and pretended to read German

with her, but really played the piano and sang Brahms without any voice. (29)

Clarissa was really shocked. This a Christian – this woman! This woman had taken her daughter from her! She in touch with invisible presences! (110)

In the first passage, we have elements of the 'stream-of-consciousness' technique for which Woolf and James Joyce, in particular, among the great modernist novelists, became known. What distinguishes stream-of-consciousness writing from free indirect discourse is that the former gives the impression of representing directly the thought processes of a character, as if we the reader could read their mind: an example appears in the second sentence of the second extract above.

The final section of Joyce's *Ulysses* (1922) is a celebrated, extended example of stream of consciousness, abandoning the normal grammar and punctuation of written language in order to represent fully the random flow of thoughts. Woolf's passages above are more orderly, but note the swift movement of thought between different objects and topics: from clothes to love to dinner and so on. The free indirect discourse element of the narration is at times difficult to identify: this is one of its advantages as a means of subtle characterisation. 'Was that possible?' is clearly a thought of Mrs Dalloway, and 'he came every summer, poor old man, for weeks and weeks and pretended to read German with her' is also hers. What makes them 'free' is the lack of authorial/narratorial interjection, and, often, the use of third-person pronouns – 'she' and 'her' – even when 'I' might seem more appropriate. The pronoun 'one' is still freer and more fluid: a phrase such as 'nothing is so strange as when one is in love' is ambiguous in its provenance. Is it the opinion of the narrator, or of Mrs Dalloway, or of both?

Such ambiguities need not be resolved: they are one of the great assets of the form, presenting the reader with rewarding textual complexity and further engagement with characters – both objective and subjective, seen from inside and out. Many first-person narratives give us, or seem to give us, direct access to a character, stimulating our interest, gaining our empathy, from the beginning. Woolf creates much the same effects in a third-person narrative. Mrs Dalloway is as much a 'she' as any other character in the novel, and yet a dazzlingly powerful centre of attention: the reader is made to feel very close to her, despite the fact that she is not telling the story. As in all third-person narratives, the characters are described, their thoughts represented by the narrating voice and so on: Woolf's novel, however, is also an exemplary instance of how free indirect discourse can open up new means of representation, new ways of building an image of reality.

METONYMY

As a genre, then, the novel is distinctively polyphonic, and in free indirect discourse has developed a linguistic method for deepening the reader's sense of a representation of real human thought. Within the confines of this chapter, it is also important to offer a brief account of another aspect of narrative language which may be seen as specific to narrative, or favoured by narrative: metonymy. Earlier, it was pointed out that a distinctive feature of the novel as it has developed as a genre – and a feature which may help explain the genre's popularity – is its attempt to invoke a sense of reality, an attempt reliant on the use made of language. While there is a deliberateness about much of this push for realism, many critics have argued that there is also something intrinsic to narrative which makes this realism almost unavoidable. This idea focuses on the establishment of an opposition between two kinds of linguistic devices: metaphor and metonymy. Admittedly, much of the critical writing on this subject is in the field of linguistics, rather than literature; however, as with Bakhtin's sociolinguistic theories, ideas about language in general may be applied to narrative language more specifically.

Poetry, as a genre, relies heavily on figural language, metaphor particularly, as Sarah Dunnigan explains in Chapter 7. All readers of poetry are familiar with metaphor, in which one thing is substituted for another comparable thing in order to produce a fresh, often unnerving perspective on the subject matter. William Blake's poem 'The Sick Rose' (1794) is a well-known example of a densely metaphorical poem; the rose might be read as a metaphor for human life, human sexuality, creativity and so on. Metaphor focuses on the similarity between things in order to express, or imply, its meaning – human life resembles a rose in that it is vulnerable to disease, at least according to Blake. One of the reasons why metaphor is particularly suited to poetry is that poetry does not rely on a chain of events, but on single instances of meaning or suggestion, such as Blake's. As narrative fiction, on the other hand, usually relies upon plot, development, storyline, coherent representation of character and so on, the trope of metaphor is not generally as prevalent.

The device often considered most germane to prose writing is metonymy. Where metaphor focuses on similarities, metonymy and the related device of synecdoche focus on proximities, habitual associations between functions, or relations between parts and wholes. 'Kiwis', for example, can be used to refer to New Zealanders; while 'the pen is mightier than the sword' succinctly (and optimistically!) suggests that writing and ideas are more effective than violence. For Roman Jakobson, one of the most influential theorists on language in literature, the difference between metaphor and metonymy sits at the core of what differentiates poetry from narrative prose. According to this thinking, metonymy offers 'the line of least resistance' for narrative, as metaphor does for poetry. This is because prose relies on contiguity, on things being next to each other, on one sentence following another; and metonymy is precisely also about contiguity.

It also about economy and directness. While poetry often offers singular insights and perceptions, sometimes even momentary ones, novels seek to encapsulate within a couple of hundred pages the sense of lifetimes of experience and entire (fictional) worlds. Economies are essential: notice when reading descriptions of a character's appearance or nature – particularly in nineteenth-century or conventionally realistic fiction – how much authors rely on their readers to develop a full, whole perspective on the basis of associations expanded from a few key details. Metonymy has a role to play in this process, as well as in shaping relations between sections of the text, and its relations to the world it represents. Woolf, for example, writes of a character in *Mrs Dalloway*: 'No, no, no! He was not in love with her anymore! He only felt, after seeing her that morning, among her scissors and silks, making ready for the party, unable to get away from the thought of her' (66). This works as metonymy because Mrs Dalloway's 'scissors and silks' are contextually realistic. Their place in the narrative is entirely consistent with their objective use in the real world: to get ready for a party. However, they also have a suggestive force, and can reasonably be read as symbolising Mrs Dalloway's elevated social position: 'scissors and silks' work much as 'sceptre and crown' in the celebrated lines – and textbook example of metonymy – 'Sceptre and crown/ Must tumble down' (from James Shirley, *The Contention of Ajax and Ulysses* (1640) I, iii).

Likewise, consider the following passage from *Lolita*:

> I marched into her tumbled room, threw open the door of the closet and plunged into a heap of crumpled things that had touched her. There was particularly one pink texture, sleazy, torn, with a faintly acrid odor in the seam. I wrapped in it Humbert's huge engorged heart. (67)

This passage begins by describing a clear action, but is heavy with metonymy, making allusions to other contiguous processes or objects: the tumbled room stands in for the child's undisciplined (free?) childishness, the closet for her invaded and abused body, Humbert's 'huge engorged heart' for his penis. The items of clothing described are contextually in their right place, the scene is in this sense realistic; however, the passage also has metaphorical or representative properties, so that the tumbled room might be interpreted as symbolising the child's temperament, beyond its metonymic fittingness. Like the example from Woolf above, the passage suggests that Jakobson's division between metaphor and metonymy may not be an absolute one, or at any rate that narrative can be as richly and sometimes as densely suggestive as the metaphoric language of poetry. Woolf's writing, and Nabokov's, perhaps make this point especially clearly. Like other key twentieth-century modernists such as Joyce, Joseph Conrad and D. H. Lawrence, each renounced many of the conventions of nineteenth-century and earlier realist fiction, including its direct, extended descriptions of character, often replaced with subtler forms of suggestion or implication. The modernist challenge to realist conventions, however, does leave intact the fundamentals of narrative prose – many-voiced, seeking to represent an idea of reality and favouring, by its linear nature, life that is close by.

NEXT STEPS

Booth, Wayne C. *The Rhetoric of Fiction*, 2nd edn. Chicago: The University of Chicago Press, 1983.

Fludernik, Monika. *An Introduction to Narratology*. London: Routledge, 2009.

Jakobson, Roman. *Language in Literature*. Ed. Krystyna Pomorska and Stephen Rudy, Cambridge, MA and London: Harvard University Press, 1987.

Lodge, David. *The Modes of Modern Writing: Metaphor, Metonymy, and the Typology of Modern Literature*. London: Edward Arnold, 1977.

12

Narrative Structure and Technique

Randall Stevenson

Tell us a story – any story! Why not the story of your life so far? This shouldn't need research. You already know the events involved. There would still be questions, though, about *how* to tell it. Which point of view would you use? Which events would you concentrate on? How would you arrange them into the most engaging, enjoyable form?

Questions of this kind confront any storyteller. They also introduce a key distinction in the study of narrative. All narratives contain events that happened – or, in fiction, are supposed to have happened – which authors shape into the form then encountered by readers. The first of these areas, the set of events to be communicated, is often referred to simply as 'story'. The second, the communication itself, is usually referred to as 'text' or 'narrative text'. Relations between the two – between story and narrative text; between what happened and how it is told – result from, and reveal, authors' technical and structural decisions. These can be roughly divided into two areas, rather as the above questions suggest: matters of perspective – of who witnesses and who describes the events of the story – and issues of ordering, timing and emphasis. These two areas are considered in turn below, using examples from Charles Dickens's *Great Expectations* (1861), Joseph Conrad's novella *Heart of Darkness* (1899) and James Joyce's short story 'The Dead' (1914). These will be supplemented with further thoughts about how you might tell your own story.

PERSPECTIVE

Who should tell your life-story? Obviously, you could just do so yourself. Life-stories are easily told in this autobiographical mode, with an individual describing her or his own experiences in the first person, in the form 'I did this, or that'. Many life-stories, of course, are instead biographical, delivered by an external observer, in the third person, in the form 'he (or she) did this, or that'. You could choose to employ, or imagine, such an observer to tell your own story. What might be gained, and what lost, if you did? No external observer, you might suppose, could know you as well as you know yourself, nor record your thoughts and feelings, if they even found out what these were, with the immediacy you could offer. First-person narrative, in other words, seems to allow a unique entry into an individual's mind and inner experience. On the other hand, what this form gains in inwardness might need to be balanced with loss of objectivity, or range of vision. Limited to your own point of view, it might be hard to record what others thought of you, to enter *their* mindset or experience or to be sure that your view of the world was shared or reliable.

As well as gaining from these opportunities the first-person form offers, novelists may also turn the form's limitations to good effect. In *Great Expectations*, for example, Pip's first-person narrative communicates very directly his thoughts, feelings and views of his world as he grows up towards maturity. Initially, though, many of these views are far from objective, but seriously limited by error and prejudice. Sharing in Pip's personal vision, and in its errors – perhaps guessing what these are, before Pip realises himself – engages readers intimately in an individual's attempts to overcome the misconceptions of youth and to reach the truth about himself and his place in the world.

Third-person narrative texts, on the other hand, seem to know from the beginning the truth about the world they describe. Such texts are often so all-knowing as to be described as 'omniscient' narratives: at any rate, they generally present events objectively, free from the limitations of individual vision. It is worth noticing that this is *only* a convention. There must always be an observer, however anonymous and aloof from the action: some individual, some 'I' who produces the narrative text we read. Conventionally, though, such observers draw little or no attention to themselves – usually eliminating the pronoun 'I' altogether – and offer instead an informed, reliable narrative text, purged of the kind of errors Pip displays. Well-established in imaginative writing, the third-person form is naturally also the most widely used in non-fictional narrative, adding authority and credibility to newspaper reporting, or historical documentation, or indeed to any text attempting to deliver reliable knowledge of the world.

Which of these forms, then, would you choose for your life-story? First-person or third? Since the former directs considerable attention to the observer, and the latter more on what's observed, your choice might be dictated by the kind of life you have led. A life of complex emotional development and private thought might lend itself, like Pip's, to the first-person form. Wide experience of fascinating personalities and world events might be better reported in the third person. Before deciding on one or the other, though, it is worth considering techniques which can add further opportunities to each, often avoiding restrictions mentioned above.

No narrative text, after all, need be delivered by the same storyteller throughout, or from the same point of view. If you chose an autobiographical, first-person form for your life-story, you could still include sections narrated by someone else. Your older brother might deliver a section of narrative text, providing details of early childhood beyond your own recall, perhaps beginning 'I remember noticing, when X was only a few weeks old . . .' Alternatively, you might choose simply to report what he witnessed of your life, in the form 'my brother noticed that, when I was only a few weeks old. . .' In the first instance, your brother takes over as a narrator, delivering a section of text in his own voice and words. In the second, you remain the narrator. You go on speaking or writing the words of the narrative text, but it is your brother, at this point, who sees and experiences the events mentioned. This witnessing and registering of the experience of the story makes him, in the usual critical terminology, a 'focaliser' at this point in the text.

Shifts in perspective of this kind can contribute to objectivity and wider vision even in the most inwardly-directed of literary narratives. The first-person narrative of *Heart of Darkness*, for example, generally confirms the view above – that this technique draws attention to the observer, sometimes almost more than what is observed. Conrad's principal narrator, Marlow, is certainly much concerned with the mysterious Kurtz, and with imperial exploitation in Africa. But his narrative, and even the difficulties he records in communicating it, draw particular attention to Marlow himself, and to the deep effects events he describes have on him. 'Do you see him [Kurtz]? Do you see the story? Do you see anything?' Marlow worries at one point. He concludes, though still doubtfully, that his audience may at any rate 'see me, whom you know' (Conrad 1909). As he suggests, readers of *Heart of Darkness* do see and know Marlow, through everything he describes.

Yet Conrad's technique ensures that this 'seeing' is varied, and includes alternative and wider views. This is achieved partly by equipping *Heart of Darkness* with more than one audience, and more than one narrator. Marlow delivers his tale to an audience *within* the novel – three companions, on a yacht on the Thames at sunset. One of them is a further narrator. Beginning the novella with his description of deepening gloom on the Thames emphasises the dark significance of Marlow's colonial misadventures for the heart of the British empire, as well as the African interior in which they occurred. This further narrator also offers some objective description of Marlow and his appearance, and his occasional comments, delivered throughout, continue to add a certain distance from Marlow's individual vision and experience.

This is occasionally extended in other ways. During his own narrative, Marlow has to rely on witnesses – as you might, in relating your childhood – to provide information about events he did not directly experience himself. Kurtz's extraordinary activities, shortly before Marlow reaches him, are described by the strange Russian whom he meets at the end of his journey upriver. Extravagant approval for Kurtz, expressed through this focaliser, provides a startling contrast to Marlow's own views, though one that probably does more to confirm than qualify them for readers. Throughout, like *Great Expectations*, *Heart of Darkness* offers a deeply inward and mostly sympathetic engagement with an individual narrator and his experience. Variations of narrator and focaliser nevertheless ensure a wider vision for Conrad's novella, and that views of its narrator are not confined too exclusively to his own views of himself.

Through long-established convention, as mentioned earlier, third-person narrative avoids any such confinement. More surprisingly, perhaps, in its literary uses it can also offer the inwardness that might have seemed a particular advantage of the first-person form. This, too, is largely a matter of convention. Almost since the beginnings of the novel, third-person accounts of observable events have extended their view, or 'omniscience', into description of characters' thoughts and feelings as well. Joyce's 'The Dead' demonstrates a range of techniques involved. Early pages give apparently straightforward descriptions of Kate and Julia Morkan, of the house where their Christmas-season party is held and of their nephew Gabriel Conroy. As often in fiction, this readily reveals inner feelings and natures through observable details of conversation or behaviour. Gabriel's blushing and fiddling with his clothes and shoes, for example, obviously register his unease after awkward words with the servant Lily. Much, too, is communicated through the convention of straightforwardly reporting thoughts and feelings – for example, that after his encounter with Lily, Gabriel 'was still discomposed', or, later, 'began to think again about his speech' (2174; 2181).

Such reports concentrate increasingly on Gabriel and his thoughts, ensuring he becomes a principal focaliser for the evening's events. But the method of presenting these thoughts often moves from report towards a form closer to recording or transcription. This can be seen in sentences such as 'He would fail . . . He had taken up a wrong tone. His whole speech was a mistake' or 'How cool it must be outside! How pleasant it would be to walk out alone . . . !' (2174; 2181). These expectations of failure, or of pleasure outdoors, and the way they are expressed, seem to belong at least as much to the character as to the author. The latter, after all, would be unlikely to exclaim, at least in these terms, over the pleasures of the snowy evening. Yet they are written in the third person, and marked neither by inverted commas used to indicate direct speech or thought, nor by cues such as 'Gabriel thought that', often used for indirect transcription of characters' reflections. Somewhere between direct and indirect forms, such sentences belong to the idiom of free indirect style, or free indirect discourse, which Keith Hughes discusses in Chapter 11. Moving subtly between the author and the voice of characters – often an inner voice, as above – free indirect style offers a flexible means of representing thoughts within third-person narrative. Examples of it appear in 'The Dead' literally from the first line.

Locally, sometimes almost line-by-line, free indirect style particularly encourages readers to consider the kind of questions raised in this section on perspective. Whose words are we reading in a narrative text? The author's, written in the third person? Or is there an identifiable first-person narrator, supposedly independent of the author? Is there a character, or characters, through whose point of view we encounter the events presented? How is the author drawing us towards sharing this point of view? Answers to these questions – likely to vary at different points even within a single narrative text – help to identify authors' techniques and the effects they create, locally and in the narrative as a whole.

ORDER AND TIMING

The events of a story occur in chronological order, like those in life. Events in a narrative text need not follow that order. It seems a natural one, but think again about your life-story. You could, obviously, just begin at the beginning, then continue, stage by stage, up to the present day. Yet this might not be as straightforward or effective as it seems. Suppose you began simply – perhaps: 'I was born on a warm June evening, in one of those brilliant summers in the 1990s', or 'X was born . . .' if you chose the third-person form. What next? You could just continue '. . . and grew up happily in leafy Loamshire', or the equivalent. But wouldn't you want to give some context first, maybe in a flashback about parents or family? Perhaps 'My [or X's] parents met at a Christmas party three years previously, surprising each other under the mistletoe . . .' As well as looking back, at this point, you might want to look forward. It might create suspense, or grab readers' attention, if you used a 'flash-forward', perhaps beginning 'Who could have guessed, on that warm summer evening, what an astounding destiny awaited the new baby?'

'Anachrony' is the name usually given to moves of this kind in narrative texts, away from chronological order, with a flashback termed 'analepsis', and a jump forward, 'prolepsis'. Certain forms of writing encourage these moves, with prolepsis a particular opportunity in first-person narratives. Throughout such narratives, storytellers are always aware of two times: the time of the event described, and the time of its description – of the storytelling itself (see also Chapter 15). An account of a past event can therefore jump forward, easily and plausibly, towards the later period in which the story is told. In *Great Expectations*, Pip looks back as a mature adult on his early experience, sometimes indicating the consequences of childhood events on later life. At the end of Chapter 9, for example, describing the effects of a first meeting with Estella, Pip remarks

> That was a memorable day to me, for it made great changes in me. But, it is the same with any life. Imagine one selected day struck out of it, and think how different its course would have been. Pause you who read this, and think for a moment of the long chain of iron or gold, of thorns or flowers, that would never have bound you, but for the formation of the first link on one memorable day.

His remarks clearly create suspense, and interest in how the story will evolve. What changes followed, what 'chain' resulted, and how did it come to bind him? Prolepsis may also encourage readers to reflect on fate – on forces forming personality and its development; perhaps forging similar chains, as Pip suggests, in life as in fiction.

Analepsis appears more frequently in both first- and third-person narrative texts, often used to fill in background, much in the manner suggested for your life story. 'The Dead', for example, immediately engages readers with vivid description of flurried arrivals at the Misses Morkan's party, then moves back in its second paragraph to offer an account of their lives and annual parties over the previous thirty years. Later stages of 'The Dead' demonstrate more complex uses of analepsis. Joyce leaves some of the earliest events of his story almost until the end of his narrative text, where they are introduced through memories triggered by chance for Gabriel's wife Gretta. Encountering a previously unsuspected part of his wife's past has a huge effect on Gabriel, creating the kind of 'epiphany' that Ken Millard discusses in Chapter 10, and the structure of the narrative text ensures that this is vividly shared by readers. Had Joyce simply followed chronological order, readers would have known of Gretta's past before Gabriel does, and might have felt distanced from him – even superior – as a result. As it is, sharing Gabriel's discovery adds to sympathy for him which has been developed throughout – perhaps alongside some amusement at his fears and foibles – by techniques discussed in 'Perspective' above. In turn, this allows the story to conclude with a larger sympathy of its own. Free indirect style engages readers fully with Gabriel's thoughts, but also allows a vision partly beyond them. The text shifts so subtly between author and character at this point that it moves almost beyond definite, individual personality. Concluding paragraphs engage instead with relationships, love and death more generally, reflecting with sad sympathy on the limitations of all thought and all earthly lives (see also Chapter 14).

Other techniques affect the timing of narrative texts as fundamentally as anachrony. Think once again of your life-story. That memorable day of your birth might demand extended description, but it would be neither feasible nor effective to accord equal attention to the thousands of days which followed. Much of your life-story might be delivered in summaries, such as 'I [or X] grew up happily in leafy Loamshire', interspersed with extended treatment of key scenes and the kind of memorable or 'selected' day Pip describes. This kind of alternation of scene and summary is a universal tactic of narrative texts, determining their pace and intensity in communicating the events of the story.

In practice, pace and intensity are almost infinitely variable, though loose distinctions can be made. The pace of events described may, firstly, roughly equate to the pace of reading the text. Gabriel's speech, included in its entirety in 'The Dead', takes about as long to read as it would to deliver. Descriptions of events can also, on the other hand, take considerably longer to read than they would to experience. In *Heart of Darkness*, the mortal injury suffered by Marlow's helmsman is inflicted in a moment, but takes several faltering sentences to describe. At the other extreme, events occupying long periods – even several years, like that childhood in Loamshire – can be described in a single summary sentence, or even omitted altogether. For example, Marlow has almost nothing to say about the period between Kurtz's death and his own return to Europe. In 'The Dead', Joyce likewise offers no account of events between the triumphal end of Gabriel's speech and the chilly leave-takings that conclude the party.

In each case, extensions and abbreviations in the narrative text crucially shape the impact of the story on readers. Gabriel's speech dominates his thoughts. Its extended description, and the chilly void it seems to leave behind, ensure once again that readers closely share his experience of the evening. Marlow's hesitant description of violence dramatises its bewildering effect on him, and his reticence about the period immediately following Kurtz's death – apparently including a life-threatening fever – emphasises the latter's profound though mysterious influence on him.

CRITICAL PRACTICE

Reflections like those above help resist impressions that structure or perspective may be dry or narrowly technical areas for literary criticism. Readers and students might well question how much is gained by suggesting that the events in a story such as 'The Dead', which might be labelled A, B, C, D, E,

F, actually appear in the narrative text in the order (roughly) C, A, D, E, B, F. Issues of order, anachrony or perspective are not ones that necessarily much occupy readers, often more interested in character, plot or action. Yet they are issues which inevitably concern authors, as you will have realised if you did think, even for a moment, about how best to communicate your life-story. Dickens could not have gone far in writing *Great Expectations* without assessing potentials and pitfalls in using a grown-up, first-person narrator to describe a younger self. Nor could Conrad, in *Heart of Darkness*, without considering the consequences of locating his narrators on the Thames rather than on the African river where Marlow's adventures took place. Correspondingly, by considering choices authors have made and techniques they have deployed, readers access factors which fundamentally shape and orient the narrative texts they read. Though techniques involved may not be immediately obvious, they are often primarily responsible for the effects fiction creates, as examples analysed above may help suggest.

Analysis of this kind is also relevant well beyond literary fiction. As discussed already, it can be applied to biography, autobiography and non-fictional narratives generally, and to an extent to other literary genres such as drama or narrative poetry. Narrative, of course, figures throughout contemporary culture in ways by no means confined to literary texts, or to written language at all. Forms of analysis introduced above can often be equally well applied to other media, such as television series, or even advertising, and certainly to film. The use of multiple camera-angles in filming, for example, might be usefully compared with changes of focaliser in a narrative text.

Thinking about structures and techniques can also contribute to an understanding of how, and why, cultures change and develop generally. For example, looking at technique in early twentieth-century novels reveals much more reliance on anachrony than figured in nineteenth-century fiction. These novels also more frequently favour forms of communicating characters' thoughts, such as free indirect style or the still more direct transcription offered by the stream-of-consciousness form Keith Hughes describes in Chapter 11. It is worth considering why such tactics predominated at this time, as part of so-called modernist changes of style early in the century, and what wider influences in the age might have encouraged this. Likewise, it is often said that first-person narrative figures unusually frequently in fiction published in the early twenty-first century. If evidence of this could be firmly established, it would be interestingly indicative – perhaps of an age in which collective, consensual vision of life and society has been replaced by more confident or exclusive interest in the individual self.

Further speculations are opened up by thinking about structure and technique, concerned not only with individual texts, but with the nature of imagination generally, and its apparently unquenchable appetite for narrative. Tactics described in 'Perspective', above, help explain this appetite, highlighting techniques authors have developed to assuage it. As well as recording the surface of experience, these techniques allow easy movement beyond it, offering more complete, quick and subtle insight into individuals' inner beings than is usually available in life itself. Joyce's tactics ensure Gabriel's character and insecurities are exposed to readers, fully and rawly, in an hour or so's reading about the single evening 'The Dead' describes. A single evening on the Thames, in *Heart of Darkness*, leads not only into the African continent but into the heart of Marlow himself, and of the imperial 'civilisation' in which he works.

Tactics discussed in 'Order and Timing', above, further explain the appeal of narrative. Its fundamental reliance on anachrony might even qualify the opinion that began that section – that life is lived in chronological order. It is, of course! Individuals are born, grow up, age and die, invariably in that order, and with clocks and calendars to measure the pace of their progress. Yet it is often remarked that life is lived forwards but experienced backwards, through memories of what has been lived. Likewise, there can be few people who experience with steady, equal attention each day of their lives, each hour of their day and each minute in each hour. Instead, memory, anticipation, boredom or enjoyment constantly create highlights, expansions, contractions, re-emphases and reorderings, much in the manner of narrative texts. As a result, and more than might be supposed, life is experienced like a narrative. At any rate, life offers much reason to *like* narrative, which can be relied on to provide the pace and order imagination desires. 'Fabulous' is a word signifying both the wonderful or amazing, and the material offered by fables or stories. Examining narrative structure and technique adds to understanding of how, and how wonderfully, narrative provides us with the shape, order, experience and excitement life itself may lack. It helps show why, in other words, there is always a desire for someone to tell us a story – any story!

NEXT STEPS

Bal, Mieke. *Narratology: Introduction to the Theory of Narrative*. London: University of Toronto Press, 1997.

Herman, David, Manfred Jahn and Marie-Laure Ryan, eds. *Routledge Encyclopedia of Narrative Theory*. New York: Routledge, 2005.

Lodge, David. *The Art of Fiction: Illustrated from Classic and Modern Texts*. Harmondsworth: Penguin, 1992.

Rimmon-Kenan, Shlomith. *Narrative Fiction: Contemporary Poetics*. London, Methuen, 2003.

13

Constructing Character

Rajorshi Chakraborti

In an essay comparing the work of novelists from across four centuries, the Czech writer Milan Kundera formulates a pair of questions which, according to him, 'all novels seek to answer': 'What is an individual? Wherein does his identity reside?' (11) Yet, directly after making such a broad, trans-historical claim, Kundera goes on to propose that writers working in different literary-historical periods respond to these same questions in distinct ways. In his view, novelists in different eras – and influenced by particular social, histori-cal, intellectual and aesthetic trends and circumstances – emphasise different aspects of character formation as being of especial significance to explore, and accordingly employ specific techniques to realise their thematic priorities. This process, Kundera also argues, is how the novel (in common with other art-forms) has evolved – through practitioners engaging in constant dialogue with, and drawing on or dissenting from, the aims and methods of their predecessors.

In this chapter we will focus on four stories (drawn from both halves of the twentieth century) by Virginia Woolf, Raymond Carver, Thomas Pynchon and Doris Lessing, each of which highlights a distinct aspect of character construction and uses narrative modes best suited for its specific aims. I will suggest, as Kundera does, that these writers prioritise thematic concerns that they share with other artists and thinkers of their time. I will also demon-strate that what raises the dramatic stakes in these stories is that each of them includes characters who are engaged in the same interpretative pursuit as us: they too are attempting to use the same techniques, and read the same details, in order to gain crucial understanding of themselves, or of others who are deeply significant to them. Thus, the exploration of the methods available to readers to penetrate and interpret the mysteries of other personalities figures as a central theme in all these stories, as well as being exemplified technically in each narrative.

VIRGINIA WOOLF'S 'THE LEGACY': A MODERNIST REFUTATION OF 'MATERIALISM'

In a well-known quarrel with the narrative methods of her older contemporaries H. G. Wells, Arnold Bennett and John Galsworthy (published as an essay entitled 'Modern Fiction' (1925)), Virginia Woolf casts them as 'materialists' who are far too 'concerned not with the spirit, but with the body' (2088). Woolf's essay expresses her own, modernist, belief that fiction should primarily evoke the inner consciousness of characters, and suggests that a faithful adherence, instead, to certain tenets of nineteenth-century realism – such as 'proving the solidity, the likeness to life' of the worlds depicted – actually results in a focus on 'unimportant things' (2089, 2088). Regarding Bennett, for instance, Woolf argues:

> His characters live abundantly . . . but it remains to ask how do they live, and what do they live for? More and more they seem to us . . . to spend their time in some softly padded first-class railway carriage, pressing bells and buttons innumerable, and the destiny to which they travel so luxuriously becomes . . . an eternity of bliss spent in the very best hotel in Brighton. (2088)

Woolf's charge against these skilled craftsmen of surfaces is that in their focus on getting right every 'single button . . . as the Bond Street tailors would have it', 'life, or spirit, truth or reality . . . the essential thing' (2089) escapes their pages. But in her story 'The Legacy' (1940), she goes further, by choosing for a central character a busy and successful man-of-the-world (a 'materialist' in an even more literal sense), and then dramatising through his own eyes his growing awareness that many 'essential thing(s)', about his wife and others around him, have entirely escaped his attention.

Through the use of free indirect style (see Chapters 11 and 12), Woolf affords us access to the inner consciousness of Gilbert Clandon (his thoughts, feelings, unvoiced instincts and reactions), who is mourning the death of his wife Angela in a recent traffic accident, as well as handling the difficult task of distributing her possessions as instructed among her friends and acquaintances. He finds this turn of affairs quite mysterious in itself, given that she had been 'in perfect health' at the time of her accident: 'how strange it was . . . that she had left everything in such order – a little gift of some sort for every one of her friends. It was as if she had foreseen her death' ('The Legacy' 2226).

Although we share Clandon's bafflement at this odd puzzle, Woolf's technique of interweaving his unvoiced memories, reflections and reactions with his speech and actions allows us to begin constructing a portrait of his own personality. At the start of the story, he is waiting to receive his deceased wife's secretary in order to give her a brooch Angela had left her. Clandon acknowledges to himself that in his eyes Sissy Miller 'was scarcely distinguishable from any other woman of her kind', but that 'Angela, with her genius for sympathy, had discovered all sorts of qualities in [her]' (2226–7). In the course of their meeting, it is only Miss Miller's dark clothes that remind him that she too 'was in mourning, of course. She too had had her tragedy – a brother . . . had died only a week or two before Angela' (2227). However, the details remain vague to Clandon: 'in some accident was it? He could remember only Angela telling him; Angela, with her genius for sympathy, had been terribly upset' (2227).

Yet, as the story progresses, we realise that Clandon, ambitious Member of Parliament, with a daily schedule full of speeches, committees and dinners, has been an inattentive reader of a character much more significant to him than Miss Miller: his late wife, whom he mentally seems to have fixed in the phrase 'with her genius for sympathy'. The device Woolf employs – that of Angela's diaries, by which Clandon finally learns of the major emotional developments in her recent life, and the reason for her death – is a relatively straightforward one for revealing some of a character's innermost feelings, secrets and motives, but it is also made clear that Angela believed nothing more subtle would have sufficed to penetrate Clandon's haze of busyness and self-absorption. Hence the diaries were her only parting legacy for him. Although Woolf shows us that Clandon had cared for Angela in his own way ('he had always been very proud to be her husband. How often when they dined out somewhere he had looked at her across the table and said to himself, she is the loveliest woman here'), she also discloses the limitations of such affection, and his attention (2228). Even as Clandon is reading the diary and learning many things about Angela for the first time, he skips the parts where 'his own name occurred less frequently. His interest slackened' (2229). When he tries to recall returning home on a particular evening during which Angela might have been in the house alone with her mysterious acquaintance B. M., Woolf tells us that 'he could remember nothing – nothing whatever, nothing except his own speech at the Mansion House dinner' (2230).

Of course, the revelations in the diaries have another tragic implication for Clandon: no matter how comprehensive they are, they can only ever be paltry when compared to all that he has failed to notice, learn and cherish about his wife while she was still an everyday living presence. The incomplete, discontinuous fragments of text that he has been left with merely emphasise the scale of his loss. Woolf has already shown us that Clandon continues to be a flawed interpreter of the people he interacts with: he misreads Miss Miller's parting avowal to be of assistance to him as a possible sign that 'during all those years when he had scarcely noticed her, she . . . had entertained a passion for him' (2228). After all, 'he could not help admitting that he was still, as the looking-glass showed him, a very distinguished-looking man' (2228).

In Woolf's story therefore, poor attention to the presence, speech and other glimpses into the emotions of another character is shown to have greatly impoverishing existential (and not just literary-critical) consequences. Her use of free indirect style to reveal, and remain close to, the workings of Clandon's inner life can be seen as not only the result of a characteristically modernist effort to 'trace the pattern, however disconnected and incoherent in appearance, which each sight or incident scores upon the consciousness' (Woolf, 'Modern Fiction' 2090). Rather, it also serves to show up the limits of his own interest in and concern for other people. By providing us with no more than his partial memories and skewed impressions of Angela and Miss Miller respectively, Woolf subversively dramatises from within Clandon's consciousness that he is in fact a novice at sympathy, and that the only character he has ever imagined with real attention is his own.

In his 1927 study *Aspects of the Novel* (1927), E. M. Forster famously distinguishes between 'flat' characters – ones based on a 'single idea or quality' which can be 'expressed in a single sentence' – and 'round' characters, those capable of more 'extended life' (75, 76, 83). Seen in these terms, it is clear that Clandon is the only 'round' character in Clandon's life, while everyone else is virtually 'flat'– reducible to a stereotype: 'there were thousands of Sissy Millers – drab little women in black carrying attaché cases', or a phrase: 'Angela, with her genius for sympathy' ('The Legacy' 2226, 2227). Only near the story's end does Clandon begin to visualise his wife in detail as an autonomous entity, at the moment when she would have chosen to end her life: 'he could see her in front of him. She was standing on the kerb in Piccadilly. Her eyes stared; her fists were clenched. Here came the car . . .' (2230). Of course, as far as his relationship with the living Angela is concerned, it is far too little, and much too late.

RAYMOND CARVER'S 'CATHEDRAL': A POSTMODERN QUESTIONING
OF CHARACTERISATION

Contrasted with Woolf, Raymond Carver deploys a wider range of techniques in order to delineate his secondary characters (longer scenes, more specific memories, much fuller renditions of dialogue and interaction as well as mood and physical detail) in his story 'Cathedral' (1984). This is because

Carver employs a narrator who, unlike Clandon, is able to use these methods attentively in observing and trying to interpret the relationship between his wife and their blind guest, Robert. Of course, as is usual with first-person narratives, we are allowed several glimpses into the narrator's unspoken thoughts and reactions (see Chapter 12), but Carver shows that the living presence and autonomous reality of other people constantly register in his mind and memories. For instance, he has clearly listened to his wife's stories of her friendship with Robert, because he recounts them in quite specific detail throughout the first half of the story:

> She read stuff to him, case studies, reports, that sort of thing. She helped him organise his little office in the county social-service department. They'd become good friends, my wife and the blind man. How do I know these things? She told me. (Carver 2198)

In contrast to the self-centred and otherwise vague memories of Clandon, Carver's narrator can recall a poem his wife had showed him years ago, about an occasion when Robert asked to touch her face:

> When we first started going out together, she showed me the poem. In the poem, she recalled his fingers and the way they had moved around over her face. In the poem, she talked about what she had felt at the time, about what went through her mind when the blind man touched her nose and lips. (2198)

Yet Carver shows us that the narrator's interest in the details of other people's experiences is not restricted to replaying anecdotes in his memory: he is also attuned to mood, conversation, appearance, significant actions, gestures and body language, as well as to how these evolve over the course of the evening when his wife's friend is actually present in their home. He notices his 'wife laughing as she parked the car', then recalls how she 'took [Robert's] arm, shut the car door, and, talking all the way, moved him down the drive and then up the steps to the front porch' (2200). The narrator notes closely their guest's appearance ('late-forties, a heavy-set, balding man with stooped shoulders, as if he carried a great weight there. He wore brown slacks, brown shoes, a light-brown shirt, a tie, a sports coat' (2201)) and goes on to scrupulously record the particular inflections of his speech ('"Bub, I'm a Scotch man myself," he said fast enough in this big voice. "Right," I said. Bub!"' (2201)). Later on, at the dinner table, in the midst of some 'serious eating' himself, the narrator finds a moment to notice their guest's table routines:

> The blind man had right away located his foods, he knew just where everything was on his plate. I watched with admiration as he used his

knife and fork on the meat. He'd cut two pieces of meat, fork the meat
into his mouth, and then go all out for the scalloped potatoes, the beans
next, and then he'd tear off a hunk of buttered bread and eat that. He'd
follow this up with a big drink of milk. It didn't seem to bother him to
use his fingers once in a while, either. (2202)

Clearly then, as a 'reader' of character, Carver's narrator has a far wider range
of skills than Gilbert Clandon in 'The Legacy'. Unlike Clandon, Carver's
narrator treats as a palpable reality the fact that other people, be they inti-
mates or strangers, have autonomous, 'rounded' lives, and share memories
and relationships in which he himself plays no part. He employs various
narrative techniques to depict his wife and their guest, and connects all that
he recalls about their past to what he observes during Robert's visit, so that
he may have as much information as possible as he tries to interpret their
friendship.

In this way, the narrator can be seen as a surrogate presence combining the
roles of both writer and reader within the story, because of his intense interest
in the processes of character-construction and character-deciphering respectively. Yet, as the story unfolds, Carver also introduces a significant degree
of doubt as to the validity of the perspective we are receiving on Robert.
Although we are impressed by qualities such as the narrator's memory and
his attentiveness to detail, Carver provides us with regular glimpses into his
(mostly unvoiced) consciousness that implicitly compel us to question his
reactions and attitudes when confronted by the unknown or the apparently
'other', and the rapidity with which his observations harden into negative
judgements about Robert.

Throughout the story, for example, the narrator gives us several hints
that he is uncomfortable in the presence of the unfamiliar. Early on, he
confesses his instinctive reaction to the fact that their prospective guest is
blind: 'I wasn't enthusiastic about his visit. He was no one I knew. And his
being blind bothered me . . . A blind man in my house was not something
I looked forward to' (2198). He is similarly uneasy about knowing that his
wife has regularly corresponded with her friend through audio-tape letters,
and that she thinks of him as a close confidante: 'After a few minutes of
harmless chitchat, I heard my own name in the mouth of this stranger, this
blind man I didn't even know! . . . Now this same blind man was coming
to sleep in my house' (2199). Even before Robert has arrived, the narrator
tries to visualise his guest's marriage based on the few details he has heard
from his wife:

They'd married, lived and worked together, slept together . . . and then
the blind man had to bury her. All this without his having ever seen

what the goddamned woman looked like. It was beyond my understanding . . . And then I found myself thinking what a pitiful life this
woman must have led. (2200)

The narrator's speculations on the subject of Robert's marriage conclude
with the word 'pathetic' (2200). Later on, when he finally has a chance
to contemplate Robert in person, he finds much in his appearance that is
disturbing, such as his beard ('A beard on a blind man! Too much, I say'
(2200)), and his 'creepy' eyes (2201). In fact, such is his level of preoccupa-
tion with the fact of their guest's blindness that throughout the story Robert
is only referred to by the narrator either as 'he', or, far more often, as 'the
blind man'.

Carver thus dramatises a character who, for all his skill at 'reading' other
people, and his awareness that they have autonomous lives, relationships and
pasts that do not always include or centre upon him, is still deeply discomfited
by any experience he cannot readily identify with or enter. The unfamiliar
unnerves him, even by its physical presence. And by inviting us to scrutinise
the processes through which the narrator accumulates what he believes to
be 'knowledge' about Robert, to regard sceptically the judgements he forms
based on a mixture of random details and instinctive prejudices and to note
the anxieties that erupt within him during this encounter with the unfamiliar,
Carver can be seen as engaging with ethical issues, as well as certain questions
about how we apprehend and interpret reality – ontological and epistemo-
logical questions, in other words. Shared with several of his contemporaries
– other writers as well as critical theorists – such preoccupations are characteristic of a sceptical 'postmodern' age. What is the status, and basis, of our
'knowledge' of other people? How open are our judgements when confronted
by forms of 'difference'? How do these judgements enrich or impoverish our
interpretations of such characters?

It is only near the end of the story that the narrator, considerably mellowed
by marijuana, is able to relax enough to allow Robert's hand to rest atop his
own while he outlines at his request the sketch of a cathedral. He even obeys
his guest and closes his eyes during the drawing, and finally permits himself to
enter a hitherto unfamiliar experience:

> So we kept on with it. His fingers rode my fingers as my hand went over
> the paper. It was like nothing else in my life up to now.
> Then he said, 'I think that's it . . . Take a look. What do you think?'
> But I had my eyes closed. I thought I'd keep them that way for a little
> while longer . . . I was in my house. I knew that. But I didn't feel like I
> was inside anything.
> 'It's really something,' I said. (2207–8)

THOMAS PYNCHON'S 'ENTROPY' AND DORIS LESSING'S 'TO ROOM
NINETEEN': THE SOCIAL SHAPING OF CHARACTER

Much post-Second World War fiction (as well as critical and cultural theory)
has explored another theme with significant implications for the construction
of literary characters: that of the impact upon our personalities of dominant
social trends, discourses, 'meta-narratives' and ideologies. By revealing the
nearly overwhelming influence of these powerful forces upon the world views
and self-conceptions of their characters, these works compel us to consider
the extent to which such continual social and discursive 'shaping' also plays
a crucial role in character formation. This will be the final theme we will
examine in this chapter, and we will do so by looking at extracts from stories
by Thomas Pynchon and Doris Lessing.

In Pynchon's story 'Entropy' (1960), an omniscient narrative voice (see
Chapter 12) is used to characterise most of the guests at a party solely by enu-
merating the consumer habits and cultural trends they favour as a group. No
further effort is made to delineate them as distinct personalities, thus implying that such a list – of the things they buy and the pretensions they affect as
a group – is both essential *and sufficient* for a reader to situate them precisely
within their niche of late-capitalist American society:

> They would stage . . . polyglot parties where the newcomer was sort
> of ignored if he couldn't carry on simultaneous conversations in three
> or four languages. They would haunt Armenian delicatessens for weeks
> at a stretch and invite you over for bulghour and lamb in tiny kitchens
> whose walls were covered with bullfight posters. They would have affairs
> with sultry girls from Andalucia or the Midi who studied economics at
> Georgetown. (Pynchon 2181)

It is as though Pynchon ironically re-adopts the 'materialism' rejected by
Woolf in 'Modern Fiction' as an adequate mode of character-shorthand to
depict his time and place. Yet the influence of popular trends and fashionable
intellectual discourses is shown to penetrate much deeper than shared group
practices. Even when Pynchon focuses on the inner world of one of his principal characters he demonstrates how Callisto is in thrall to the vocabulary of
thermodynamics and feels that he has discovered through the study of entropy
'an adequate metaphor to apply to certain phenomena in his own world'
(2184):

> In American 'consumerism' [he] discovered a similar tendency from the
> least to the most probable . . . from ordered individuality to a kind of
> chaos. He . . . envisioned a heat-death for his culture in which ideas, like
> heat-energy, would no longer be transferred'. (2184–5)

However, while trying to revive a dying bird at the end of the story, Callisto finds his all-encompassing 'meta-narrative' to be entirely inapplicable and inadequate as a response, though it is the best he can offer:

> 'I held him,' he protested, impotent with the wonder of it, 'to give him the warmth of my body. Almost as if I were communicating life to him, or a sense of life. What has happened? Has the transfer of heat ceased to work?'(2190)

The first half of Doris Lessing's story 'To Room Nineteen' (1963) examines a related problem – that of measuring the nuances of a character's actual experiences against the expectations created by dominant discourses and value-systems. Susan and Matthew, whose self-image is one of being 'well-informed and responsible people' (2546), reassure themselves about their increasingly troubled marriage by reiterating the most varied and up-to-date thinking that they have absorbed about people in their situation. Lessing employs free indirect style to show how these characters now sound just like the books they have read even when they speak or think: 'So what did it matter if they felt dry, flat? People like themselves, fed on a hundred books (psychological, anthropological, sociological), could scarcely be unprepared for the dry, controlled wistfulness which is the distinguishing mark of the intelligent marriage' (2546). Later on, as with Pynchon's entropy-obsessed protagonist Callisto, we see the effects of the almost-voluntary entrapment of Susan and Matthew within the terms of their favoured discourses, as they seek to react to the specificities of their deteriorating relationship:

> There was no need to use the dramatic words, unfaithful, forgive, and the rest: intelligence forbade them. Intelligence barred, too, quarrelling, sulking, anger, silences of withdrawal, accusations and tears. Above all, intelligence forbids tears.
>
> A high price has to be paid for the happy marriage with the four healthy children in the large white gardened house.
>
> And they were paying it, willingly. . . (2547–8)

Both stories bring out the ready availability – virtually as consumer options in their own right for the educated middle classes – of a wide array of fashionable or intellectually prestigious discourses within mid-to-late twentieth-century Western society. Yet, exhibiting a scepticism characteristic of much postmodern writing and thought, they go on to satirically explore the dangers of rigid adherence to the terms and categories of any such 'meta-narrative' or ideology, especially as their characters are confronted by the test of responding to new, unpredictable and particular experiences.

CONCLUSION

In his essay on 'The Art of Fiction' (1884), Henry James makes the claim that there is no part of a narrative 'that is not [also] of character' (862). He substantiates:

> What is character but the determination of incident? What is incident but the illustration of character? What is . . . a novel that is *not* of character? What else do we seek in it and find in it? It is an incident for a woman to stand up with her hand resting on a table and look out at you in a certain way . . . At the same time it is an expression of character. (862)

This essay has shown, in a Jamesian vein, how we can glean direct or implied character insights from several interrelated aspects of any fiction: not only the reported details of physical presence, inner life and social interaction, but also their styles and narrative voices as well as the priorities (and limits) of their guiding points of view. As the examples discussed demonstrate, authors frequently draw on intellectual, philosophical and aesthetic preoccupations characteristic of their wider period, and turn them into distinct ways of constructing literary characters, each of which raises different questions, and gives us new human views.

NEXT STEPS

Forster, E. M. *Aspects of the Novel*. Harmondsworth: Penguin, 1971.

James, Henry. 'The Art of Fiction'. In *Norton Anthology of Theory and Criticism*. 855–69.

Kundera, Milan. 'The Day Panurge No Longer Makes People Laugh'. In *Testaments Betrayed*. London: Faber, 1995, pp. 1–32.

Woolf, Virginia. 'Modern Fiction'. In *Norton Anthology of English Literature* 2. 2087–92.

14

Narrative, Society and History

Aaron Kelly

Thinking about fiction in terms of its various forms and genres usually involves well-established expectations about what is appropriate to each of them. We are encouraged to think that a particular genre, such as the novel or short story, has an appropriate subject matter and context, while various forms or styles of writing – such as realism, the gothic or fantastic – are suitable for specific kinds of experience; also, in each case, following appropriate rules and priorities. These priorities, and expectations about the nature of the novel and short story generally, have evolved through history, and as a result of authors' responses to the societies in which they lived. This chapter explores various forms and genres of fiction in relation to this historical evolution, looking at the ideas of critics who have sought to explain it, and examining the social roles of writing and narrative imagination.

The novel is usually considered to have emerged in the eighteenth century, at a time when Europe, under the influence of various nationalist movements, developed into modern, bourgeois nation states. Critics such as Benedict Anderson, in *Imagined Communities* (1983) propose that the novel played a formative cultural role in this process – in cementing the development of cohesive modern nations. Anderson contends that the novel offers such nations a form in which individuals can imagine themselves as part of a unified national community, replacing older regional, cultural or linguistic divisions. Central to this process, according to Anderson, is the development of print technology, a literate population and a standardised national language through which this new unity may be expressed (see also Chapter 9). Anderson's views do emphasise one of the novel's characteristic strengths: its potential to explore relations between individuals and wider societies. But there is also a risk: that his views suggest only mature, unified societies produce novels, while more backward or less developed ones produce only the more fragmentary, fractured form of the short story.

Some widely-accepted accounts of the short-story form seem further to support such views. The Irish writer and critic Frank O'Connor defined the short story as the primary mode of expression for 'submerged population groups' (18). In other words, short stories may be especially appropriate for people at the margins of society, unable to gain access to mainstream media and dominant forms of representation. This thinking was based on O'Connor's account of the short story's role in literature in the United States, where, he claimed, continual waves of immigration and settlement had established a whole range of divergent ethnic groups and ghettos. These 'submerged population groups' struggled both to express their own experience on the social margins, yet also to enter a mainstream which itself, in the USA, was subject to transformation and not necessarily clearly or coherently unified. Comparisons can be made here with Ireland. Collisions between Irish and British culture provide a further example of a fractious society which might be more suited, in O'Connor's eyes, to producing short stories rather than novels. In his view, the short story is ideally suited to confronting a shifting, fragmentary society, such as Ireland's, experiencing uneasy tensions between folk and cosmopolitan traditions, between old and new.

These suggestions have been taken further by other critics. In their view, there is more than just a general correspondence between novel or short story and historical phases of a society or nation's development. This correspondence also extends into relations between a society's development and specific forms of writing *within* the genres of novel and short story. In this view, the forms of writing most closely corresponding to a society's advanced development and historical maturity are historical fiction and the realist novel. For the Hungarian Marxist critic Georg Lukács, the historical novel often deals with great and disturbing moments of upheaval and change, but it still manages to present a society coherently and in its entirety. Events depicted are likely to involve antagonism and struggle, but historical fiction usually still shows diverse social groups integrated within a harmonised, collective narrative ordering of the world. The historical novel, in other words, encourages us to accept what seems a plausible, objective and realistic representation of history, and, in turn, to accept our place within a connected, shared understanding of history itself.

While the historical novel affords us a coherent view of the history which has made us and our societies, Lukács sees this process completed by the realist novel – the form that reproduces most convincingly for us the real world that we live in, providing a rounded, all-encompassing reflection of our present life. In realist writing, the individual is usually reconciled with a society, represented as a coherent whole. This capacity to view the whole is important to Lukács, whose Marxist politics made him an adversary of capitalist economic systems, and of the competitive individualism, class divisions – and hence fractured, divergent perspectives – that they create. Realist novels, for Lukács, at least offer a full overview of these divisions and divergences, and of the society in which they operate, placing individual experience in meaningful relation with the society which shapes it. A tension nevertheless arises between content and form, or, if you like, between realism and reality. Many realist novels do expose all sorts of social inequalities and divisions, in ways of which much Marxist criticism would approve, yet Lukács diminishes the force of this exposure by suggesting that the literary form of the realist novel can transcend these fractures by offering a continued wholeness: in the shared, coherent, objective viewpoint of the novel itself. Realist fiction seems to offer in this way a fair and full view of everyone: real societies do not.

This tension between content and form is further highlighted by some of Terry Eagleton's views in his critical study *Heathcliff and the Great Hunger* (1995). This work develops the idea introduced above – that some societies produce the novel (with realism as its highest achievement) while others are unable to. In Eagleton's thinking, England offers an example of a successfully-achieved realist literary tradition, while Ireland lacks the conditions necessary for this achievement. Eagleton associates realism with the kind of 'liberal impartiality' he finds in novels such as George Eliot's *Middlemarch* (1871–2) – novels that 'alternate in their pages the perspectives of higher and lower classes' (150–1). Eliot, in this view, allows upper and lower classes to speak within the same shared field of representation, shifting her perspective between these divergent social groups within what remains a cohesive, democratic, narrative ordering of experience. This rounded mode of representation is possible, Eagleton argues, because of what he terms England's social 'settlement and stability' (147).

A fairer view might reconsider some of the tensions between form and content mentioned above. Instead of alternating equally between the perspectives of upper and lower classes, novels such as *Middlemarch* may instead be translating the experiences of the latter into the register of the former. This is not democracy but domination, and suggests realism may be less representation than ruse. Because realist writing *seems* so persuasively representative of experience, it allows what is actually a dominant ordering of the world to be mistaken for objective reality itself. Social pressures, conflicts and antagonisms which shape the actual world can be suppressed within literary form: a convincing picture of a stable, consensual society obscures the difficult conditions of contemporary life itself – including, around George Eliot's time, industrialisation and convulsive social conflict and change.

Eagleton substantiates his views of England as a settled, stable society, reflected in successful realist writing, by making contrasts with Ireland. Because it lacks the social stability and development of England, Eagleton maintains, Ireland lacks a tradition of novelists such as Eliot, Henry Fielding, or Jane Austen: 'art demands serenity, stable evolution, classical equipoise; and an island racked by rancorous rhetoric is hardly the appropriate breeding ground for these virtues' (*Heathcliff and the Great Hunger* 151). Such views overlook challenges to 'serenity' which undoubtedly occurred in England, and reduce Ireland's complex situation to one simply lacking stability and development. They also return us to the idea considered earlier: that mature societies produce novels whereas others do not develop beyond the fractured form of the short story.

Let us use James Joyce's short story collection *Dubliners* (1914) as a test case for these arguments. Joyce's own rationale for his collection seems to confirm the idea that early twentieth-century Ireland lacks the wholeness required to produce novels, especially realist and historical novels. 'My intention', Joyce remarks, 'was to write a chapter of the moral history of my country and I chose Dublin for the scene because that city seemed to me the centre of paralysis' (Gilbert and Ellmann II, 134). So at the centre of Irish society is paralysis, not stability. There is no shared, objective centre from which a form of representation that accounts for everyone is possible. Joyce, indeed, associated three guiding words with his collection: 'paralysis', 'simony' – the material debasement of spiritual things – and 'gnomon': a term signifying a missing piece or a ghost form not quite there; or a smaller shape taken away from a larger one. Throughout *Dubliners* there are missing bits, absences, things not quite there. There are unfinished sentences in 'The Sisters', a deleted stanza of a poem in 'Clay', frustrated desire in 'Araby', the silences of 'A Painful Case'. All this culminates in 'The Dead' where Gabriel is constantly missing things, including the truth about his own marriage (see Chapters 10 and 12 for further discussion of Joyce's stories).

Rather than accept these gaps and fragmentations as a reflection of Ireland's failure to live up to someone else's literary norms – of unity and coherence in particular – we can reverse our thinking and observe that *Dubliners* picks apart exactly those representational standards, and to good effect. Gabriel's experience stands as a reminder that narrative as a form of representation is an ordering of the world and not a reflection of it. When preparing his speech, Gabriel continually meditates on what he is expected to say, on what is appropriate. In addressing these expectations Gabriel looks to words already written by others and by himself to help to structure his thoughts. However, he is notably aware that every narrative ordering of the world which he assembles will always leave things out: each selection is also an exclusion of others. In particular, much as he strives to make his wife Gretta a mere character in his own narrative, Gabriel finally comes to accept that she has her own story, one which he will never fully know. Gretta's subjectivity, her past experiences and feelings, disrupt Gabriel's effort to order the world in his own terms. Although those sonorous passages which conclude 'The Dead' are usually considered to be one of the most hauntingly beautiful expressions of individual consciousness in fiction, this story, if anything, points to the limits of that consciousness.

Gabriel's thoughts, like *Dubliners* as a whole, acknowledges what is not known, and cannot be known. So instead of considering this short story collection as a failure – and Irish society's failure – to live up to someone else's standards and norms, we can rethink *Dubliners* as a radically 'decentred' fiction. That is, *Dubliners* undermines the notion that there is some central, governing form of representation which can know and include everything and everyone objectively and consensually. Each attempt to impose a form or frame on the world is haunted by the ghosts of other forms and frames. A singular frame or world view in *Dubliners* is disordered specifically by the experiences of women, a host of inferences to repressed sexualities in both male and female characters more widely, and by the whole collection's aggregation of those at the margins of representation. The depiction of the central character in 'Eveline', for example, reveals the constraints placed upon her by both literary and social conventions. 'Eveline' is important as much for what it does not or cannot say as for what it can. Eveline's depiction is disrupted by insinuations of the unsaid or unspeakable: her father's violence, the social and religious outlooks which brutally constrain her life, her personal dissatisfactions. So the reader is left not with the rather passive, inert portrait of Eveline as a complete characterisation, but with a strong sense that there are other, much darker truths about her experience of the world which conventional representation cannot confront.

Other stories work similarly. Even though the series of snapshots of Dublin in the collection seems at first glance to be a realistic depiction of the dreariness of life there, *Dubliners* undermines realism by suggesting other, competing realities. One key method by which Joyce suggests deeper realities and underlying structures is through his use of a symbolic framework. The first sentence of *Dubliners* – 'There was no hope for him this time' – deliberately echoes Dante's *Inferno* (1308) and the inscription over the gates of Hell: 'Abandon hope all ye who enter'. So as readers enter *Dubliners*, they are instructed by a symbolic code, rather than realistic detail, that this will be a journey through a modern inferno. Across the stories, symbolic hints or references to other texts are able to say and infer things which the realistic cannot. So rather than being a miscarried version of an English norm, *Dubliners* is instead a form of radical difference. Instead of supporting some supposedly shared, singular world view, along with a mode of representation which speaks for everyone, *Dubliners* shows that each effort to frame the world in one way is always troubled by other, competing or lost perspectives and experiences.

Resisting in this way any singular world view, *Dubliners* can be seen to contest the 'monologic', in Mikhail Bakhtin's sense of the term. Bakhtin uses this term (also discussed by Keith Hughes in Chapter 11) to refer to the idea that a society might employ a unified, common language, equitably shared by all. As Bakhtin suggests, any monologic, unitary aspects of language and culture are brought into being only through processes of hierarchy and stratification that entail forms of suppression –

> the victory of one reigning language (dialect) over the others, the supplanting of languages, their enslavement, the process of illuminating them with the True Word, the incorporation of barbarians and lower social strata into a unitary language of culture and truth, the canonization of ideological systems. (*The Dialogic Imagination* 271)

The processes Bakhtin identifies here are similar to those Colin Nicholson discusses in Chapter 9 in relation to the competing language forms, accents and dialects at work within poetry, and the social, class or other divisions these represent. In Bakhtin's terms, the idea that a society is stable and undivided – and reflects this homogeneity in literary forms and narratives expressing a single, shared reality – deliberately suppresses hierarchies and antagonisms in both life and literature. For Bakhtin, language is fundamentally dialogic: a continual conflict between dialects; a continual resistance by those deemed 'barbarians' and 'lower social strata' to their subjugation and containment by a standard language of power. Dialogism within any society inevitably extends into literary language and forms as well. Any literary effort to present the world in terms of orderly, singular vision struggles, ultimately in vain, against the inherent dialogism of language itself. Dialogism ensures that any apparently objective reflection of reality in narrative is in fact a complex struggle to order competing dialects, languages and the world views that accompany them.

This leads to further questions about realist writing and its relation to other forms of fiction. Realism, obviously, claims to represent reality more fully and fairly than any other literary genre. Yet it should be clear from suggestions above that realism – just as much as fantastic or gothic fiction – practises its own distortions and exclusions. Fantastic or gothic writing is like a fairground mirror, showing us a world transformed into the kind of weird or monstrous shapes – vampires, ghosts and demons – usually repressed from waking consciousness and found in nightmares instead. But the mirror of realist writing is also a selective, particular one: what it shows depends on the direction in which it is held and what it is allowed to frame. Think again about that earlier, easygoing definition of realist fiction, as 'the form that reproduces most convincingly for us the real world that we live in'. Who might 'we' be in this formulation? Might there be a 'them' that it deliberately excludes? How do individual readers' languages or dialects fit into hierarchies of linguistic register, from Standard English to vernaculars, which realist fiction offers? How far, in short, can we accept realism's fictional ordering of the world as a shared, acceptable one?

In view of such questions, genres such as the gothic or the fantastic may seem less a thorough alternative to realism than a kind of realism under duress; a mirror stressed, cracked or distorted by the pressures of history. Gothic fiction is often thought to emerge in periods of revolutionary upheaval or rapid social change: the French Revolution, war, *fin-de-siècle* malaise, extensive shifts in gender relations and so on. Such periods make the kind of questions above more pressing, and the reassuring, coherent, consensual answers realist fiction depends on harder to provide. Realism, the gothic or fantastic all grapple with the same social materials, while differing in their modes of narrative ordering. Labels such as 'realism' or 'gothic' programme – often usefully? – expectations and responses of each genre, in terms of the forms they adopt and the experiences and characters they offer. But the genres themselves have uncertain boundaries, and can collapse into each other – often revealing, in doing so, the importance of experiences that each has sought to exclude.

In the case of a work such as R. L. Stevenson's *The Strange Case of Dr Jekyll and Mr Hyde* (1886), for example, the reader encounters the monstrous eruption of the fantastic or gothic. But, in order for this text to engage us, it must claim some elements of realism, persuading us that this is 'really happening'; that Hyde's character might exist. Stevenson's device – the split or dual self – is a key means by which to draw out what is repressed or excluded by realism, or by established society: 'it came about that I concealed my pleasures', Jekyll remarks (1675). Divided or multiple selves which populate gothic or supernatural fiction help express a range of repressed desires and anxieties which could not be publicly acknowledged in the late Victorian context in which Stevenson wrote (especially, in this instance, concerning issues of masculinity and sexuality). Jekyll and Hyde is strikingly dialogic in that the two selves and the narratives they produce are virtually unable to coexist. Rather, the one threatens the other, to the extent that both realms of experience would obliterate the traces of each other. As Jekyll says of his manuscript: 'Should the throes of change take me in the act of writing it, Hyde will tear it in pieces' (1685.) In other words, one narrative ordering of the world fears being overturned by another. Jekyll knows that his monstrous reality – the very thing that people will find unreal or unbelievable about him – is a threat to his attempts to document his experiences in writing. Thus, his reality will destroy the very narrative by which Jekyll seeks to convince people of that reality. Jekyll's dispute with his society about what can be said or admitted as true extends into the complete incommensurabilities of his divided selves – alternate realities unknown to one another, the one existing in place of the other. And there is no overarching, all-knowing narrative perspective able to reconcile these antithetical existences: the text remains creatively dialogic.

A comparable dynamic occurs in James Hogg's *Confessions of a Justified Sinner* (1824), which seems to divide itself straightforwardly between the modern, enlightened consciousness of George and the fanatical, evil con-sciousness of Robert, in league with the devil (Gil Martin). But the very form of this novel undermines the straightforward view that it is a satire of Calvinist dogmatism and self-righteousness, contrasting the decent, reasonable instincts of George with Robert's unpleasant idea of himself as one of the elect. There is no omniscient narrator to evaluate the competing narratives representing the characters or to arbitrate finally about the truth of either. Instead, these narratives are presented by an uneasy 'Editor' who constructs George's per-spectives for us but does not intrude upon or explain Robert's narrative. The Editor claims to be merely recording events known to most Scottish people – insinuating they will know who to believe – but the form of *Confessions* does not grant the Editor a superior position or final authority. Instead, the com-peting, dialogic narratives are maintained in tension with each other, and the Editor is positioned almost in parallel with Robert. Both are trying to justify, as it were, their versions of events; both seek to impose upon the past a pre-ordained narrative pattern. Ultimately, the supposedly enlightened rationality of the Editor is confronted by something which it cannot explain or order. In this sense, the Editor's claims to a consensual, complete and objective truth are rendered a fiction – a narrative; a story – just as much as Robert's, because the text cannot finally resolve its competing voices: it cannot, as it maintains it will, explain or know everything.

As with Joyce and Ireland, Hogg's work should not be construed as a Scottish failure to mature into the supposedly serene stability that produces novelists such as Jane Austen or George Eliot. *Confessions* does not disappoint literary norms but disputes them in refusing a consensual, omniscient narra-tive. Like Joyce's work, *Confessions* reminds us that a static notion of form or genre is almost the antithesis of literature, which should not be about fore-closed labels or order, but rather a continual, rebellious recasting of what can be thought, said or registered by a society – particularly by people excluded from what prevailing logic deems appropriate, by people who wish to disagree. Notions of form and genre seem helpful in shaping our approaches to literature, but there is also a sense in which all of this is about people, society and history as much as form, style or technique. That is, if literature had only ever done what was deemed appropriate then there would be no writing by women, by working-class authors or by those who were slaves or formerly colonised people, because at various junctures throughout history all these groups were considered inappropriate writers or even readers of literature. If we are, paradoxically, to find a truth in fiction perhaps it should be this: that literature thrives through people breaking the rules, disputing what can be said, felt and registered in a society.

NEXT STEPS

Bakhtin, Mikhail. *The Dialogic Imagination*. Austin: Univerity of Texas Press, 1981.

Lukács, George. *The Historical Novel*. London: Merlin Press, 1989.

Lukács, George. 'Realism in the Balance'. In *Aesthetics and Politics*. London: NLB, 1977. 28–59.

O'Connor, Frank. *The Lonely Voice: A Study of the Short Story*. London: Macmillan, 1963.

15

Life Writing

Laura Marcus

In recent years, 'life writing' has become a familiar term in literary and cultural studies. The term, and the related category 'personal writing', covers a broad range of texts, including autobiography, biography, letters, memoirs, diaries and travel-writings. Genres such as biography and the diary form might previously have been placed in the category of 'non-fictional prose'. The emphasis now, however, is less on the fiction/non-fiction divide and more on the ways in which such literatures represent the lives of individuals, whether those of another or others, as in biography, or of the self, as in autobiography, journal or diary. Indeed, the recently coined term 'auto/biography' is intended to show the permeable boundaries between the literature of the self and the literature of the other. The category of 'personal writing' raises further issues: writing need not have made its mark in the public sphere, or have achieved publication and wide dissemination, to count as 'literature'. This has opened the way for the study of a range of women's writings, in particular, from earlier periods and for a recognition of the significance of 'personal' or 'private' writing, including family memoirs, diaries and journals.

AUTOBIOGRAPHY

While the category of 'life writing' suggests a broad and inclusive approach to the study of literature and culture which we might associate with our contemporary moment, it was in fact a familiar appellation in the eighteenth century, used alongside 'biography', whose usage can be dated from the seventeenth century. 'Autobiography' did not come into existence as a term until the beginning of the nineteenth century: critics and commentators might refer instead to 'self-biography' or 'the biography of a man written by himself'. This suggests that it was still perceived as unusual in secular contexts for a writer to turn his or her regard inward, though this principle guided many earlier spiritual and religious texts. St Augustine's *Confessions* (written in the fourth century) marks, for the Western literary tradition, the origin of autobiographical writing. The concept of 'confession' would later be used in a secular context by Jean-Jacques Rousseau, whose *Confessions* (1782) are often held to mark the birth of modern autobiography, and by Thomas de Quincey, in his *Confessions of an English Opium-Eater* (1821/2).

A number of the most influential texts of modern autobiographical writing – Rousseau's *Confessions* and Wordsworth's *The Prelude* (1850) among them – begin with the claim that their writers are embarking on an unprecedented endeavour. Rousseau opened his *Confessions* by asserting the uniqueness both of his autobiographical enterprise and of his being: 'I am made unlike anyone I have ever met; I will even venture to say that I am like no one in the whole world' (17). In 1805, when Wordsworth completed the first full version of the poem that would become *The Prelude*, he was writing to a friend that it was 'a thing unprecedented in Literary history that a man should talk so much about himself' (Wordsworth and Wordsworth 586). By 1850, when his long poem was posthumously published as *The Prelude*, the autobiographical mode in which he had been working had become a far more familiar one. Autobiographers from the mid-nineteenth century onwards would be less likely to introduce their texts with justifications for their autobiographical acts. None the less, autobiographies to the present day might well contain discussion of how it was that they came to be written and of the kind of work they represent. Autobiography, as a literary form, thus tends to exhibit a marked self-consciousness about its generic identity. This is linked, in turn, to the very question of its literary status. Autobiography, like biography, might be seen as a form of historical rather than literary writing, or at least, as occupying a space between the two modes. Both autobiography and biography have a particular bearing, then, on definitions of the literary and on the question, around which all literary theory could be said to revolve: 'what is literature?'

Not all autobiographers are writers by profession, though there is a widespread assumption that the literary writer's autobiography best defines the genre, and that it is less the particularities of the life-story that are of interest than the ways in which they are remembered and recounted. The life, indeed, is being recreated in words, and the method and means of its representation are of as much significance as the experienced events themselves. The term 'autobiography' breaks down into its component parts – 'auto' (self), 'bios' (life), 'graphia' (writing). The element of writing or text is inscribed in the term itself, unlike any other literary designation (apart from 'biography' and, of course, 'life-writing'). Language, as well as the workings of memory, shapes the past. The literary writer's autobiography also bears on, and frequently comments upon, his or her other works. Such texts will often recount the ways in which a writer entered into the profession or 'vocation' of literature. The life thus becomes identified as a 'literary life'.

Edmund Gosse's *Father and Son* (1907) is a classic example in this context. Gosse, who would become a highly influential literary critic and commentator in the late nineteenth and early twentieth centuries, was the son of Philip Henry Gosse, an eminent Victorian scientist who found himself torn between his religion (he belonged to the strict Christian sect the Plymouth Brethren) and the intellectual appeal of evolutionary thought, which radically undermined the doctrine of Creation. A central thread of Gosse's narrative (which lies somewhere between autobiography, biography and memoir) is of Edmund's gradual turning away from the religion of his childhood towards literature. (Many Plymouth Brethren held that fictional writing operated as a delusion and a snare, telling 'untruths' about the world.) The youthful Gosse's 'turning' to literature (and, finally, away from 'the artificial edifice of extravagant faith') is represented in a language of 'conversion' which echoes, rewrites and, ultimately, subverts the powerful conversion moment in Augustine's *Confessions* – 'it was as though the light of confidence flooded into my heart and all the darkness of doubt was dispelled' (Augustine 178).

This moment of epiphany, or revelation (see also Chapter 10), was imitated by many of the spiritual autobiographers who followed in Augustine's wake. Conversion is indeed central to the narrative structure of autobiography: the writing 'I' finds a stable point (in Augustine's case, an imagined state outside the flux and flow of earthly temporality) from which to look back on the past as it moves towards the present. As a central and repeated trope, it indicates the extent to which we can locate a 'tradition' in autobiographical writing in which autobiographers will look back to their predecessors. Each life may be unique, but the means of its telling exist within a recognisable literary form and will follow at least some of its conventions.

Father and Son ends with Gosse on the threshold of his new life. Like a number of modern autobiographies, it shares many of the features of the *Bildungsroman*, the 'novel of formation', or 'novel of education', which typically traces the youthful development of an individual, and the shaping of his (and less usually her) mind and character, as he or she moves towards maturity and the taking up of a place in the world. Gosse ends his story as his young adult self enters into (productive) time (rather than, like Augustine, moving out of linear or narrative time into timelessness). He represents his father, who continued to deny the logic to which evolutionary science would have led him, as one of a dying species. Biographers and autobiographers writing in the wake of Gosse would understand him to have performed an act of symbolic parricide (the killing of the father) which was, in turn, inseparable from the ways in which the innovative writers and artists of the early twentieth-century modernist movement would seek to differentiate themselves from their Victorian predecessors: family relations (or, to borrow Sigmund Freud's term, 'family romances') are also social and historical structures.

Virginia Woolf's autobiographical text 'A Sketch of the Past' was written towards the close of her life and not published until many years later. Its composition at the end of the 1930s, when world war was becoming an increasing threat, ran parallel to an engagement with Freud's writings which she had earlier resisted. She was most struck with the term 'ambivalence', a new term in the language, definable as the coexistence of 'love' and 'hate', and she applied it to her feelings towards her father, the critic and biographer Leslie Stephen. 'Two different ages', she wrote, 'confronted each other in the drawing room at Hyde Park Gate [her childhood home]. The Victorian age and the Edwardian age . . . We looked at him with eyes that were looking into the future' (Woolf, *Moments of Being* 149). Looking back at this time, and at her childhood more generally, Woolf makes explicit the dual or double time frame, and the dual or double identity (the 'I' of the present writing self and the 'I' of the past self whose story is being recounted), which underlies autobiography as a genre. As Woolf records:

> 2nd May . . . I write the date, because I think I have discovered a pos-
> sible form for these notes. That is, to make them include the present – at
> least enough of the present to serve as platform to stand upon. It would
> be interesting to make the two people, I now, I then, come out in con-
> trast. And further, this past is much affected by the present moment.
> What I write today I should not write in a year's time. (87)

Woolf's 'platform' is very different from Augustine's autobiographical standpoint and his vision of an eternity outside human temporality: hers is a temporary stopping-point within the flux and flow of time. This, in turn, is connected to daily time or diary time, echoing her use of the diurnal or 'dailiness' in many of her novels. Woolf also used her memoir to explore the ways in which childhood experience shaped her identity as a writer, focus-ing on her 'scene-making' capacity, which comes to define the workings of childhood vision, of memory and of fiction-making.

The opening passages of 'A Sketch of the Past' recall 'the first memory' (two memories in fact vie for primordiality) 'of red and purple flowers on a black ground – my mother's dress' and

> of lying half-asleep, half-awake, in bed at the nursery at St Ives . . . It is of
> lying and hearing this splash [of the waves] and seeing this light [behind
> a yellow blind], and feeling, it is almost impossible that I should be here,
> of feeling the purest ecstasy I can conceive. (78–9)

The second ('first') memory seems to mark the emergence of self-consciousness,
of the sense of identity which is the precondition for autobiographical consciousness, and, in turn, for autobiographical writing. The first, highly visual
memory is of the mother, who fills the child's vision: the mother, like the
pattern on her dress, is both foreground and background. Such representations
have been of profound importance for an understanding of women's life-
writings, including their representations of mother–daughter relationships and
the shaping of selfhood. More broadly, autobiographical writing is seen to act
as a window onto concepts of self, identity and subjectivity, and into the ways
in which these are themselves determined by time and circumstance.

Autobiography as a genre became of central significance to literary theory
as it emerged in the latter decades of the twentieth century. The critic
Philippe Lejeune, whose work on life-writing has been highly influential,
defined autobiography as a 'retrospective prose narrative produced by a real
person concerning his own existence, where the focus is his individual life, in
particular the story of his personality'(4). Lejeune's central concern was with
the question of 'identity' in autobiographical writing, and with the 'pact' that
is set up between text and reader, whereby the latter can be assured that the
author's name designates a real person and that the narrator and the protagonist are one and the same. The value of Lejeune's approach lay in its attention
to the textual aspects and generic markers of autobiography (he has written
extensively, for example, about the various uses of first, second or third person
narrative in autobiographical writings). His concept of 'the autobiographical
pact' also focused on the relationship between the author, the text and the
reader as the guarantor of autobiographical authenticity. Rather than defining
the autobiographical form on the basis of textual properties alone, it provided
a flexible model of generic identity and an understanding of the historical
and institutional contexts in which a given work will be received and read as
autobiographical.

Lejeune's seemingly 'legalistic' vocabulary of 'pact' and 'contract' was,
however, strongly critiqued by commentators such as the deconstructionist
Paul de Man. Following from the work of the French philosopher Jacques
Derrida, deconstructionist criticism generally challenges possibilities of creating reliable truth or coherent meaning in the unstable medium of language,
and for de Man the attempt to define autobiography was a fruitless endeavour: 'autobiography . . . is not a genre or a mode, but a figure of reading or

of understanding that occurs, to some degree, in all texts' (70). The drive to define and demarcate autobiographical writing was thus countered by an equally strong sense that autobiography escapes final definition. For one thing, any narrative of the self and its life-story will entail a reconstruction, subject to the vagaries of memory, which renders the division between autobiography and fiction far from absolute. De Man offered a radical reversal of the relationship between life and work: although we assume, he argued, that the life produces the autobiography, it is equally possible that the autobiographical project produces and determines 'the life'.

The critical focus on autobiography in the 1970s and 1980s, including the work of Paul de Man, ran alongside, and was a dimension of, the re-evaluations of Romantic literature in the same period. The deconstructive reading of Romanticism emphasised its ironies, its self-consciousness and the complexities of the ways in which it brought together philosophy, literature and history. Wordsworth's *The Prelude*, with its splitting and doubling of selves (past and present 'I', the writing and the written self, the mirroring that brings the self as other into being) became a central text here.

De Man also wrote extensively on Rousseau, exploring the drive to, and the inexhaustibility of, 'confession': his argument is that confession breeds the desire for yet more confession, and that Rousseau exhibited a particular pleasure in the production of confessions intended as penitential discourse. This understanding has been central for the contemporary South African born writer J. M. Coetzee. In Coetzee's best known novel, *Disgrace* (1999), David Lurie, an academic whose specialism is Romanticism, is called before the authorities at the university at which he teaches after he has had sexual relations with one of his students. He refuses to confess and to seek exculpation, pointing out the futility of the exercise, and he leaves his academic post. Underlying the narrative are the complex, troubled relationships to the past with which post-apartheid South Africa has had to deal, and Coetzee's sceptical stance towards its Truth and Reconciliation Committee. In his most recent work, Coetzee has taken up various modes of autobiographical writing, creating a series of alter egos. In *Youth* (2002), he presents his former self in a cold, dispassionate prose that seems to break the threads of identification and continuity between the present, writing 'I' and the past, written self: he uses the present tense and third person narration to express this distance between, in Woolf's words, the 'I now, I then' of autobiography or memoir. *Summertime* (2009), which again resists generic classification, is written through diary entries and as a series of interviews with those who knew, and in some cases loved, a now deceased writer called John Coetzee, who shares at least some of the living J. M. Coetzee's biography. Like many of Coetzee's novels and essays, the text is occupied by the concept of the double, echoing representations of a writer's work, in the Romantic movement (and in the Transcendentalism which followed in the mid-nineteenth century in the USA), as his 'corpus', as his shadow figure, and working with the division between the writing self and the written self.

The complexities and paradoxes of the autobiographical mode thus become, in Coetzee's work, the substance of the 'autofiction' itself. For other recent writers, memory – its recovery and its loss – has been placed at the heart of autobiographical writing. With increased longevity, there is both more memory and more memory to be lost: many contemporary autobiographers have turned to writing family stories which shore up memory as their parents forget their pasts.

Since the 1970s, at least, autobiographical texts have become containers for multiple narrative and interpretative approaches to identity and time, competing for an ever-receding 'truth' of the self and the past. The widespread interest in autobiography since then has emerged in part as a result of feminist criticism and its demands for a different kind of public/private articulation, but also as a result of the fracturing of the would-be seamless narratives of assimilation in twentieth-century culture. In many postcolonial autobiographies (significant examples include Wole Soyinka's *Aké: The Years of Childhood* (1981) and Shirley Geok-Lin Lim's *Among the White Moon Faces: Memoirs of an Asian American Woman* (1996)), the autobiographical 'I' is split and doubled by the experience, and the representation, of cultural translation and dislocation, while narratives recounting stories of marginality, exclusion or unstable social identity have become a dominant autobiographical mode.

BIOGRAPHY

Like autobiography, biography continues to play a complex and shifting role in the study of literature. At times, biographical criticism (the study of the lives of authors, understanding of the part played by an author's identity and experience in shaping their literary works) has been at the heart of literary study. At other junctures, biography has been largely excluded, on the grounds that we understand literary texts best by reference to their uses of language, their relationship to other texts and/or their bases in history and culture and not through biographical interpretations. Literary biographies – that is, those which record the lives of writers – will also vary in the extent to which they make the biographical subject's writings a significant focus. Biographers who do elect to discuss their subject's written works will need to confront the question of how 'autobiographically' they should read them. We thus return to the question of the relationship of the work to the life of its author: for all the contestations between them, biography and the study of literature are clearly deeply interrelated.

If Rousseau and Wordsworth are central texts in the formation of modern autobiographical writing, James Boswell's *Life of Johnson* (1791) has a foundational role in the development of modern biography. Boswell, born in Edinburgh and initially trained as a lawyer, met Samuel Johnson – poet, essayist, lexicographer – in 1763, and, within the next decade, was developing plans to become his biographer: to this end he started to keep increasingly detailed journals. The *Life of Johnson* has a particular immediacy and dramatic quality, which arises in large part from Boswell's 'verbatim' recordings of Johnson's conversations. He also quotes at length from Johnson's letters, so that the voice, and the words, of the great man are at the heart of the biography. 'Indeed', Boswell wrote, at the opening of his biography,

> I cannot conceive a more perfect mode of writing a man's life, than not only relating all the most important events of it in their order, but interweaving what he privately wrote and said, and thought; by which mankind are enabled as it were to see him live, and to 'live o'er each scene' with him, as he actually advanced through the several stages of his life. (22)

Boswell thus expresses his commitments to chronology, to detail, to completeness, to honesty and to the creation of a subject who lives, in the biography, after his death.

Elizabeth Gaskell's *The Life of Charlotte Brontë* (1857) is also a 'companionate' biography, the life of one woman writer told by another, and by one who knew her in life. Like Boswell, Gaskell drew extensively on the letters of her biographical subject: Brontë's own words thus form a significant part of the story Gaskell tells. The biography opens, however, not with Brontë's presence but with her absence: not with her birth but with the record, inscribed in stone, of her death. In a remarkable first chapter, Gaskell takes her reader on the journey, by rail and road, through the Yorkshire landscape, into Haworth village, surrounded by the moors, on through the village churchyard, passing by the Brontë parsonage, and into the church. She leads the reader up to a set of inscriptions which mark, in the order of their deaths, the site of 'the remains' of Charlotte Brontë's mother and of her four sisters and brother (two of whom died in childhood and none of whom lived beyond the age of thirty), coming finally to rest on the inscribed words which identify the burial site of Charlotte herself. The chapter as a whole, and those that follow, reveal Gaskell's commitment, everywhere apparent in her novels, to the realist representation of place and space, and to the significance of the environment in shaping an individual's character. The focus on the inscription also raises

broad questions of the relationship between biography and the genres of obituary or epitaph, and between biography as life-writing and as death-writing
or 'thanatography'.

In the immediate post-Victorian age, the nineteenth-century preoccu-
pation with death and, in particular, with the 'death-bed scene' was both
pilloried and parodied by the modernists, who also took issue with what
they perceived to be the hagiographical aspects of Victorian life-writing
('hagiography' is the term for the writing of the lives of saints). The so-called
new biography of the early twentieth-century, whose most prominent expo-
nent was the historian and biographer Lytton Strachey, stood for modernity
against the previous century. In his *Eminent Victorians* (1918), Strachey took
a debunking, satirical approach to historical figures as a counter to Victorian
'hero worship'. His written lives were often 'brief lives', in contrast to the
multi-volumed works which had come to characterize nineteenth-century
biographies. His approach, while seen as startling in its time, brought to the
fore questions which had long accompanied the writing of biography: its
aesthetics (biography becomes defined as an art in which the selection and
shaping of facts is all-important) and its ethics (for example, the degree of revelation or concealment the biographer adopts in relation to his or her subject's
hidden life or relationship with others).

Later twentieth-century biography has continued to explore these questions. The issue of form and the narrative shape given to, or imposed upon,
the life as lived remains a vexed one. While most biographers continue to
observe the conventions of chronological narration espoused by Boswell,
they will often find ways of qualifying, or stepping aside from, the time-
boundedness of the genre. In Hermione Lee's *Virginia Woolf* (1996), to
take one example, space and the perspectives that accompany it precede
and succeed time. The biography opens with a chapter which discusses the
difficulties of writing biography, and follows it with one entitled 'Houses',
showing how Woolf's consciousness of self came into being in rooms inside
the houses of her childhood. The biography closes with a section in which
Lee stands in the garden of Talland House in St Ives, Woolf's holiday home
in her childhood, and looks out at the view: 'I can allow myself to suppose
that I am seeing something of what she saw. My view, overlays with, just
touches, hers' (772).

Lee's sense of identification with her subject lies at the heart of biographical
representation and experimentation in the twentieth century. As we have seen,
the relationship between biographer and subject was central to eighteenth-
and nineteenth-century writers, such as Boswell and Gaskell, but in recent
decades it has been framed much more substantially in terms of quest, 'haunt-
ing' and detection. The biographer Richard Holmes, for example, developed

the 'footsteps' mode of biographical writing: "'Biography,'" Holmes wrote in his *Footsteps: Adventures of a Romantic Biographer* (1985),

> meant a book about someone's life. Only, for me, it was to become a kind of pursuit, a tracking of the physical trail of someone's path through the past, a following of footsteps. You would never catch them; no, you would never quite catch them. But maybe, if you were lucky, you might write about the pursuit of that fleeting figure in such a way as to bring it alive in the present. (27)

NEXT STEPS

Autobiography

Anderson, Linda. *Autobiography*. London: Routledge, 2001.

Jay, Paul. *Being in the Text: Self-Representation from Wordsworth to Roland Barthes*. Ithaca, NY: Cornell University Press, 1984.

Marcus, Laura. *Auto/biographical Discourses: Theory, Criticism, Practice*. Manchester: Manchester University Press, 1994.

Moore-Gilbert, Bart. *Postcolonial Life-Writing: Culture, Politics and Self-Representation*. London: Routledge, 2009.

Smith, Sidonie and Julia Watson. *Reading Autobiographically: A Guide for Interpreting Life Narratives*. Minneapolis: University of Minnesota Press, 2001.

Biography

France, Peter, and William St Clair, eds. *Mapping Lives: The Uses of Biography*. Oxford: Oxford University Press, 2002.

Lee, Hermione. *Body-Parts: Essays on Life-Writing*. London: Chatto and Windus, 2005.

Lee, Hermione. *Biography: A Very Short Introduction*. Oxford: Oxford University Press, 2009.

Section IV – Drama

16

Introducing Drama

Roger Savage

English literature must be about the only long-established literature to have as its Absolutely Top Writer a professional man of the theatre who did a certain amount of acting, had shares in a successful playhouse-company and wrote around 95 percent of his surviving work in play-text form. With William Shakespeare looming over them, then, people involved with literature in English have little excuse for brushing drama aside and asserting that poetry and narrative fiction are the really important forms. Yet it has to be said that drama is something of an uneasy bedfellow to poetry, the short story and the novel when it comes to literary study. This becomes clear as soon as one attempts to give it a comprehensive definition – one like this perhaps:

> *Drama:* An artistic medium in which physical impersonation is used to present the actions and situations of fictive characters to an assembled audience that hopes to be beguiled, stirred, amused, provoked or affected in some more profound way by the spectacle created.

This foregrounds two elements seemingly foreign to poetry and narrative fiction – the impersonators and the assembled audience – as well as hinting at the diversity of activity drama embraces; it certainly has been active in a remarkably wide range of places and a great variety of modes.

The places, geographically speaking, have been all around the planet, and drama's locales in those places have been very various too. It has thrived in the open air (fields, forest clearings, the squares and streets and inn yards of towns and cities); in religious buildings and their precincts; in royal courts and private houses; and in specially built structures ('theatres': from the Greek *theatron*, an observing place), sometimes with roofs, sometimes without:

structures that allow people to gather together close to 'live' performers or to range themselves in front of two-dimensional screens for shadow-puppet shows or multi-million-dollar movies. As for drama's modes, it can happen with visible human performers, with invisible ones (in radio plays for instance) or, in the case of puppets again, with no apparent human agency involved. If visible, its human performers may wear their own faces or transform them with bold face-paint or with attachable-detachable masks (*personae* in Latin, whence 'impersonation' and so on). It can work well without words, for instance in mime-theatre, classical story-ballet and some dance-theatre, or it can make much of them: words in prose or verse, words spoken or sung, words largely improvised during the show or written, learned and rehearsed before being delivered live or recorded by a camera.

English drama has involved itself in all these modes and locales, and this is worth stressing to counter the assumption quite common among Western or West-leaning theatre-goers that drama is by definition and exclusively something scripted from words before the event and performed by live, speaking human actors in purpose-built, generally roofed theatres. It is not, not exclusively. This type of drama simply constitutes one successful team in a global league whose other teams and their tactics are well worth studying. It is a situation which should remind us that, however much the dramatic texts we are most likely to be reading in an English literature course may seem on occasion to cosy up to poems and novels, they are linked just as closely with a Broadway musical, a south Indian dance play, a Punch and Judy show, a military tattoo.

Drama has two outstanding characteristics. One is the apparent absence of the author from the play. Though there are some interesting exceptions, poems and novels tend to make us aware of a continuous, controlling voice: the author's own voice or a voice the author has created. Drama very largely dispenses with such voices: the appearance of characters living independently through events is essential to it. True, there can be suggestions of a direct authorial voice in some plays: those, for instance, that include 'choric' figures (since part of the role of a dramatic chorus – as in ancient Greek tragedy – can be to express the author's opinions) and those that feature characters known as *raisonneurs*: people blessed with plain common sense who aren't carried away by the passions swirling around them and may sometimes put what appears to be the author's view of what's going on. But such figures cannot be relied on to Tell It How It Is, or even to be there at all. More often, it is as if the dramatist sets up the characters, sets events in motion – and then leaves the scene, letting them work out their own destinies. Which raises the important question of Drama and Truth. Does the playwright set these things running in a particular situation so as to convince us in the audience of some truth which he or she holds to, or to allow us to experience that situation so that we can find our own – and possibly quite different – truth in it?

Mention of an audience leads to the other characteristic feature of drama: staging. By intention at least, the great majority of play-texts in the drama of the spoken word, the sung word too, are primarily *scripts*: that is to say they are there to make a contribution to a theatrical event which is bigger than the script itself, even if it is also more transient. Away from that event, dramatists may put such word-books into print for several reasons: for cash or prestige; to provide a souvenir of the event; to encourage further performances; to allow enthusiasts to look into the detail of how the script was made. But aside from instances of 'closet drama', that quite small sub-group of play-texts designed simply to be read, scripts exist to be brought to fruition by the rich interrelation of the elements of theatre: a sense of occasion; the assembled audience; an acting area with particular dimensions and facilities for the dramatist to exploit; telling decor; music perhaps (in small or large quantities); a certain unstoppable pace and rhythm to the whole thing; and a troupe of performers who have rehearsed the script in advance, have found apt characterisations for their roles and know how to inject such characterisations into everything they do from their very first appearance. All of which compounds the Drama and Truth issue. Is the performers' job to locate and communicate the author's central truth in a script, or to pursue and promote some truth of their own that work on it has led them to?

If we wanted to see the elements of drama effectively laid out in a very small space, we could take as an example a tiny English play, a 'proto-play' perhaps, dating from about a thousand years ago and generally known, like others of its sort at the time, as *The Visit to the Sepulchre*. In his book, compiled around the year 970, on the proper rites for a Benedictine monastery, the Bishop of Winchester, St Ethelwold, requires that this playlet be performed in monastic churches as an integral part of the order of service near the end of the dawn ritual of Matins on Easter Day: the ritual that celebrates the resurrection of Jesus Christ after his crucifixion. It is in Church Latin; so here is my translation. The playlet is designed to be given, by the brethren for the brethren, near the church's altar and close to the monastery's choir and assembled clerics. (There would be no 'lay' congregation.) Prominent is a 'sepulchre', which might be part of the permanent architecture of the building or be set up on or near the altar especially for Holy Week. It has a veil over it and, within, folded linen that at a ritual two days before had been wrapped around a crucifix. Now St Ethelwold:

While the Third Lesson is being read, let four of the brethren vest themselves. Then one of them, wearing an alb, should come in as if intent on some quite other thing, go unobtrusively to the place of the sepulchre, and quietly sit there, holding a palm in his hand. And during the singing of the Third Responsery, the other three should follow, all wearing cloaks, carrying thuribles full of incense in their hands. They should come cautiously to the place of the sepulchre in the likeness of seekers after something. These things are done in imitation of the Angel sitting at the tomb and of the women coming with spices so that they might anoint Jesus' body. So, when the seated one shall see the three coming near him as though they were wandering about and searching something out, he shall begin singing sweetly in a moderate voice:

Whom is it you seek [in the sepulchre, O Christians]?

When this is fully sung, the three should reply in unison:

Jesus of Nazareth [who was crucified, O heavenly one].

He to them:

He is not here; he is risen, as he prophesied. Go, announce that he is risen from the dead!

Once this command is uttered, the three should turn to the choir, saying:

Alleluia; the Lord is risen. [Today Christ, the strong lion, God's son, is risen.]

This said, sitting again as though calling them back, he should speak the antiphon:

Come and see the place [where the Lord was laid; alleluia].

Saying this, he should stand, lift up the veil, and show them the place divested of the cross, yet with the linen cloths still in place in which the cross had been wrapped. When they have seen this, they should set down the thuribles they have been carrying in that same sepulchre, take the linen, open it up in the sight of the clerics and, as though showing that the Lord has risen and is no longer wrapped there, sing this antiphon:

The Lord has risen from the sepulchre [who hung on the cross for us; alleluia].

Then they should lay the linen on the altar. At the end of the antiphon the Prior, joining in their rejoicing at the triumph of our king who has risen, conquering death, should begin the hymn 'We praise thee, O God'. When it has begun, all the bells should sound out together. (Ethelwold 249–50)

We might be tempted to think of AD 970 as decidedly 'Dark Ages' and only likely to produce fairly primitive play-texts; but this one suggests the contrary. It does so by bringing together two idioms. One is that of the traditional service-book: a book of rites laid out with great care in the conviction that they will only be effective if they are performed just so. The other is that of a group of actors, which, being rather unusual in the context of a religious ceremony, needs to be spelt out clearly. Hence the careful explanation that the monk-performers are presenting something 'in imitation of' a particular episode in the biblical life of Jesus. Hence the specifying of a particular space as the acting area, with the sepulchre as focus but with clear lines to the altar and the places of the clerics and choir. Hence the stress on distinguishing between a character's entrance when its function is just to help set the scene, the actor of the angel sidling in, in the hope that no one will notice his arrival, and an entrance that is part of the action, as with the Marys and their sad searching. Hence, too, the alb, an enveloping white cloak which the angel-actor puts on to become a shining being, and the cloaks (or 'copes') worn by the others, with their hoods up perhaps, so that three choirboys or maybe grown men can become the Marys of the Gospel story. And hence, crucially, the appeals to the acting-skills of the cast: 'as if intent on . . .', 'in the likeness of . . .', 'as though wandering', 'as though calling', 'as though showing'.

One could say that these things exemplify the dramatic basics: audience, locale, chain of events, decor, impersonation through words and movement. But in its small way our playlet also exemplifies other things in play-making and stage presentation that are often seen apart but happen here to be brought together. Thus, when the Marys are looking for Jesus's body and the angel talks with them, we seem for a moment to be in the world of what would later be called 'realism'. Yet a few moments later it is clear that the *Visit* is also a ritual of demonstration: the Marys turn outward to address the choir, and later show the linen 'shroud' to the clerics, placing it on the altar as the presiding prior joins in and leads everyone in a familiar hymn, the *Te Deum Laudamus*. And this mix of life-likeness and presentational self-consciousness goes along-side a blending of illusionism and symbolism in the decor. The angel-actor's alb makes him a plausible heavenly being, but the palm he carries needs to be read as a symbol of victory (that of Christ over death). The Marys bring spices to Jesus's tomb, as well they might, but in the form of incense-filled thuribles of the sort used in church rituals of 'censing'. The sepulchre and grave-linen can be seen as realistic (970s-fashion); yet the veil seems, quite daringly, to allude to the great stone sealing the sepulchre in the Bible story, while the body of Christ, embarrassing, impious and probably impossible to show real-istically at that time, is symbolised powerfully but very abstractly by a crucifix that had been placed in the linen with great ceremony on Good Friday and is now miraculously gone.

It is a sophisticated and rewarding text, but it has its problems: problems which have a wider relevance, as we shall see. Firstly, what is the extent of its dialogue? The words put in square brackets in our translation are not in Ethelwold's book but have been added by modern editors because they appear in many other Easter enactments of that age and later, and they serve to round things out here. Ethelwold, the argument runs, felt that he didn't need to set down more than the first few words of each 'cue' because the rest would be familiar to everyone taking part and so would be uttered accordingly. Maybe; but perhaps the text he recorded was *all* he wanted uttered. Next, how was the dialogue delivered? We are told that the angel 'sings' at first, but later the Marys 'say' that the Lord is risen and the angel 'speaks' when he calls them back to the sepulchre, at which they 'sing' to the clerics. Outside information tells us that at the time most of a monastery's liturgy tended to be intoned or sung, though it was song without harmonisation or the support of instruments. Quite possibly Ethelwold meant this to be the case here, done in such a natural way as to justify those 'speaks' and 'says' directions. Such singing, though, might seem to turn our playlet into an opera: a scripted, rehearsed story with words and characters but sung pretty much from end to end. Does it help to think of it as an opera (another perfectly valid mode of scripted drama but one in which the script becomes the 'libretto'), or does that confuse the issue? And while we are categorising, does it help to think of this play/opera/ceremony as part of a dramatic genre? If so, arguably it would have to be a comedy, a 'divine comedy' so to speak: not a matter of laughs but of something fitting the time-honoured comedic pattern of a movement from darkness to light, from conflict to resolution – in this case from the wretchedness of the Marys looking for their cruelly crucified master to the moment when all the monastery's bells sound out together.

What is there to be gathered from all this by the student of English literature who wants to read play-texts? First and foremost that it is valuable to build a 'theatre of the imagination' in your mind, so that plays on the page can begin to generate the sort of life they have inherent in them. If that 'theatrical event bigger than the script' is not about to take place in the world outside you, let it happen in your head. This is not so very difficult to bring about, though there are some things it might be useful to remember so as to ensure that your internal theatre functions efficiently. For instance, it helps if you establish what sort of document the script you have in your hand is. Scripts as printed in library books can vary quite a lot in this way and so may need different areas of your imagination brought into play to compensate for what they leave out. Is the script you are looking at a transcript of the play's dialogue to the exclusion of almost everything else, with only the most minimal indication (if any at all indeed) of entrances, exits, scenes, costumes, music? Or is it a set of bald technical instructions in backstage jargon aimed solely at jobbing actors and stage-crew? Is it an attempt to turn the script into a self-sufficient 'book-work' which can be relished almost as a novel with little thought of practical theatre? Or is it something else again? (In the case of *The Visit to the Sepulchre*, for instance, we have a set of 'rubrics' laid out for men who are professional as monks but amateur as actors.) It may also be worth while to assure yourself of the state of the text you are holding. Are you reading what the performers actually said and did or what the author wanted them to say or do? And have there been problems with verbal transmission? (Conflicting scripts from the author's lifetime? Scribes' misreadings? Printers' mistakes?) With our *Visit*, we clearly have pretty much what the author wanted – and since Ethelwold was both a bishop and a saint it is likely that he got it from his monks at Winchester. Yet it's doubtful whether we will ever know if his angel sang 'Whom is it you seek in the sepulchre, O Christians?' or only 'Whom is it you seek?'

Next, for your imaginary-imaginative theatre to flourish as you read such a text, you need to bear in mind those performance-characterising elements of pace, unstoppability, pre-thought-out characterisation, stage-configuration, atmosphere and 'occasion'. (They contribute to the sense of unfolding mystery and momentousness in *The Visit to the Sepulchre*.) And, though quite possibly you would want to return to this idea and modify it later, you might find that it helped in the first instance to envisage the play you were reading as being performed on the stage for which it was originally conceived. There have been so many changes in the conditions of English drama over the 1,000 years since Ethelwold's time, even in the 600 of them in which scripted plays have largely been given *in* English: changes in the type of audience for which a play is framed, in the sort of stage space and theatrical apparatus available to the playwright, and in the degree of importance his or her words have in the total theatrical experience. A notion of original context could be valuable. That monastic church in Winchester at the beginnings of English recorded drama provides a case in point: a sacred space; a single-sex gathering; the expectation of sung Latin; costumes and props familiar through their use in church rituals; the *frisson* when the normal service mode in which choir and clerics have been taking part suddenly flowers into a dramatic impersonation which they witness. Similarly, the coming phases of scripted and spoken English-language drama have homes and clienteles it is worth becoming familiar with. Broad-brush sketches of five of them should help us to do this.

Thus, when reading the 'mystery' cycles of the fifteenth and sixteenth centuries – sequences of short religious plays making up a history of the world in medieval Christian terms – it helps to imagine the open-air environments and temporary stages they were scripted for, the festival days they helped celebrate, the audience of often illiterate town and country people gathering around the pageant-wagons and scaffolds they were done on, the amateur performers from the town's guilds who acted them, and the carrying power and memorability of the sturdy rhymed vernacular verse they were written in. With the post-Reformation drama of the decades around 1600, written by Marlowe, Shakespeare, Jonson, Webster and the rest, the image changes to Britain's first purpose-built, permanent theatre-buildings: playhouses manned by professional companies that performed in them for many months of the year; in most cases big places open to the sky housing a thousand and more spectators of all sorts and conditions who wanted plays to match, where gallery-goers and groundlings surrounded three sides of a thrust-stage on which an all-male company presented a drama of word and gesture (with the words often in blank verse) against the unchanging façade of their backstage building or 'tiring house' rather than against what we might think of as scenery.

That image doesn't outlast the theatre-less Commonwealth of the mid-seventeenth century. Indeed, at the new 'Restoration' theatres from the 1660s onwards – roofed, candle- and oil-lit places, much smaller than the Shakespearean 'wooden O', more exclusively for the high bourgeoisie, gentry and aristocracy – two of the major selling points were 'scenes and women' (as the phrase went). We need to imagine the fascination of audiences and drama-tists in the late seventeenth century and into the eighteenth with female roles being played by actresses and with scenery made up of painted symmetrical sliding wings and back-'shutters' which changed speedily before the audi-ence's eyes within a proscenium arch. Witty and knowing prose-comedies of modern life did especially well in this clubby environment; however, a lot of this would change under the impact of the Industrial and Romantic Revolutions. The industrial one made for a big shift of the rural population to the towns and cities, which in turn swelled audiences, led to the building of bigger theatres and created the demand for audience-friendly plays (romantic 'tales of mystery', pictures of lower-class life) where wit and knowingness were no longer at a premium. It also revolutionised theatre technology. Stages were fitted with the newly developed gaslight and limelight showing off elaborate illusionistic scenery which needed a lowering of the curtain between the acts to hide the setting up of so-called box-sets for indoor scenes and striking 'set pieces' for outdoor ones. And this in plays where the dialogue in very functional prose was supported and enhanced by a great deal of music from the orchestra pit: the *melos* which gave the age's representative drama its name, melodrama. And from this comes later Victorian and Edwardian theatre, partly by continuation (realistic decor, social concerns) and partly through an earnest reaction influenced by Continental ideas of 'naturalism' in acting and an interest in a cooler analysis of modern life. To be there, imagine yourself sitting among quite sophisticated, quite well-off people in a darkened auditorium, looking at a picture-frame stage (lit by the new electricity) which reflects back aspects of the audience's own world, shaping it into 'well-made plays' and 'plays of ideas' which tangle more or less intensely with the big issues of the day.

From around 1910 on, there are so many valid and valued traditions of theatre running side by side that it is no longer really possible to say that the age can be characterised by one playhouse mode. Rather, it is as if the whole century is moving towards the point near its end when one could take a short walk up-river on London's South Bank from 'Shakespeare's Globe', lovingly reconstructed and encouraging 'historical' performance, to the National Theatre, which is a multiplex of three differing auditoria with differing stages to match, and so a home to almost any kind of drama. However, one movement took an important place alongside the others from about 1910 on: the drama of modernism. This deployed a range of styles but had a few common characteristics where performance was concerned. One of these was the support of 'studio' audiences: the intrepid, the truly curious, those interested in cutting-edge, state-of-the-art theatre. Small acting spaces, chamber-theatres, churches, even drawing rooms, often provided the venues, and in them there was a strong reaction in acting and decor against the picturesque spectacle or photographic naturalism of the previous century. With this went a foregrounding of the sheerly theatrical, which might involve song, dance, cabaret turns, image projections, scenic abstraction, masks, formalised gesture, stylised verse – in an attempt to reveal areas of experience that for some centuries Western drama could not reach: dream-states, the archetypal, the transcendental.

All that may seem a long way from St Ethelwold's monastery in the 970s; but we can bring monasticism and modernism alongside each other finally if we think of that line of the Angel's from *The Visit to the Sepulchre*, 'Go, announce that he is risen from the dead!', and take the Bible story on to its next episode: the Disciples' uncertainty after the Marys' message, followed by Jesus's appearance to them. This is the subject of a brief modernist play by W. B. Yeats, *The Resurrection* (1934). The scene: a bare room. Three Christians younger than the biblical twelve talk excitedly as they guard an inner hideaway where many of their seniors are gathered. Outside, we are told, excited mobs surge around Jerusalem while bands of devotees of the god Dionysus, obsessed with *his* death and resurrection, roam the streets. Eventually the risen Jesus passes momentously across the stage and goes into the inner room – which pretty much ends the play.

In contrast to Ethelwold's piece, Yeats's doesn't proclaim, confirm and rejoice in a great truth. It seems to accept that an act of potent magic has taken place at the first Easter and hints that, like a change of the moon, this heralds a change in the world order. But mainly the play raises issues for us as spectators to ponder: issues of belief and doubt, mysticism and humanism, the rational and irrational, the cycles of history and the connections between the world's great religions. And though it does this for a lot of the time in quite a talky way, it is pure theatre none the less. The presence of three musicians who share the stage with the three speaking actors; their mysterious choric songs 'for the unfolding and folding of the curtain'; their evocations of the cries of the Dionysiacs; the sound-effects and intensifications of atmosphere they contrive with their drums and rattles; then the climactic presence of a silent Jesus traversing the stage in a stylised mask: it is as if a strain of traditional East Asian theatre had been grafted challengingly onto a stem of late nineteenth-century Drama of Ideas. The reader in the library needs, in the words of an earlier Yeats play, to call it all to the eye of the mind.

NEXT STEPS

Brown, John Russell, ed. *The Oxford Illustrated History of Theatre*. Oxford: Oxford University Press, 1995.

Dukore, Bernard, ed. *Dramatic Theory and Criticism: Greeks to Grotowski*. New York: Holt, Rinehart, 1974.

Meisel, Martin. *How Plays Work: Reading and Performance*. Oxford: Oxford University Press, 2007.

Trussler, Simon. *The Cambridge Illustrated History of British Theatre*. Cambridge: Cambridge University Press, 1994.

17

Text and Performance

Olga Taxidou

The complex and interdependent relationships between play-text, stage and performance have always been an integral part of theatre history and theatre criticism. Ever since Aristotle wrote *Poetics* (c.335 BCE), theatre has been understood and experienced as an *event*. This event is defined both by contingent historical circumstances but also by a sense of its 'liveness', the immediacy and ephemerality of the moment of performance and this seems impossible to recreate, let alone make the basis of a critical theory. For all these reasons, the study of theatrical play-texts has tended to focus on their literary dimension as if they were already completed works of art. However, even written play-texts are always dynamic, blue-prints for performance that at once acknowledge the staging conventions within which the play was first produced and offer the possibility of creating a new, original event every time the play-text is performed, as the last chapter has suggested. And this dynamic relationship between text, staging and performance is where the uniqueness of theatre lies.

Furthermore, in order to be fully realized, theatre needs an audience. All this makes for an experience that extends far beyond the activity of imagining a world proposed by reading a play-text. This power of the performance event to engage us physically, intellectually and emotionally, individually and collectively has at times accorded theatre a privileged position in society, for example, in the use of theatre in political propaganda or in ancient Athens, in the classical drama of Aeschylus, Sophocles and Euripides in the fifth century BCE. At other times, however, it has made theatre a target of censorship and persecution. All this is testament to the sometimes overwhelming impact that a theatrical event may have on its audience. This derives from the fact that it is not simply written, but also made, staged and performed.

Every period of major theatrical achievement has developed its own mechanics of production, a set of practices that facilitate the transition from text to stage. Every performance requires stages of preparation, casting, setting the play to scenery and usually music, laborious rehearsals that also demand systems of funding. In ancient Athens, this process of production was supported by the *polis* (the state) itself, and also funded by wealthy Athenians. As performances of tragedies took place within the Great Dionysia, the greatest civic and religious festival of the time, Aeschylus, Sophocles and Euripides functioned not simply as dramatic poets but as prototype directors. They were responsible not only for the writing of the script but also as trainers of the chorus (*chorodidaskaloi*) and the actors. This training involved singing and dancing as well as acting. In creating these performances these great tragedians also relied on a set of dramatic conventions, but these were also modified and reformulated throughout their work. Archaeologists, classicists and theatre historians have helped to recover and define the function of some of these conventions: the use of masks, the function of the chorus, the use of music, the stylised setting, the use of stylised gesture, the function of myth, the all-male *hypocrites* (the Greek term for actors) and the (probably) all-male audience.

That 'probably' is indicative here: we are certain about some of these conventions, but others are still matters of debate. The crucial issue, however, is that the classical Athenian tragedies were written with these conventions in mind, and the three tragedians who helped to define tragic form at once worked within these conventions and helped to modify them, for the process was not simply mechanical but imaginative and creative. These conventions were not simply formal devices but also reflected contemporary philosophical, aesthetic and socio-political attitudes and sensibilities about matters such as the role of women, the relationships between history and myth and humans and the Gods, and the function of political representation, as theatre functioned in the words of the contemporary Athenian ruler, Pericles (495–29 BCE), as the great school of Athenian democracy. The collective term for all the activities that help to facilitate the transition from text to stage is *mise en scène*. This term was not used until the beginning of the nineteenth century, but the process itself is a constituent element of every school of theatre. The term refers to a set of formal devices – in effect, a creative process that makes the theatrical event present and visible. At the same time it contributes to the power of the stage to create a world view, projecting an image of itself back to the audience and so creating a metaphor of itself and its world.

When approaching a play-text as a piece of literature it is vital, therefore, to be aware of these historical conventions. They help us to realise that the play we are reading is part of an intricate set of relationships and cannot really exist outside these. In turn, this 'tool kit' of production that almost every play-text comes with reflects the systems of belief of the society it represents. The varying cast of actors – perhaps including chorus-members – as well as of impresarios, movement and voice coaches, stage- and actor-managers (functions often later absorbed into the work of the modernist director; see below) reveal to us the developing nature and role of theatre professions and their contribution to contemporary performance. These changing, developing roles – the appearance of the first English actresses, for example, in late seventeenth-century Restoration drama – also indicate much about contemporary society and the place of the theatre professions within it. All these factors are crucial as matters of scholarly research and debate and in understanding influences on playwrights. But how important are they when we approach historical play-texts for performance today? Can we ignore the conventions according to which the plays were written and simply approach them for the ideas and issues they raise about human nature? Are we in danger of producing a 'museum' performance if we adhere too strictly to the historical conventions of a piece? And are these ever fully recoverable? All these questions became particularly pertinent during the modernist period in English literature after 1910 – a period characterised by the urge to 'make it new', in the words of Ezra Pound. In the field of theatre, this often heralded the complete 'emancipation' of the notion of performance from the 'tyranny' of the literary text.

To help look further into these concerns, useful evidence is offered in the performance history of one of Shakespeare's greatest tragedies, *King Lear* (c.1605; printed 1608 and 1623), written within the conventions of early modern drama, the period roughly between 1500–1700. Like Greek drama, Elizabethan and Jacobean drama was not straightforwardly realistic but highly conventional. These conventions included the use of verse for dramatic speech, asides spoken from stage to audience, characters apparently talking to themselves in soliloquies, boys playing the roles of women, the use of different levels of the stage, props and elaborate costumes. The performances themselves were framed by extra-theatrical activities such as a jig after the play, sometimes offering a parodic commentary on contemporary events. All these factors informed the first staging of *King Lear* and later developments of them would have continued to shape its reception by audiences throughout its staging history. Another factor in this history is that *King Lear* has often been burdened with a reputation of being unperformable, on account of its supposedly apocalyptic, bombastic or overly-philosophical language and its bleak, relentlessly pessimistic ending. Notoriously, Charles Lamb, Leo Tolstoy and Henry James all believed it was impossible to stage.

The first problem we encounter in considering the play's relationship to its original conditions of performance is that two versions of the play-text exist, and these present different versions of the play. The play was probably first performed in 1604–5, and although the first printed version, the Quarto of 1608, appeared in Shakespeare's lifetime, most scholars agree that the playwright was not involved with the production of this edition. After Shakespeare's death, a Folio version of his complete works appeared in 1623, probably through collaboration between printers and two members of his company. This included a different version of *King Lear*, perhaps intended primarily to be read; it is this text, though, that is mostly used for performances today. Christie Carson claims that the textual differences between the Quarto and the Folio versions of the play result from audience responses during Shakespeare's lifetime (Carson and Bratton 10). However, it is not certain whether Shakespeare would have approved or even been aware of these differences. Carson's claim endows the audience with extraordinary power. Furthermore, the Folio version dramatically rewrites the ending of *King Lear*, giving a more optimistic tone to the Quarto's bleak conclusion. This is significant in a play that has often been read as post-apocalyptic (probably written after the death of Queen Elizabeth in 1603), relentlessly nihilistic in its study of masculine power and lineage and deeply troubled about the 'nature' of women.

The quest for a 'happy ending' seems to haunt the reception history of this play. As early as 1681 the Irish playwright Nahum Tate wrote a version deleting many of Shakespeare's lines, getting rid of the fool altogether and creating a love interest for Cordelia in the role of Edgar (see Chapter 3). In 1742 the actor David Garrick reinstated some of Shakespeare's lines but kept Tate's uplifting ending. Another celebrated actor-manager, Edmund Kean, tried to go back to Shakespeare's full text in the early nineteenth century but this performance only lasted for three nights as again it was deemed 'unbearable' for the audience. It was not until 1838 that Shakespeare's text was performed more or less in full by William Macready. Yet again the question remains whether this 'full' text was the Quarto version or the Folio.

Modern productions of the play do not shy away from its bleak, apocalyptic atmosphere, but rather revel in it, as did Peter Brook's groundbreaking production of 1962. Despite the charges of unperformability and antitheatricality *King Lear* has proved to be one of Shakespeare's most adapted and adaptable plays on the stage and on the screen (notable examples of the latter include the Russian version of 1970 directed by Grigori Kozintsev with music by Dmitri Shostakovich and the Japanese version *Ran*, directed by Akira Kurosawa in 1985). In a sense, every contemporary or future performance of the play is in dialogue with its staging history and forms part of this on-going negotiation between play-text and reception. The historical conventions of production, the material conditions that helped to create Shakespeare's own performances, are not simply a matter of empirical historical fact but exist in the ways the plays themselves are written; they help give shape to the world of the play.

This world is primarily expressed and embodied through the function of the actor. This is all the more the case when it comes to Elizabethan acting, which was not psychological and character-based, the modes we are most familiar with today through naturalism (see below) and film. Rather than expressing the inner world of the role or character the acting was stylised, exaggerated and external in mode as it had to express highly rhetorical language in demanding performance conditions. Plays could command audiences of up to 2,000 spectators who gathered in an open-air auditorium in the middle of a busy London afternoon. Hence the emphasis on costumes, which were detailed and highly codified denoting such categories as the class or rank of the role portrayed. How, then, is a contemporary actor approaching the role of Lear to engage with these conventions, taking on board that most actor training today is psychologically-based and does not rely solely on such stylised conventions?

It is helpful at this point to introduce a set of terms used by contemporary performance theorists when attempting to describe the function of the actor, keeping in mind that this function is primarily based on the physicality of the performing body. There is a distinction between the actor's 'phenomenal body'(her/his physical bodily being-in-the-world) and the actor's 'semiotic body'(what the performer is representing or attempting to embody). Throughout the history of acting, it is only really in the tradition of naturalism where the two converge, where the actor is asked to 'be' the role, physically and significantly psychologically. In most acting traditions, this relationship between the 'phenomenal body' of the performer and the 'semiotic body' is a conventional one, delineated by rules and forms that the actor acquires and importantly the audience is able to decode. In this sense, the actor performing Lear is not asked to 'be' Lear, but to portray, exhibit, demonstrate him (and his world), through a mode of acting that celebrates its artificiality, its theatricality, and does not try to hide it. Significantly, it also portrays clearly the interpretation of Lear that the particular actor brings to the role in the process of demonstrating it to the audience. This mode of acting also allows the actor to perform asides, to directly address the audience and step in and out of the world of the play, something that was common on the thrust stage of the Elizabethan playhouse. A thrust stage protruded out onto the audience across its three sides and it blurred the boundaries between the world of the audience and the world of the stage. The reconstruction of the Globe Theatre in London has provided performers, directors and scholars with very useful insights into how Shakespeare's theatre worked in performance. In turn, these insights have informed contemporary stagings of the plays (see Carson and Karim-Cooper).

In the 1997 National Theatre production of *King Lear* directed by Richard

Eyre, with Ian Holm in the leading role, there was one of those electrifying, epiphanic theatrical moments where an actor creates 'presence'. In the words of Patrice Pavis,

> 'To have presence' in theatrical parlance, is to know how to capture the attention of the public and make an impression; it is also to be endowed with a *je ne sais quoi* which triggers an immediate feeling of identification in the spectator, communicating a sense of living elsewhere and in an eternal present. (301)

This was the scene on the heath (III, iv) where actor and director decided to enact literally Shakespeare's words 'Off, off you lendings' and present a naked, slight-figured Ian Holm, stumbling about extremely vulnerable, like a 'bare forked animal' on the bleak stage (III, iv, 104–5). The nakedness of Lear/ Holm appears shocking but at the same time can be read as a sophisticated way of acknowledging historical performance conventions and creating a modern reading of the play, bringing out its existential bleakness (although Eyre used the Folio text). The total absence of costume, clothing and the seeming confla- tion of the phenomenal and semiotic body, could be said to pay homage to the Elizabethan and Jacobean emphasis on what can be signified through costume or appearance. In this instance, however, the costume has become the naked body of the actor, which now lacking meaning and reason becomes itself a mask that enacts the word 'nothing', so emblematic in this play. The actor's nakedness enacts the lines uttered by the fool in Act One: 'thou art an 0 without a figure. I am better than thou art now; I am a fool thou art nothing' (I, iv, 186–8). It is this non-figure of 0 that we see enacted on the stage. In a sense, this contemporary performance still remains faithful to Shakespeare's poetry, bringing to the stage a version of the actor's phenomenal/semiotic body that would have been incon- ceivable for the Elizabethan audience. To see a king naked or in rags is to witness the destruction of state power. In the words of Pavis, this moment communi- cates to the audience a sense of both 'living elsewhere and in an eternal present' (301); an awareness of the languages of staging helps the performer to create this double movement. In turn, this unique moment of presence has now become part of the reception history of *King Lear*; the 2007 Royal Shakespeare Company production also had a naked Ian McKellen as Lear. And this creative interaction between past and present also takes place every time we read or study a play-text. Our awareness of the historical contexts of production of the play and its history of reception serves to create the sense of 'living elsewhere', while, at the same time, the freedom that we have – as members of an audience, as theatre-makers or simply readers – to change, re-imagine or redirect it, makes the play-text alive for us in the present.

Another instance of an incongruous relationship between the performer's phenomenal and semiotic body is cross-gender casting. This, of course, will always refer to the Elizabethan convention of boys playing women, but crucially, as contemporary scholars claim was the case with this historical convention itself, it serves as a vehicle to examine, portray and sometimes critically analyse gender relations, the position of women and the absence of actresses. Since 2000, we have had many male actors play Shakespeare's female roles and vice versa. Casting a female performer as Lear may initially appear at odds for a play so concerned with kingship, fatherhood and masculinity. On the other hand, the particular gendered perspective that the female performer brings also helps highlight and scrutinise what has been read as a complex and somewhat difficult position that the feminine occupies in this play. These issues are discussed further by Suzanne Trill in Chapter 21.

All these casting and staging decisions are not solely the domain of the actor but derive from a creative encounter between actor and director. Although we tend to take the figure of the director for granted today (mainly because of his/her prominence in film) and although there has always been a mediating figure between play-text and stage throughout theatre history, it is within modernism, as an aesthetic, socio-political movement of the avant-garde in the early twentieth century, that this role is clearly defined, acquires independent artistic status and comes to bear almost sole responsibility for the creation of a performance.

The crucial staging relationship for theatrical modernism and the historical avant-garde is that between the playwright and the in-between, mediating figure of the director. The battle was one of authorship, not of the play-text, for that incontestably belonged to the playwright, but of the performance. In 1911, Edward Gordon Craig – the son of Ellen Terry, the famous Victorian actress and the acting pupil of Henry Irving, the equally famous actor-manager of the Lyceum theatre in London – published his manifesto-style book *On the Art of the Theatre*, heralding a new concept of theatre, making a strong and impassioned plea for the total independence of performance. In it he wrote,

> the Art of the Theatre is neither acting nor the play, it is not scene nor dance, but it consists of all the elements of which these things are composed: action, which is the very spirit of acting; words, which are the body of the play; line and colour, which are the very heart of the scene; rhythm, which is the very essence of dance. (Craig 138)

And this 'new' art demands a new 'artist of the theatre', to use Craig's phrase. This figure was the director who, 'when he will have mastered the uses of action, words, line, colour and rhythm, then . . . may become an artist' (148). Out of this conflict between the playwright and the director, performance itself emerges as an independent artistic activity, no longer compelled to remain 'faithful' in any way to the play-text or to its historical staging conventions.

Within all the experiments of theatrical modernism it is as if the whole notion of stage conventions is re-addressed and the job of the mediating figure, which may have been simply to stage a play-text, becomes the job of the director and is elevated into a creative activity in its own right. Much of this experiment is facilitated by new stage technologies of the period (the introduction of electric lighting, new concepts of scenic space etc.) and new methods of actor training. Many of the modernists we study in English Literature – including T. S. Eliot, W. B. Yeats, W. H. Auden and Christopher Isherwood, D. H. Lawrence, Joseph Conrad – wrote plays, but significantly most also wrote essays about the relationship between plays and performance. In a sense, they wrote their plays not only as playwrights, but also *as if* they were directors. They were concerned both with 'the poetry in the theatre' and 'the poetry of the theatre', to borrow the French author, playwright and film director Jean Cocteau's phrase (96–7).

Samuel Beckett, who in many ways continues the modernist experiments in poetic drama and the stage, can also be said to merge the roles of playwright and director, not only because he often directed his own plays, but because his plays come with detailed staging directions and are in a sense 'ready made' for performance. These directions, however, are not interpretive, they neither serve to explain the roles or the play, but rather clearly and precisely signify how these roles are to be transferred to the stage. *Endgame* (1958) opens in the play's single set with Clov drawing the curtains on two windows (the sea window and the earth window), uncovering two dustbins (containing the 'accursed progenitors', Nagg and Nell) and then uttering the first lines, 'Finished, it's finished, nearly finished, it must be nearly finished' (Beckett 2395). He is the 'carer' of Hamm: seated, blind, covered in a blanket, a figure that could itself be seen as a reading of *Lear* after the apocalypse. Although the first productions directed by Roger Blin in Paris and George Devine at the Royal Court were unsuccessful, the play has come to occupy a privileged position in the history of twentieth century theatre, both as a completed performance piece (for the relationships it establishes between playwright, director and actor) and for the nightmarish, post-apocalyptic world it evokes. This image of the Beckettian stage has almost invariably been interpreted as resulting from the devastation and horror of the post-Second World War period, and this is discussed in more detail by Dermot Cavanagh in Chapter 20.

Throughout his life, however, Beckett had always objected to literal, psychologising and freely interpretive visualisations and stagings of his plays, when they diverge from his own directions. 'Anybody who cares for the work couldn't fail to be disgusted by it' was the phrase he insisted be added to the programme notes of JoAnne Akalaitis's 1984 production (with the American Repertory Theatre) of *Endgame* set in a New York subway tunnel after a nuclear war (Oppenheim 139). It is as if the most experimental playwright/ philosopher of the twentieth century was denying the director his/her creative autonomy, an autonomy fought for and mostly achieved throughout the first decades of the same century. An argument could be made that in order for plays to survive they have to be performed, sometimes successfully, sometimes not. The concept of performance also should allow for the concept of failure. At the same time, Beckett himself was inconsistent in his attitudes towards directors. Alan Schneider, the director he met in 1950s Paris and who is known for faithfully 'serving' him throughout his life, had almost total freedom to do what he wished with his plays. For what mattered for Beckett was that Schneider (born in 1917 during the October Revolution, the son of Russian Jews, whose aunt died in Auschwitz) shared the same sensibility towards the horrors of his age. Beckett was equally generous towards many actors and directors he worked with and he would change the play-texts numerous times himself during the rehearsal process. As many contemporary scholars claim, the works of Beckett will survive through to the twenty-first century, not necessarily through meticulous reconstruction, but through creative re-imaginings that will be always be contingent upon the historical contexts of their audiences, whether this is intentional or not.

On the one hand, the so-called emancipation of performance from the literary text, heralded by modernism and the avant-garde, allows for the total freedom of the performance event. On the other, this event always takes place within a historical context and always relies on audience reception. The success or failure of a performance might be measured not by the degree to which it remains faithful to a play-text (which in some postmodern performances is discarded altogether), but possibly to the degree it re-imagines that text within its historical context, providing through an embodied, live experience insight and pleasure for its audience. The study of play-texts as dynamic performance events, informed by their history of production and reception, may offer us a similar experience of insight and pleasure.

NEXT STEPS

Bentley, Eric. *The Life of the Drama*. New York: Applause Books, 1991.

Fischer-Lichte, Erika. *History of European Theatre*. Trans. Jo Riley. London: Routledge, 2001.

Pavis, Patrice. *Dictionary of the Theatre: Terms, Concepts and Analysis*. Trans. Christine Shantz. Toronto: University of Toronto Press, 1999.

Shepherd, Simon and Peter Womack. *English Drama: A Cultural History*. Oxford: Blackwell, 1996.

18

Tragedy

Simon Malpas

THE IMPACT OF CATASTROPHE: TRAGEDY AND AFFECT

Nowadays, the term 'tragedy' is as often used to refer to events in the world as it is to identify a particular genre of drama. Every day we hear news of occurrences from across the planet ranging from individual personal crises to national, regional or even global disasters that are identified with the epithets 'tragedy' or 'tragic'. The sudden death of a well-loved public figure, fatal accidents on the roads or plane or train crashes that cause injury and suffering, natural disasters such as hurricanes, earthquakes or tsunami that devastate the lives of vast numbers of people, all are presented in the media and experienced as 'tragedies'. Such events are reported with solemnity and produce reactions of shock, horror, pity, fear, awe and sympathy. These types of reaction are the responses commonly associated with the term 'tragedy' in both its dramatic and more general usages and serve as a means to begin to understand the term.

Used in relation to the examples above, 'tragedy' identifies an affect: the witnesses feel shock and horror at the event, experience pity for the suffering of the victims and identify with their plight however different or distant they might be and even imagine the reactions they themselves might have had should they have been caught up in the crisis. In this way, the tragic affect focuses on the sense of a potential for shared feelings between spectator and victim – 'It's so sad', 'They must have felt wretched', 'If I'd had to go through that, I'd be devastated' – rather than an examination of the causes of the disaster, the analysis of which might come later but is not part of the immediate response that says of an event 'That's a tragedy'. The affect of tragedy thus forges a link, creates a sense of sympathy or empathy, between spectator and victim as the former attempts to comprehend the impact and consequences of the catastrophe.

In its narrower and more specialised sense as a term designating a particular mode of dramatic writing, this idea of affect is still central: tragedy is a genre that sets out explicitly to evoke responses of fear, horror, sympathy and pity from the reader or audience. The earliest and most influential definition of tragedy, produced in the fourth century BCE by the classical Greek philosopher Aristotle in his *Poetics* (c.335 BCE), makes this point clearly:

> Tragedy is a representation of a serious, complete action which has mag-
> nitude, in embellished speech, with each of its elements used separately
> in the various parts of the play; represented by people acting and not by
> narration; accomplishing by means of pity and terror the catharsis of such
> emotions. (95)

In other words, tragedy seeks, by means of representation, to present a partic-ular course of action in such a way that it elicits feelings of pity and fear in its audience in a manner that will somehow resolve them through catharsis. The concept of 'catharsis' is complex, and has proved extremely controversial in analyses both of Aristotle's work and tragedy more generally, but it is crucial to any definition of the genre. For the purposes of this introduction, it might be generally understood as indicating that the experience of pity and fear in the face of some tragic catastrophe has the therapeutic effect of rebalancing or harmonising the spectator's emotions. In other words, the excess of emotion brought about by the terrible event portrayed in the text leads to a renewed balance of feeling once there is time to reflect upon it.

Aristotle's work has influenced profoundly all subsequent understanding of tragic affect. For example, the seventeenth-century poet John Milton presents it as a form of homeopathy in the preface to his poem *Samson Agonistes* (1671). In his account, tragedy has the effect

> by raising pity and fear, or terror, to purge the mind of those and such-
> like passions, that is to temper and reduce them to such measure with a
> kind of delight . . . for so in physic [medicine] things of melancholic hue
> and quality are used against melancholy, sour against sour, salt to remove
> salt humours. (Milton 355)

In other words, the pity and fear felt by an audience stimulate their emotions in order to calm them, turning terror into 'a kind of delight'. For Aristotle and Milton, then, tragedy is a mode of drama that presents its subject matter in such a way that it provokes a cathartic response from its audience so as to bring about some sort of psychological balance by purging excesses. An even grander sense of the role of catharsis is given by the Romantic poet Samuel Taylor Coleridge who, acknowledging that primarily 'tragic scenes were meant to *affect* us', asserts that tragedy's real aim is

> to transport the mind to a sense of its possible greatness . . . during the temporary oblivion of the worthless 'thing we are', and of the particular state in which each man *happens* to be, suspending our individual recollections and lulling them to sleep amidst the music of nobler thoughts. (192)

Catharsis, by evoking particular instances of pity and fear, serves to ennoble the spectator who empathises with the dignity and courage displayed by the victim in the face of her or his downfall and thereby recognises the greatness of the tragic action as a whole. Just as with real-world tragedies, the defining feature of dramatic tragedy for the Aristotelian tradition is the affect a text has on its audience and its formation of a sympathetic emotional bond between spectator and victim.

ACHIEVING CATHARSIS: ARISTOTLE'S TRAGIC FORM

If the aim of tragedy is to provoke catharsis, it is important to explore how a work of drama might be structured in order to bring such a response about. How, in other words, can a story be presented in a manner that persuades an audience to respond to the suffering and downfall of a character with pity, fear and catharsis?

A key task Aristotle sets himself is to identify and define the formal structures of a tragedy that generate a cathartic response. In *Poetics* he argues that the most crucial feature of tragic drama is the plot, it is 'the origin and as it were the soul of tragedy' (96), and it is by means of an analysis of the structure of tragic plot that his argument proceeds. The plot should contain a series of elements that work together to generate catharsis: it must centre on a protagonist whose *hamartia* (error or flaw) gives rise to *peripeteia* (a reversal of fortune) in the narrative, which in turn leads to a moment of *anagnorisis* (recognition) of the *hamartia* by the protagonist, before the final terrible moment of *catastrophe* that evokes the audience's *catharsis*. It is worth spending a moment exploring each of these elements in some more detail.

Aristotle defines the elements listed above, and shows how they work together to create the tragic affect, in the following way. A tragedy begins with the introduction of a protagonist, a heroic public figure who displays a range of virtues with which the audience might want immediately to identify, a character representing a person who is, says Aristotle, 'better than we are' (103). So, for example, the tragic protagonist might be a ruler such as

Agamemnon, Oedipus, Cleopatra or King Lear, a noble such as Antigone or Hamlet, or even a character presented as exemplary of a particular trait as Doctor Faustus might be of intelligence or Coriolanus of bravery and military honour. But this protagonist also displays some form of *hamartia*: either they make a fatal error, such as Lear's decision to split his kingdom on the basis of who claims to love him best or Oedipus's unwitting murder of his father and marriage with his mother, or they present some other kind of flaw; this might be, as with Othello's jealousy, a psychological propensity or, like Romeo and Juliet or Antony and Cleopatra or other 'star-crossed' lovers, they might fall in love in circumstances that turn out to be disastrous.

For Aristotle, the attractiveness of the virtues that have encouraged the audience to identify with the protagonist also urge them to acknowledge their capacity to share the error or flaw: they empathise with the hero, simultaneously admiring the character's grandeur and projecting their own feelings and personality onto that character in order to identify with them; thereby they are urged to acknowledge their own propensity to fall prey to the *hamartia*. As the narrative of the tragedy develops, the *hamartia* brings about a moment of *peripeteia*, a radical reversal of the protagonist's fortunes, which generally serves to hurtle them towards disaster, suffering and even death: Oedipus's crimes are revealed by the soothsayer, Lear is cast out into the storm, Othello is deceived by Iago and Pentheus is fooled into spying on Dionysius's revels. In each case, the character begins to suffer from the consequences of *hamartia*, and a sense of the impending disaster starts to emerge. This is the moment at which an audience might be tempted to dis-identify with the protagonist, to lose their empathetic link, distance themselves and refuse to recognise their propensity to share the hero's error or flaw. However, Aristotle's invocation of a moment of *anagnorisis* serves to counter this: at this point the protagonist heroically recognises his or her *hamartia*, acknowledges it and passes 'from ignorance to knowledge' in a manner that 'such a recognition and reversal will contain pity or terror (tragedy is considered to be a representation of actions of this sort), and in addition misfortune and good fortune will come about in the case of such events' (99). Oedipus recognises his guilt, accepts his fate and chooses banishment; Mark Antony acknowledges that his desire has led him to fail politically and falls on his sword; Juliet forsakes a loveless life and chooses to die beside Romeo. In each case, the protagonist has the opportunity to reflect upon what has happened, recognise their own part in the events and show courage in the face of the impending disaster. The nobility of such a gesture serves, according to Aristotle, to renew the audience's identification with the protagonist and restore the sense of empathy: despite their error or flaw, the protagonist still provides a heroic model with which to identify. As a consequence of this renewed identification, the moment of catastrophe which follows will produce in the audience the required affects of pity for the hero and fear that they too might share an analogous fate, and the catharsis that results from the release of these emotions seems to bring them back into balance. Tragedy, according to Aristotle, is thus at once a moral warning about the dangers of a particular *hamartia*, and also a safety valve that allows excessive emotions to diffuse harmlessly.

Poetics illustrates this structure by citing a wide range of plays, some of which have now been lost, but ends up focusing most closely on a single example of tragedy, Sophocles' *Oedipus the King* (c.429 BCE), which Aristotle frequently describes as the most effective example of each aspect of the tragic plot. Before the play begins Oedipus has been elected king of Thebes for defeating the Sphinx by solving its riddle and thereby liberating the town that it had been holding hostage. He is called by his citizens to use his wit once again to free them from a plague. Learning that the plague has been sent as punishment by the gods because one of the Thebans has committed unspeakable crimes, Oedipus determines to discover the identity of the criminal. The opening scenes of the play present him as heroic: the brave, intelligent and wise saviour of the city to whom his people turn in their distress. The audience is encouraged to appreciate and empathise with his noble virtues, to admire him and see him as a model to emulate. The subsequent revelation that Oedipus is himself the criminal, that he has murdered his own father and married his mother, is the moment of reversal that precipitates him towards a tragic fall. However, Oedipus's courage in acknowledging his guilt (even though his crimes were committed without his knowledge) reasserts his nobility and virtue, holding the audience's sympathy. And, thus, at the moment of catastrophe where Jocasta his wife and mother commits suicide, and Oedipus blinds himself and accepts banishment from Thebes, the audience are suitably shocked and experience pity 'for a person undeserving of his misfortune, and the latter terror for a person like ourselves' (Aristotle 100). This excess of emotion leads to catharsis as the final lament by the chorus of Theban citizens accompanies Oedipus's exit into exile.

On the basis of its analysis of *Oedipus the King*, *Poetics* thus presents a straightforward account of the key constituents of plot that serve to create a tragic affect. Unfortunately, however, although Aristotle's model is clear and concise, problems arise when one attempts to read other tragedies in terms of its categories: not all classical Greek tragedies fit its strict criteria and neither do more than a few subsequent works. How useful, then, is a model of tragedy with which so few actual tragedies appear fully to comply? In addition to this, questions also arise about the political implications of Aristotle's account, especially with regard to the apparently coercive nature of catharsis. To what extent is an audience manipulated into identifying with the hero? What are the consequent political effects of tragedy as a genre? The aim of the next section is to discuss some responses to these questions.

PROBLEMS AND ALTERNATIVES: CRITIQUES OF ARISTOTLE'S THEORY

The question of how accurate and exhaustive a model Aristotle provides for tragic form is helpful for exploring the ways in which tragedy has changed over time. While there are clear continuities, especially with regard to affect, there have also been some key changes to ideas of the structure and role of tragic drama. As a genre of dramatic performance, tragedy originated in Greece towards the end of the sixth century BCE. Plays were performed in open-air theatres at public festivals, and all members of the community were expected to attend: the plays were part of a coming together of the community to celebrate its identity and worship the gods, a form of social ritual rather than simply private entertainment. The immediate social function of the tragedies was reflected in their form: a small number of characters interact with each other and with a larger chorus who often reflect the thoughts and beliefs of the audience. By the time Aristotle came to write his *Poetics*, almost a century and a half later, the writers we now associate with Greek tragedy, Aeschylus, Sophocles and Euripides, were long dead and tragic drama no longer played such a central role in society. Written in the aftermath of the great age of classical tragedy, *Poetics* aims to describe the genre and identify features shared by the texts rather than provide a single prescriptive model for 'correct' tragedy. As Clifford Leech suggests, 'Aristotle was not generally pre-scriptive: he wanted primarily . . . to describe what he found' (14). Although he cites *Oedipus the King* as a model of the most successful form of tragic drama, Aristotle also makes an effort to acknowledge the wide range of differ-ent possibilities for tragedy – including, for instance, tragedies with multiple heroes or even with happy endings. However, as the quotations from Milton and Coleridge above suggest, for many subsequent critics, how closely a text fits the structural criteria Aristotle presents in his discussion of *Oedipus* is often taken as a measure of how good a tragedy it is.

Subsequent interpretations of what Aristotle meant have led different cultures to set out different versions of his rules for what might constitute 'correct' tragedy. For example, in a continuation of the passage cited earlier, Milton contrasts the 'correct' tragedy of the ancients with the 'small esteem, or rather infamy' in which more recent tragic drama is held because of the 'poet's error of intermixing comic stuff with tragic sadness and gravity; or introducing trivial and vulgar persons, which by all judicious hath been counted absurd' (356). The practice of Renaissance and Restoration dramatists of producing sub-plots, non-aristocratic characters and comic interludes, which serve only 'corruptly to gratify the people' (356) is rejected by Milton as improper for tragedy. In response to this sort of view, Milton's contemporary, John Dryden in his *An Essay of Dramatick Poesie* (1668) finds himself having to argue strenuously that the freedom and flexibility of form to be found in the work of English writers such as Shakespeare and Jonson does not make their tragedies less successful than those of much more formally Aristotelian French playwrights such as Pierre Corneille and Jean Racine. Dryden is at pains to point out explicitly that 'the irregular Playes of *Shakespeare*' have more 'fancy and greater spirit in the writing, than there is in any of the *French*' (54). In fact, he asserts, it is precisely in the 'irregularity' – the freer and more apparently anarchic practice of English Renaissance playwrights who were prepared to break up the tragic action of their plays with sub-plots, spectacular scenes and even comic interludes – that the greatest tragic impact could be made. Dryden, a playwright himself, is much more focused on what works to create a cathartic affect than with the precise detail of Aristotle's theory.

In this and many other periods, the meaning and definition of tragedy was produced by the conflicts between the formal classicism of scholars and playwrights who wished to stick rigidly to an interpretation of Aristotle's 'rules' and those who were more concerned with adapting Aristotle's 'suggestions' to suit contemporary circumstances. As a result of this, the formal structures of individual tragedies tend to tell us as much about the expectations and beliefs of their particular contexts as they do about some sort of ideal tragic form. The modern critic George Steiner is not, then, simply being dismissive when he concludes that, rather than slavishly following Aristotle, the best classification of tragedy 'must start from the fact of catastrophe. Tragedies end badly' (8). The bad end, and the cathartic affect this produces, is probably the limit of a formal definition of tragedy.

The second question raised about Aristotle's model of tragedy at the end of the last section related to its politics. Critics have often claimed that his definition of catharsis is politically problematic: the affect of tragedy, they argue, seduces the audience into identifying with characters, actions and circumstances that are politically questionable and ought to be challenged. Catharsis relies on the production of an immediate emotional response in the audience rather than allowing space for the sort of reflection that might question the necessity of the tragic events.

Perhaps the most influential rejection of catharsis comes from the twentieth-century German playwright, director and theorist Bertolt Brecht, who develops his own account of a directly political 'epic theatre' in explicit contrast to Aristotle. Brecht asserts that his own drama is

anti-metaphysical, materialistic, non–aristotelian . . . [It] relates differently to certain psychological effects, such as catharsis . . . Anxious to
teach the spectator a quite definite practical attitude, directed towards
the changing world, it must begin by making him adopt in the theatre a
quite different attitude from what he is used to. (57)

Writing here in 1932, Brecht rejects the identification and empathy on which
catharsis is based in favour of a 'practical attitude' that allows the audience to
judge critically events they see, questioning their necessity and the possibility
of other types of reaction rather than becoming swept up in the emotional
flow that is the basis of Aristotelian tragedy. For Brecht, the Aristotelian spectator is anything but critical: appealing to identification and empathy produces
instinctive feelings that are reactionary by their nature rather than engaging
the audience with arguments they can assess rationally. In contrast to this,
Brecht's own plays seek deliberately to distance the audience and prevent
empathy from overcoming reason. *Mother Courage*, written in 1938–9 while
Brecht was in exile from Nazi Germany, certainly deals with potentially tragic
events. The play tells the story of how Courage, a trader who makes her
living by selling goods to the opposing armies during the Thirty Years War
that consumed Europe during the seventeenth century, loses her daughter
and two sons to that war. Although each child's death is a possible subject
for tragic treatment, Brecht takes care to break up the action in ways that
make immediate empathy impossible, and forces the audience to reflect on its
social and political causes. For example, Mother Courage's daughter Kattrin
is shot while beating a drum to warn a nearby town that its citizens are about
to be massacred. This is very moving, but the subsequent discussion of her
daughter's actions between Courage and some peasants undercuts any sense of
heroism by exploring the commercial consequences of her death and paying
off the peasants for the 'inconvenience' she caused. The central gesture of the
scene is not one of heroic grief at the death of a daughter but of financial transaction as Courage is forced to part with money. By refusing catharsis, Brecht's
play seeks to refocus the audience's attention on the politics of the events.
Instead of lulling the audience 'to sleep amidst the music of nobler thoughts',
as Coleridge put it, the play focuses explicitly on the material conditions that
produced the events depicted.

   Brecht's diagnosis of the conservative effects of catharsis is not inaccurate.
Many scholars argue that the *Poetics* presents tragedy as having a clear, even a
reactionary, political aim: the preservation of order in the Greek state. Most
now argue that the text was written to defend poetry against the criticisms of
its harmful effects on society presented in Plato's *Republic* (c.360 BCE). Plato
argues that drama is inherently immoral as its presentations of vice and error

serve only to encourage such behaviour in the audience. *Poetics* seeks to demonstrate that rather than being a disruptive force that excites an audience's antisocial passions, tragedy serves to rebalance them, therapeutically allowing for excessive feelings but, through catharsis, restoring balance and order as it delivers a moral message about the sufferings generated by a particular *hamartia*. Catharsis contains threats to the social order presented in the play, and purges antisocial sentiments by eliciting the audience's pity for the punished hero and fear that they might themselves suffer an analogous fate should they step outside of the social norms.

One result of this recognition of tragedy's political stance is that some contemporary criticism has sought deliberately to read tragedies 'against the grain' to explore whether anything escapes cathartic containment. As Jonathan Dollimore puts it in his influential book on English Renaissance theatre, *Radical Tragedy*:

> It is true that some of the most intriguing plays of the period do indeed rehearse threats in order to contain them. But to contain a threat by rehearsing it one must first give it a voice . . . Through this process the very condition of something's containment may constitute the terms of its challenge: opportunities for resistance become apparent, especially on the stage and even as the threat is being disempowered. (xxi)

If tragedy, as Aristotle presents it, contains antisocial impulses by manipulating an audience into affectively identifying with the negative consequences of an error or flaw, one aim for contemporary criticism is to explore such containment, the structures of power that produce it, and the possibilities of resistance in tragic drama.

NEXT STEPS

Drakakis, John and Naomi Conn Liebler, eds. *Tragedy*. London: Longman, 1998.

Leech, Clifford. *Tragedy: The Critical Idiom*. London: Methuen, 1969.

Williams, Raymond. *Modern Tragedy*. Ed. Pamela McCallum. Peterborough, ON: Broadview Press, 2003.

19

Comedy

Jonathan Wild

The perennial problem with comic drama is that critics have proved reluctant to take it seriously. While tragedy has long held an established place at the forefront of academic study, comedy has singularly failed to acquire this high intellectual status. The main difficulty for comedy in this context has been its perceived role as providing mere entertainment to its consumers. Tragedy is conventionally associated with portraying some of the most significant experiences of our lives, and it explores how we might cope with these. It sets out, as Simon Malpas noted in Chapter 18, to evoke responses of fear, horror, sympathy and pity from the reader or audience. In contrast to the solemnity of this task, comedy appears designed simply to amuse us and take us out of ourselves for a brief period. But although comic drama has remained the poor relation to tragedy among critics and students of literature at least over the last 2,000 years, it has never lost its popularity on the stage. During eras in which tragedy has moved out of fashion with audiences, comedy has continued to fill theatres and keep playwrights and actors in work. Furthermore, apart from its staying power as a discrete theatrical genre, comedy has also found its way into all other distinct theatrical modes including tragedy. Shakespeare's most serious works of tragic drama such as *King Lear* (1605) and *Macbeth* (1606) include considerable comic elements: Hamlet himself proves to be an adept comedian when the occasion requires. An understanding of the function and technique of dramatic comedy is therefore vital to our study of English Literature.

The roots of comedy's academic image problem can be traced back to classical writings on this topic. W. K. Wimsatt usefully sums up Plato's negative thoughts on comedy as expressed across various books of the *Republic* (c.360

BCE): 'the actions performed in comedy are a frivolous and giddy experience, demoralising to the spirit of serious citizenship' (7). Aristotle's discussion of comedy in Chapter V of his *Poetics* (c.335 BCE), is similarly perfunctory and dismissive, but it does at least provide a bedrock for future critical attempts to classify this dramatic form:

> Comedy is . . . a representation of people who are rather inferior – not, however, with respect to every kind of vice, but the laughable is only a part of what is ugly. For the laughable is a sort of error and ugliness that is not painful and destructive, just as, evidently, a laughable mask is something ugly and distorted without pain. (94)

Aristotle establishes comedy here in direct opposition to tragedy. The characters in comedies, he claims, are drawn from lower sections of society than those in tragedies and are involved with ridiculous rather than sublime elements of life. In addition, comedy is categorised – in contrast with tragedy – by the lack of authentic violence and suffering experienced by its characters. Although Aristotle devotes relatively little space to comedy in his *Poetics* (leading some critics to suspect the loss of a volume of *Poetics* dedicated to comedy) he does manage to classify the key features by which we continue to recognise this enduring dramatic form.

These key features certainly typify the golden age of English stage comedy during the early modern period, roughly between 1500–1700. The period is also marked by the variety of different types of comic productions that appeared at this time. We can classify these varieties of comedy into four broad generic types: farce, satiric comedy, comedy of manners and romantic comedy. The first of these categories, farce, forms the central element of what is generally recognised as the earliest English stage comedy, *Roister Doister*, written by Nicholas Udall in about 1553. This comic mode typically includes much physical interplay between characters and the often knockabout action that ensues almost always takes place between stereotypical character types. In *Roister Doister*, for example, the title character courts a widow, Christian Custance, who is already betrothed to an absent merchant, Gawin Goodlucke. At the end of the play, the widow and her maids beat off the unwelcome advances of Roister, and order and happiness are restored when Custance and Goodlucke are reconciled. While the slapstick elements of farce comedy are usually designed to provoke uproarious laughter from audiences, this unbridled amusement is often licensed by a moral element in the play which is usually included in a prologue or epilogue. In *Roister Doister*'s Prologue, for example, comedy is promoted as a life-enhancing force rather than a potentially destructive one: 'For Mirth prolongeth life and causeth health, / Mirth recreates our spirits and voideth pensiveness, / Mirth increaseth amity, not hindering our wealth' (Udall 93). This desire by dramatists to justify farce comedy by emphasising the positive role it might perform in society was a common feature of the form that lasted until the twentieth century.

One form of comedy had a more enduring association with moral purpose: satire. The satiric comedy of the early modern period has its roots in the classical drama of writers such as Aristophanes. Like Aristophanes, later satirical dramatists attempted to challenge political and philosophical orthodoxies (or challenge unorthodox thought depending on the political persuasion of the playwright), and they achieved this aim by making the individuals and issues that they satirised appear ridiculous. Ben Jonson is probably the most renowned satiric dramatist of the seventeenth century, and his plays, including *Volpone* (1605–6), *The Alchemist* (1610) and *Bartholomew Fair* (1614), provide excellent examples of this mode of comedy. The first of these works, *Volpone*, satirises the avarice of modern city society via a cast of unscrupulous characters. In the plot, a nobleman (Volpone) pretends that he is dying while several greedy members of middle-class society (including a lawyer, miser and merchant) pay court to him in the hope of gaining an inheritance. By making all of his seemingly respectable characters appear either corrupt or ludicrous (or often both), Jonson intended that his audience scrutinise themselves for similar faults. In making the play's action into a virtual mirror of their own daily lives the audience might then successfully guard against the contagious vice that they had witnessed on stage.

The comedy of manners also features satire as its driving force. But rather than focusing on broader political or philosophical matters, this form of comedy instead targets the domestic world, attacking in particular the pretensions of polite society. Like farce, the comedy of manners dates back to classical times, and early examples of this genre can be found in the Roman comedies of Plautus and Terence in the second century BCE. Their work, often featuring star-crossed lovers thwarted by a cast of stock character types, was recycled by Shakespeare (among other dramatists) in the early modern era. In *Much Ado About Nothing* (1600), Shakespeare offers a neat twist on the Roman plots from which he has borrowed by tricking Beatrice and Benedict into admitting their love for each other. The parallel love plot in this play, between Claudio and Hero, has a different focus, being primarily concerned with the issue of infidelity outside marriage. The defamatory charge of sexual unfaithfulness brought against Hero before her wedding by the jealous Don Pedro allows Shakespeare to question attitudes to this perennially contentious issue. In the process, conventional beliefs regarding gender and sexual hierarchy are interrogated and are placed in a new and revealing light. The opportunity for audiences to transfer this new light from the world of the play to their own experience of life affords the comedy of manners (like broader satiric comedy) a potential interrelationship with society.

The last of these key categories of early modern comedy drama, romantic comedy, includes several features which overlap with the other types of
comedy discussed above. But romantic comedy has proved perhaps the most
popular and enduring of all forms of drama, remaining today a staple element
of the film industry in its modern guise as 'romcom'. Like these latter-day
romantic comedies, the basic plot of their seventeenth–century counterparts
might best be summed up in the following simple formula: 'boy meets girl,
boy loses girl, boy gets girl and then marries her'. Shakespeare's repertoire
of comedies includes several which might be classified as romantic, including *A Midsummer Night's Dream* (1596) and *As You Like It* (1599). But his
most accomplished work in this area is generally regarded to be *Twelfth Night*
(1601). This play provides a number of features which might be considered
typical of the form. Its unfamiliar geographical setting, Illyria, for example,
allows the play's action to take place outside the 'real' world of everyday
concerns. Northrop Frye has identified examples of the use of this extraordinary space across a number of Shakespeare's romantic comedies: you will,
for example, recognise this dramatic shift of location in *A Midsummer Night's
Dream*'s transition between the aristocratic world of the court and the forest
world ruled over by fairy characters. In this location, which Frye has termed
the 'green world', unconventional forms of behaviour are licensed and consequently much comic potential is released. For Frye this festive 'green world'
provides a key aspect of what he argues is the archetypal function of comic
drama. In these terms, the significance of the move from the 'normal world'
to the 'green world' is connected with 'the victory of summer over winter'
(Frye 183): cold winter is here defeated in a festive summer environment in
which all things become possible. Whether or not we follow Frye in recognising this underlying mythic function of comedy, the movement into Illyria
in *Twelfth Night* allows scope for fundamental shifts in the existing attitudes
and patterns of behaviour of the play's characters. In the process, the move
into the 'green world' permits characters to see themselves and others in often
unexpected and transforming ways.

In *Twelfth Night* this shift in perspective is extended by the cross-dressing
of one of the central characters. Viola, who is shipwrecked along with her
brother Sebastian in the opening section of the play, decides to adopt male
dress so that she might act as Duke Orsino's page. In this guise, Viola (now
acting under the assumed name of Cesario) acts as a go-between for the
Duke and the woman, Olivia, whom he wishes ardently to marry. While
the Duke and Olivia independently discuss the nature of love with the cross-
dressed Viola/Cesario, they both become emotionally attracted to her/him.
The resulting comedy works on a number of different levels, all of which
are accessible for the audience via their privileged knowledge of the gender

deception taking place here. In his early encounter with Viola/Cesario, for
example, the Duke remarks upon her/his feminine qualities without realising
the truth behind these suspicions:

> Diana's lip
> Is not more smooth and rubious: thy small pipe
> Is as the Maiden's organ. Shrill and sound,
> And all is semblative of a woman's part.
> Shakespeare, *Twelfth Night* I, iv, 31–4

On one level, the dramatic irony occurring here is too obvious to require
further comment. But we do need to recognise the ways in which the masculine register in which the Duke addresses an individual he assumes is another
man intensifies the scene's comedy. In particular, the writer's freedom here
to introduce potentially bawdy material in dialogue between male and female
characters imbues these scenes with comedy underscored by sexual frisson.
The comedic potential of *Twelfth Night* to question assumptions about sexual
identity is discussed in much greater detail by Suzanne Trill in Chapter 21.

Aside from this primary comic plot of love and mistaken identity, *Twelfth
Night* also includes a separate block of comic characters grouped around
Sir Toby Belch, Olivia's drunken relative. In contrast with the largely high
comedy of wit and wordplay that takes place in scenes involving the Duke,
Viola and Olivia, the episodes with Sir Toby typically act out a low comedy
which is fuelled by drunkenness and misrule. The Russian formalist critic
Mikhail Bakhtin has identified this sort of festive behaviour as representing
the spirit of Carnival. This concept draws upon our knowledge of those feast
days in the Christian calendar in which eating, drinking and often sexual
freedoms were permitted to take place, including Twelfth Night itself when
Shakespeare's play was first performed. For Bakhtin, these periods of temporary liberation for the proletarian people marked 'the suspension of all hier-
archical rank, privileges, norms, and prohibitions. Carnival was the true feast
of time, the feast of becoming, change, and renewal. It was hostile to all that
was immortalised and completed' (*Rabelais and his World* 10). In *Twelfth Night*,
Shakespeare distils this anarchic spirit and relocates it to a domestic and seemingly bourgeois setting, thus offering a slightly different twist on Frye's notion
of the 'green world'. But while the harnessing of Carnival in this way might
appear to divorce it completely from its original functions (leaving behind
only the excuse for drunken horseplay) the political implications of this stage
business become evident as the play progresses. The festive revelling of Sir
Toby and his confederates (Maria the maid, the cowardly fop Sir Andrew
Aguecheek and Feste the fool) bring them into direct conflict with Malvolio,
Olivia's steward. This conflict on its localised level offers a comedy of class:

the social climber Malvolio's attempt to dictate behavioural rules to Sir Toby is greeted with the withering rejoinder 'Art any more than a steward?' (II, iii, 106–7).

But the clash between these characters is equally concerned with the larger conflict between puritans and those with more traditional or mainstream religious and social attitudes. These ideological battle lines emerged from the increasing power of 'puritan' beliefs at this time: among these beliefs was a desire to prohibit theatrical performance. These tensions are exposed in the lines that immediately follow those quoted above: 'Dost thou think because thou art virtuous, there shall be no more cakes and ale?' (II, iii, 114–15). This remark would resonate with those traditional members of a seventeenth-century audience who had themselves been subjected to prejudice by fundamental religious factions opposed to putatively frivolous pastimes. The new historicist and cultural materialist literary critics of the 1980s and 1990s sought to reconstruct original political and social contexts in which drama of this type was performed. These critical movements attempted to expose the contemporary power relations underpinning play texts which had been obscured by the passage of time.

The roles played by Malvolio in representing both petit bourgeois upstart and puritan killjoy offer excellent examples of elements in *Twelfth Night* that have lost much of their original resonance. These aspects of the play are fully elaborated in two key scenes which expose differing aspects of Shakespeare's comic technique. In the first, Sir Toby and his friends gull Malvolio into believing that a letter that they have forged was actually written by Olivia. This letter, which Malvolio discovers while walking in the garden, includes an apparent declaration of Olivia's love for him, along with a number of her individual requests: these include her desire to see him dressed in yellow stockings with crossed garters while wearing a perpetual smile. Furthermore, the letter includes a direct appeal to Malvolio's social ambitions in its request that he 'be not afraid of greatness': 'Some are born great, some achieve greatness, and some have greatness thrown upon 'em' (II, v, 144–6). The immediate comic potential of this gulling of the ambitious Malvolio is extended by setting this scene in a public space from which the audience might witness the reactions (and hear the whispered interjections) of the eavesdropping Sir Toby. Audiences used to the dramatic convention of eavesdropping scenes in comic plays were quite prepared to suspend their disbelief regarding the improbability of stage action of this kind. In addition to the comic action that takes place within this self-contained scene, Olivia's apparent requests regarding Malvolio's future dress and demeanour set up the pleasurable expectation of a further comic set piece. This duly occurs in a later scene in which the unenlightened Malvolio presents himself to Olivia suitably smiling and cross-gartered. Olivia who has no knowledge of the trick reacts with incomprehension and assumes that Malvolio has been affected by 'midsummer madness':

OLIVIA	Wilt thou go to bed, Malvolio?
MALVOLIO	To bed? Ay, sweetheart, I'll come to thee.
OLIVIA	God comfort thee! Why dost thou smile so, and kiss thy hand so oft?

(III, iv, 30–3)

The opportunity for visual and verbal comedy that emerges in this scene is designed to provoke uproarious rather than thoughtful laughter and as such it draws heavily on the tradition of farce comedy discussed above.

Farce is also much in evidence in the other key scene in which Sir Toby's group take revenge on Malvolio. In this episode, the suspicion of Malvolio's madness (initially established in the cross-gartered scene) is fully exploited by his adversaries who use this as a pretext to imprison him in a darkened cellar. Trapped here with no means of escape, Malvolio is mocked by Feste the fool who uses verbal trickery to elicit a confession of lunacy from the imprisoned man:

FESTE	Master Malvolio?
MALVOLIO	Ay, good fool.
FESTE	Alas, sir, how fell you besides your five wits?
MALVOLIO	Fool, there was never man so notoriously abused: I am as well in my wits, fool, as thou art.
FESTE	But as well? Then you are mad indeed, if you be no better in your wits than a fool.

(IV, ii, 87–93)

While this sort of inhumane treatment may have been less disconcerting to an early modern audience, today's playgoers often find this abuse of 'mad' Malvolio unpalatable. Indeed, actors in several recent stagings of the play have recognised these shifting attitudes towards the insane in the nature of their performance. This is an example of changing social behaviour altering the ways in which comic material is performed by players and received by audiences across different eras. What we might now regard here as an uncomfortably black comic episode in the play would, in the seventeenth century, have probably been viewed as a straightforwardly farcical episode. Malvolio's desperate claims for his sanity and pleas for his release evidently affect us now in quite different ways from those in which they struck our play-going forebears.

While we might broadly categorise *Twelfth Night* as a romantic comedy it also clearly draws upon a wide variety of comic modes (including farce, satire, comedy of manners) to achieve its ends. In addition, the many different comic techniques used in this play (including cross-dressing, mistaken identity, wordplay, stock characters, 'green world' locations and eavesdropping) suggest the variegated nature of a drama that is broadly classified as comedy. All of the comic forms, modes, locations and techniques evident in *Twelfth Night* remained staple features of the genre during subsequent eras. Through the Restoration comedy of manners in the later seventeenth century, the eighteenth-century comedies of Richard Brinsley Sheridan and the early Victorian works of Dion Boucicault, stage comedy relied upon the familiar and the recognisable for its success. Only in the 1890s with the emergence of Oscar Wilde's comedies including *Lady Windermere's Fan* (1892), *An Ideal Husband* (1895) and *The Importance of Being Earnest* (1895) can we recognise the arrival of something distinctively different in this field. In making this claim for the freshness of Wilde's work we need to recognise that all of these plays appear, at least on the surface, to follow forms of conventional stage comedy. They include characters drawn from the polite society of the day; they include plots of mistaken identity and moments of high farce; they are largely predicated on the difficulties involved in love and marriage; and they end up with an apparently happy resolution of their often complex stage business. But Wilde manages to make these hackneyed elements of comedy new by refusing to obey a number of the 'rules' that had previously governed their use on stage. In doing this he arguably reinvented this genre for the modern era.

A brief examination of what is perhaps Wilde's most successful comedy, *The Importance of Being Earnest*, suggests the ways in which he achieved this feat. One key way is through his use of characterisation. While Wilde's cast includes several of those characters whom Frye observes provide the stock types of comedy, in *Importance* these individuals fail to conform to their predestined roles. The hero and heroine figures, for example, whom Frye suggests are typically played down and made to appear 'rather neutral and unformed in character' in comedy (173), are in Wilde's play fully engaged in the comic action. Similarly, for Frye the traditional 'blocking characters' of comedy who try to thwart the lover's union are frequently lacking in 'self-knowledge' and consequently tend not to gain the audience's sympathy. In the case of Wilde's Lady Bracknell (a seemingly stereotypical blocking character in her desire to prevent the marriage of Jack and Gwendolen), her wit and verbal dexterity ensure that she sidesteps the traditional villain status the audience anticipate from this role. We can recognise this facility in Lady Bracknell during the following exchange in which she tests Jack's suitability as a husband for her niece:

LADY BRACKNELL	Are your parents living?
JACK	I have lost both my parents.
LADY BRACKNELL	Both? To lose one parent may be regarded as a misfortune; to lose *both* looks like carelessness. Who was your father? He was evidently a man of some wealth. Was he born in what the Radical papers call the purple of commerce, or did he rise from the ranks of the aristocracy?

(Wilde 1709)

Rather than finding comedy in the misguided nature of this blocking character's behaviour, we instead admire the inventive and intelligent wit evident in her dialogue. It is perhaps this question of audience sympathy that sets Wilde's comedies apart from many of their predecessors. The democratic involvement of all of the play's characters in its sparklingly witty dialogue ensures that traditional groupings of empathetic and antipathetic comic characters are deliberately resisted here.

More significant, however, than this freedom of characterisation is the play's unwillingness to conform to a recognisable moral code. Instead of the conservative status quo of morality being restored in the last act, the flippancy which has marked the cast's attitude to prevailing social mores throughout the play is simply reinforced in its ending:

JACK	Gwendolen, it is a terrible thing for a man to find out suddenly that all his life he has been speaking nothing but the truth. Can you forgive me?
GWENDOLEN	I can. For I feel that you are sure to change.

(1740)

This exchange is typical of the play's refusal to take anything seriously, including marriage. Just when the audience feel that they are about to witness the lovers retreat into seriousness or sentimentality, the heroine neatly sidesteps this anticipated change in register. While we have grown familiar in more recent years with sardonic and self-aware stage comedy, its Victorian audience recognised in drama of this kind a departure from what had gone before. The shock of the new that plays such as *Importance* delivered in the 1890s was registered by Wilde's contemporary playwright George Bernard Shaw. His feelings that the play was 'really heartless' and 'essentially hateful' offer a revealing perspective on the play's contemporary impact (Shaw 286, 287).

While it would be misleading to overstate the revolutionary effects of Wilde's comic drama, it did mark a shift towards a new freedom in this field that emerged in the twentieth century. This lack of restraint is recognisable, for example, in the work of modern dramatists who have arguably pushed the limits of this genre: this group might include Samuel Beckett, Harold Pinter, Tom Stoppard and Caryl Churchill. But while comedy and tragedy often appear inextricably intertwined in these stage manifestations, modern comic drama of this type still largely relies on many of those forms discussed above. As Alexander Leggatt argues in relation to one aspect of stage comedy, 'Through the changing properties, tastes and social conditions of different periods, the comedy of the disruptive body carries on, changing its language but not its essential statement' (14). Roger Savage's note in Chapter 16 of the 'time-honoured comedic pattern of a movement from darkness to light, from conflict to resolution' conveys eloquently the nature of this 'essential statement'. This is also manifestly true of comic drama at large, which appears set to retain its prominent place in stage history irrespective of its continuing lack of academic regard.

NEXT STEPS

Frye, Northrop. *Anatomy of Criticism: Four Essays*. New York: Atheneum, 1966.
Leggatt, Alexander. *English Stage Comedy 1490–1990*. London: Routledge, 1998.
Stott, Andrew. *Comedy: The New Critical Idiom*. London: Routledge, 2005.

20

History and Politics

Dermot Cavanagh

This chapter will consider how theatre engages with and is shaped by the world beyond the stage. It will emphasise that although not all plays express a political argument all drama is both implicated in and takes a view of political experience. 'Politics' is a word with complex implications, of course. Theatrical practices and institutions are themselves political in the sense that they are embedded deeply in a particular society's hierarchies and structures along with its norms and values. Still, plays also engage with political contexts and ideas by the forms and techniques they use. These can challenge as well as affirm prevailing ideas concerning, for example, relationships of power between different groups in society or the just exercise of authority. In this respect, dramatic forms are not simply determined by the circumstances around them; they also reflect upon and intervene into their historical surroundings.

In Chapter 16, Roger Savage raised the question of drama's relationship to truth, and this provides one starting-point for this chapter. Savage noted that some playwrights convey their view of the world explicitly. For example, in *The Permanent Way* (2004), the contemporary British playwright David Hare depicted the impact of privatisation upon the public transport system. The text of the play consisted of a sequence of dialogues and monologues derived from interviews with a range of those most affected by this change of government policy: passengers, railway workers, civil servants, survivors of accidents. This exposed privatisation as a symptom of how badly contemporary British society has been damaged by its inability 'fully to commit to the notion of living together' (Hare 65).

However, many plays do not reveal their viewpoint so clearly, and this means that deducing their political attitudes is not so straightforward. For example, many kinds of drama do not engage in a naturalistic or realistic representation of society and may evidence little concern with matters of governance. As we shall see in this chapter, theatre may represent experience in an abstract manner largely devoid of a substantial social or historical context. The latter technique is intended to be non-specific and might suggest that the playwright intends a universal or timeless account of experience. Some traditions of drama take place in a largely imaginary or fantastical world, as in Shakespeare's 'late plays', such as *Pericles* (1609) or *The Tempest* (1623). What are the 'politics' of these kinds of plays? Dramatic form itself does not always invite straightforward conclusions. Plays contain multiple voices and perspectives which invite performers and audiences to experience these in their own terms. Studying theatrical history compounds some of these problems of interpretation because this involves reconstructing the context and viewpoint of past theatre, sometimes from very remote periods; this is a difficult and sometimes contentious process.

Some practitioners and critics of theatre would stress that we should not be overly concerned to place theatre-works in context anyway and that their political implications should certainly not be constrained by this. For example, as Olga Taxidou notes in Chapter 17, the rise of the director in modernist theatre coincided with a powerful insistence on the autonomy of theatrical performance. On this view, play-texts are better conceived of as musical scores that provide a set of cues and notations for an almost infinite variety of performative emphases and interpretations. As performances, plays have a continuing life that allows them to adjust to new theatrical conditions and historical circumstances; they are not singular events whose 'truth' was fixed at the moment of their first performance and then embodied for good in a printed text. The meaning of a play, including its political viewpoint, is determined primarily by its realisation in the immediate moment of performance and this will change over time. Such a dynamic process should not be arrested by attaching excessive importance to a moment of origination.

In contrast to these views, this chapter will contend that we lose something of great value when the critical understanding of drama and its performance neglect historical context. Of course, directors must be free to interpret plays in a multitude of ways. However, as students of theatre it is equally important that we are able to evaluate and even inform that process by acquiring an understanding of the historical conditions from which dramatic works emerge. In particular, awareness of a play's historical moment provides the key to unlocking its political significance. To ignore this is to obscure how plays comprehend the worlds from which they come as well as how their concerns might still speak to the present. Considering the critical methods and practices we can use to understand the context and politics of a theatrical work will be the subsequent concern of this chapter, especially when, as happens so often in relation to theatrical history, these are not retrieved easily. The analysis will consider the historicity and politics of two plays from very different periods, the anonymous late medieval morality play *Everyman* (c.1530) and Samuel Beckett's *Endgame* (1958). These plays present a particular challenge to historicist criticism and seem remote from a highly topical and committed work like *The Permanent Way*. Neither of these plays is set in a specific time or place and neither expresses a directly political viewpoint. As we shall see, this does not mean that these plays are without history, far from it, nor does it mean that they have no politics. On the contrary, there is a crucial connection between the two.

EVERYMAN

Everyman was printed about 1530. It is a morality or 'moral' play, a popular mode of late medieval European drama; indeed, *Everyman* is not an original composition but a modified translation of a Dutch work, *Elckerlijc* (c.1475). These plays ask the audience to contemplate their spiritual lives. Morality theatre depicts the choices of a protagonist who stands for all Christians, and there is little interest in establishing a specific setting or context in which this process takes place. Over the course of the play, an 'everyman' figure encounters personifications of forces and values, both worldly and spiritual, which will either aid or impede his salvation. The message of such plays is intended to be spiritually challenging but optimistic: the protagonist may decline into despair or sinful indulgence but, in the end, he finds his way back to God's grace and to a righteous way of living or, in Everyman's case, dying.

Each morality play is defined by its concern with a crucial facet of experience. In *Everyman*'s case this is evident: how should we face death? At the outset, the messenger invites us to reflect on life from the perspective of its ending: *Everyman* will confront this prospect by teaching us to distinguish what is truly valuable and enduring from what is merely transitory. This crucial lesson of the play has been forgotten. God speaks at the outset of the play to express his anger and frustration at human worldliness and summons Death, the first of the play's many personifications, to call Everyman to account for his life, provoking the latter's lament: 'O Death, thou comest when I had thee least in mind' (*Everyman* l. 119). Death will not be bargained with or delayed and he will not return us to the world despite Everyman's anguished petitioning that he do so.

This dramatic situation has one crucial consequence: who or what will accompany Everyman as he advances towards the grave? In this way, the play reveals what surrounds and absorbs us in life from the perspective offered by our mortality. Everyman appeals to a sequence of symbolic figures to accompany him in his plight: his friends, Fellowship, his family relations, Kindred and Cousin, his wealth and property, Goods. In each of these encounters and dialogues Everyman is abandoned and betrayed. This is how the play's first sequence concludes, and, in essence, it presents a spiritual language lesson in which the protagonist begins to learn the unreliability of words and promises. Gradually, the dying Everyman comes to understand what words truly matter as well as what they mean because worldly illusions are named and distinguished from spiritual realities.

In this respect, the play seems to turn in a much more positive direction when Everyman meets the weak and badly neglected personification of Good Deeds, who introduces Everyman to Knowledge, meaning awareness of one's sins; the latter leads him to the sacrament of confession (see Ryan 728–9). By undergoing a process of penitential reflection and mortification Everyman begins to restore his own spiritual integrity and to reinvigorate the strength of Good Deeds. In the play's final movement, the protagonist is joined by a new set of personal qualities and attributes to accompany him on his pilgrimage: Discretion, Five-Wits, Strength and Beauty. Five-Wits testifies strikingly to the power of the church's sacraments as administered by the priesthood: 'God hath to them more power given / Than to any angel that is in heaven' (ll. 734–5). Everyman receives offstage the last sacramental rites of the church for the dying (Extreme Unction) and he then approaches the mouth of his grave. At this point, the play takes a surprising turn. Those same bodily faculties that have emerged to guide and support him in his progress towards death desert him. In the end, only Good Deeds accompanies Everyman to meet God's judgement, although the play stresses that these good actions are not sufficient in themselves; they will only lead to redemption for the Christian who has achieved a state of grace through penance. Knowledge survives as well to comment approvingly on Everyman's final commitment to virtue and achievement of salvation.

On this account, it may well seem superfluous to speak of *Everyman*'s historical context let alone the play's politics. Its message concerns mortality, seemingly the most universal aspect of experience. The play might be considered as historical in a broad sense inasmuch as it testifies to a vanished period when Catholic beliefs dominated European culture. In this respect, we perhaps misjudge the play if we see it as 'abstract'. Its view of reality is simply different from ours because it emphasises how our narrow temporal experiences only make sense in terms of a transcendent spiritual world to which we are all eventually summoned (see King 242). The play is closer to ritual than our ordinary understanding of theatre. Its performance enacts a highly structured process or pattern to which all of its elements contribute and this affirms a set of commonly held Christian beliefs concerning the pathway to salvation.

Yet there is a clue within the text of *Everyman* that the play does have a historically specific as well as a broad sense of human worldliness and this has a political aspect as well. As was noted above, when Five-Wits helps to prepare Everyman to receive the sacrament of Extreme Unction he commends the priesthood. Priests are ordained to administer the sacraments and these offer the cure of the soul. Knowledge echoes this insight and both personifications concur in affirming the necessity of obedience to the clergy: 'follow their doctrine for our souls' succour' (*Everyman* l. 765).

This is a curious moment of excess in an otherwise spare and concentrated drama. We can discover in these insistent passages a glimpse of the passions and conflicts of the play's historical world as well as those experienced by its protagonist. Why is the play so committed to defending the clergy? Surely a medieval play and its audience would be at one in taking their value for granted? These questions provoke more curiosity about the play's date and context than a reading of it as essentially ritualistic or universal in import might inspire. For example, *Everyman* is often studied and performed as an archetypal instance of 'medieval' drama. Yet its text was first printed during the Tudor period; no manuscript exists before that date. This means it was first published and more widely circulated during the initial phase of the European Reformation when the institutional power and teaching of the Catholic Church was subject to a challenge that was to split the Christian world irrevocably. The play's publication is significant, in part, as an attempt to defend Catholic beliefs concerning good works and the efficacy of the sacraments. These ideas and practices were being challenged by Protestant thinkers as part of a broader assault on the church's institutional and ideological dominance. Of course, *Everyman*'s moment of publication is not quite the same as its 'date', and the printed text was likely to have had a substantial legacy of performance that predated the Reformation. Whether this text was expanded or modified is unknown, but the decision to print the play at this particular time reveals a crucial feature of its social and political concerns that might otherwise be obscured if it is considered simply as a 'medieval' play. Rather than seeing its concerns as wholly abstract or universal we can see them as highly specific: an attempt to sustain the church's role as the uniquely ordained institution responsible for Christian salvation.

This context also alters understanding of the play's potential connotations in performance. *Everyman* is often interpreted as a ritualistic affirmation of shared and incontestable truths but its printing in 1530 also reveals it as an impassioned and polemical argument whose vibrancy has been enhanced by an increasingly antagonistic public world. Awareness of some of the religious and polemical writing and debate that surrounded the play deepens this understanding. For instance, in 1529, perhaps only a few months before the publication of *Everyman*, copies of the English reformer Simon Fish's incendiary tract *A Supplicacyon for the Beggers* began to circulate in London. Fish's work was satirical and sensational and it provoked the famous Catholic humanist Thomas More into composing an orthodox reply, *The Supplicacyon of Soulys* (1529), that was ten times the length of its target. Fish assailed the clergy as treacherous, greedy and corrupt and derided the doctrine of purgatory that underlay the sacrament of penance:

> there is no purgatory but that it is a thing invented by the covetiousnesse of the spiritualtie onely to translate all kingdoms from other princes unto theim and that there is not one word spoken of hit in al holy scripture. (Fish sig. 6^r)

For Fish, the church's insistence on confession served to extend its temporal dominion.

How does this awareness of context change our understanding of the play? Firstly, it demonstrates that *Everyman* is not an 'innocent' text whose performance is akin to a religious ritual. Identifying an area of tension in the play's dramatic structure reveals that it is also shaped by the pressure of dissent and disagreement. This is why the play insists that the sacraments are independent sources of grace which are offered to us regardless of the spiritual condition of those who administer them (see *Everyman* ll. 763–9). It was precisely on this issue of clerical privilege that so much anti-Catholic polemic was beginning to explore not only the gap between ideas and realities in the church but the inadequacy of its foundational doctrines. In its apparent digression on the priesthood, the play reveals itself as a plea from a divided and turbulent world where categories of orthodoxy were under severe pressure. This approach offers us a method for practicing historically informed criticism of drama: sensitivity to moments of insistence or excess in play-texts helps reveal those problems that defined their context as well as the political attitude they take towards these.

ENDGAME

It is a mark of the puzzlement evoked by Samuel Beckett's *Endgame* that it is not susceptible to a summary of its action or events in the way outlined above for *Everyman*. This bafflement is shared by those within the play. When one of its protagonists repeats the question, 'What's happening, what's happening', the precise, if not exactly helpful, response is: 'Something is taking its course' (Beckett 2399). In one sense, what is taking its course in *Endgame* is perfectly straightforward. We are watching a play: characters appear and interact with

each other, speeches are made, there are extensive passages of staccato dialogue, questions are asked and answered (not always satisfactorily), demands
are made, memories are recollected, the protagonists experience and articulate
a range of emotions – frustration, anger, nostalgia, aspiration, despair – and
undergo bodily experiences, usually of a discomfiting and sometimes of an
alarming kind. All of these things happen in traditional theatre as well, including in *Everyman*. However, in *Endgame* there is a crucial difference inasmuch
as there is no overarching narrative or pattern which connects together or
explains the purpose of these linguistic and theatrical exchanges.

Consequently, *Endgame* makes it surprisingly difficult to settle questions
that we expect a theatrical work to resolve. Where is the play set? The action
unfolds in a single interior space, although we hear of a kitchen adjoining
this and a world, of a kind, that is (barely) visible through the room's two
small windows. However, there is no sense of where this space exists or in
what period. Admittedly, there allusions to recognisable properties and com-
modities like painkillers and bicycles and references are made to Lake Como,
the Ardennes and Sedan but these are of little help. It is similarly difficult to
discover who the people in this room are. Are they 'people' exactly? (One of
them appears to have no pulse.) We encounter four protagonists: Clov, who
acts as a kind of servant to the chair-bound and seemingly blind Hamm and
two figures immured in ashbins, Nell and Nagg. We receive fractured hints
at relationships between these figures – for example, Nell and Nagg appear to
be Hamm's parents and Clov has been adopted by Hamm – but these fail to
cohere into a recognisable shared history.

One common way to explain this disconcerting theatrical experience is to
stress how the play's mode is a typical instance of the Theatre of the Absurd.
This kind of drama expressed a general acceptance of the senselessness of life
which was shared by a range of mid-twentieth-century intellectuals. 'In a
universe suddenly divested of illusions and lights', wrote Beckett's contemporary Albert Camus, philosopher of the Absurd, in 1942, 'man feels an alien, a
stranger . . . This divorce between man and his life, the actor and his setting,
is properly the feeling of absurdity' (13). The world of the play is undoubtedly a stricken and purposeless one, and what can be done about this, apart
from enduring it, is far from clear. Certainly, the capacity of religious faith to
illuminate and clarify experience is an unthinkable prospect. *Endgame* can be
grasped as a statement about a world where we merely exist or even fail to
exist, a world without meaning. Any religious consolation would only betray
a fantasy of self-importance: 'Do you believe in the life to come' asks Clov;
'Mine was always that' replies Hamm (Beckett 2410). Any attempt to imbue
experience with broader significance is as absurd as Hamm's attempt to have
Clov wheel him to the exact centre of the room. After his pointless efforts to

do so, Clov declares 'If I could kill him I'd die happy' (2403). The protagonists of *Endgame* appear incapable of change or development, although they
can undergo physical decline. All they can do is to engage in absurd routines
that pass the time to which they are condemned. The protagonists appear to
desire nothing more powerfully than the play's ending; unfortunately, this
wish seems unlikely to be fulfilled. What unfolds in *Endgame* has no conventional beginning, middle or conclusion. The play finishes but there is no
apparent ending for the experience it has portrayed. In contrast to *Everyman*,
Beckett's protagonists seem incapable even of dying, indeed, the categories of
life and death are not established clearly. On this view, the play is a disturbing,
if often comic, message about the futility of human experience and the ludicrous inadequacy of our attempts to bestow significance upon it. Although this
view of experience is not stated by the play as a clearly articulated 'message'
it can be deduced from its puzzling dramatic form, especially its insistence on
abandoning any coherent narrative sequence.

What we experience in *Endgame*, put simply, is a refusal to play by conventional theatrical rules and to satisfy the expectations these sustain. Yet this too is
a form of response to the world from which it comes. 'What we see in his work
is not some timeless *condition humaine*', Terry Eagleton observes, 'but war-torn
twentieth-century Europe' ('Political Beckett?' 69). Approaching the play as a
post-war work illuminates a way of considering the style and mode of *Endgame* as
both deeply historical and political. Indeed, it is striking to compare a work that
is often deemed to express resignation or despair with Beckett's own war-time
commitment, like Albert Camus, to the French resistance (see Knowlson 297–
339). One way of understanding Beckett's refusal to return to dominant theatrical
conventions is that they simply cannot do justice to the indescribable experiences
of world war: totalitarianism, global conflict, mass slaughter, genocide, nuclear
weaponry. None of these events are portrayed in *Endgame*, of course, nor is the
play well-served by being treated as an allegory of the consequences or aftermath
of such events. But the play does express a broader sense of ruination and catastrophe; it attempts to portray a world that has undergone an almost incalculable
degree of damage. In contrast, a traditional drama with identifiable characters, a
seemingly logical sequence and a shared framework of reference cannot capture
a world whose traditions and values have been smashed.

The Marxist critic Walter Benjamin observed that after the First World
War 'the ability to exchange experiences' had diminished (83). This was
because the technological transformation of society and, especially, the trauma
of mass warfare were simply incommunicable by those who had undergone
them. The contradiction between one's inherited assumptions and the reality
of world war was simply impossible to overcome or express. In Benjamin's
view, the result was that human experience itself had 'fallen in value' (84).

This offers an insight into Beckett's *Endgame* as a response to historical events and experiences whose scale exhausts the ability to communicate their nature and it intensifies understanding of Beckett's abandoned world where the 'whole place stinks of corpses' and which has endured some barely imaginable affliction (Beckett 2409).

In *Endgame*, language itself fails to convey meaning; it has becomes exhausted and inert: 'All life long the same inanities' (2409). This is less a comment on the immutable pathos of the human condition and more a way of confronting how life has simply lost the significance once attached to it, given a world where so many human lives had been designated as worthless. There is a politics as well to this vision of calamitous deprivation. For example, it renders Hamm's attempt to dominate Clov as ludicrous, an exercise of power that is especially farcical given the meagreness of the means and the results. In contrast to these botched attempts at compulsion, Beckett's theatre is a ragged and unfinished one that does not convey a clear meaning. Traditional theatrical conventions decompose in Beckett's plays not simply as part of an experiment with 'absurdity' but because such depletions and disconnections reveal the damage inflicted upon experience and language in a world that has endured the most drastic diminishments of freedom.

Recovering the historical contexts in which plays appeared does not mean that their range of implication is constrained. On the contrary, understanding of the different contexts in which plays have appeared enriches and extends awareness of their concerns. Of course, if plays are to survive in performance they are bound to sustain a variety of theatrical approaches. To do otherwise is to turn them into museum-pieces rather than works that can yield new implications. Equally, to set aside the social and political contexts that shaped plays is to choose instead to treat them as interchangeable examples of drama and to forget a crucial ingredient that explains how these works became what they are. In both *Everyman* and *Endgame*, even the most abstract portrayal of the human condition also provides a way of addressing the specific social and historical worlds from which they come.

NEXT STEPS

Dillon, Janette, ed. *The Cambridge Introduction to Early English Theatre*. Cambridge: Cambridge University Press, 2006.

Esslin, Martin. *The Theatre of the Absurd*, 3rd edn. Harmondsworth: Penguin, 1980.

Krasner, David, ed. *Theatre in Theory 1900–2000: An Anthology*. Oxford: Wiley-Blackwell, 2007.

Pilling, John, ed. *The Cambridge Companion to Beckett*. Cambridge: Cambridge University Press, 1994.

21

Sex, Gender and Performance

Suzanne Trill

The 1998 movie *Shakespeare in Love*, directed by John Madden, publicised a fact well known to scholars of theatre history: that is, on the public stage in Renaissance England all roles were played by male actors. Preparing for bed, Viola (Gwyneth Paltrow) and her nurse (Imelda Staunton) discuss the all-male performance of *Two Gentlemen of Verona* they have just seen at Queen Elizabeth I's court. During this exchange Viola launches into an attack upon 'Sylvia', whom she 'did not care for much. His hands were red from fighting, and he spoke like a school-boy at lessons'. Following this, Viola observes indignantly that 'Stage love will never be true love while the law of the land has our heroines played by pipsqueak boys in petticoats!' (Norman and Stoppard 20).

While explicitly acknowledging the historical practice in which boy players enacted female roles, Viola's statement privileges the modern predilection for 'naturalistic' performances in which actors predominantly play roles which accord with their own, physical sex. Critiquing the actor's physique and his 'pip-squeak' voice, Viola cannot entertain the notion that early modern audiences may have accepted 'boys' as 'female' characters. Indeed, she suggests that clothing 'pip-squeak boys in petticoats' is not enough to erase the difference between the actor's body and the female role. In seeking such verisimilitude, the supposedly 'Elizabethan' Viola is expressing a desire for a more modern and naturalistic performance style. Furthermore, by asserting that while such transvestism is in place, 'stage love will never be true love', Viola simultaneously articulates a thoroughly modern assumption of normative – or compulsory – heterosexuality (see Rich, 'Compulsory Heterosexuality and Lesbian Experience'). Indeed, this statement turns out to be central to the narrative trajectory of the film as the wager concerning a play's capacity to show us 'true love' is judged to have been achieved only when the naturalistic representation that Viola desires actually occurs; that is, when she, as Viola (rather than as 'Thomas Kent'), plays 'Juliet' to Shakespeare's 'Romeo' (Joseph Fiennes) at the Curtain (see Norman and Stoppard 137–49). Although the film flirts with the potential for homoeroticism insofar as Shakespeare is depicted as desiring 'Thomas Kent', the audience is never allowed to forget that 'Thomas Kent' is Viola in 'disguise'. In parallel with 'Sylvia', it takes more than male attire to make 'Viola' convincing as a 'boy'.

Thus the film reinforces the concept of a 'natural', binary division of the sexes, in which one's physical sex determines one's being, identity or essence. This is curiously at odds with over fifty years of feminist and queer theory and activism, which, since at least the publication of Simone de Beauvoir's *The Second Sex* (1953), has interrogated the relationship between one's biological sex and one's cultural identity: as de Beauvoir famously put it, 'one is not born a woman, one becomes one' (qtd in Moi, *What is a Woman?* at 5). In its most recent guise, emerging from the work of Judith Butler, this debate has focused on gender as performance (see Butler, *Gender Trouble* and *Bodies that Matter*). In *Gender Trouble*, Butler argues that 'drag' performance – when a male performer dresses and acts like a woman or vice versa – draws our attention to the distinction between the performer, their anatomical sex and their gendered performance. This parodies the idea of a stable, fixed gendered identity and challenges our assumptions that a particularly 'sexed' body should behave in a specifically 'gendered' way. This chapter will focus on two plays which explicitly examine the potentially disruptive effects of cross-dressed actors on conventional sex-roles: Caryl Churchill's *Cloud Nine* (1979) and William Shakespeare's *Twelfth Night* (1601). While for Shakespeare, of course, this was partly the result of the material use of all-male acting companies, for Churchill it was a self-consciously political act which aimed to question contemporary assumptions about (un)natural sexual and gendered acts. Taking into account the historical circumstances of these two plays' productions, this chapter will concentrate on the sexual politics of cross-dressing in order to consider whether either of these plays 'enact and reveal the performativity of gender itself in a way that destabilizes the naturalized categories of identity and desire' (Butler, *Gender Trouble* 139).

CLOUD NINE

Britain in the 1970s is often perceived as a decade marked by disputes, with 'weak' governments kowtowing to over-zealous trade unionists, culminating in the 'winter of discontent' (1978–9) and the election of Margaret Thatcher as Britain's first female Prime Minister (4 May 1979). If the 1970s was a period of discontent, though, this was not confined to the predominantly male political arena but was also apparent in the growing influence of a Women's Liberation movement. Its agitation and ideals were, of course, not wholly new, continuing in some ways the demands for equal rights and social justice for women made during a 'First Wave' of feminism early in the twentieth century by 'New Women' and the Suffragettes. The extension of such concerns to literary criticism is arguably embodied in Virginia Woolf's *A Room of One's Own* (1929). The early 1970s, though, saw the publication of two further landmarks which helped develop the feminist movement into a widely influential 'Second Wave': Germaine Greer's *The Female Eunuch* (1970) and Kate Millett's *Sexual Politics* (1971). Although originally published in the USA, Millett's vitriolic attack on D. H. Lawrence in *Sexual Politics* set the tone for much feminist literary criticism of the decade. As their titles indicate, the decade's leading feminist writers were particularly engaged with the politics of female sexuality and with the idea that 'The Personal is the Political' (a phrase which became a mantra for the feminist movement as it gained strength during the decade). While not always in alignment, feminists' concern with rights and social roles, and with extending sexual liberation, coexisted with the emergence of the Gay Rights movement in the UK, consolidated in the establishment of a Gay Liberation Front in 1970. Like the feminist movement, Gay Liberation engaged strongly in forms of literary or cultural criticism, eventually referred to as 'Queer Theory'.

As literary theory developed during the 1980s, feminism and feminist criticism advanced into a 'Third Wave'. Its ideas have often been criticised as essentialist – that is, as ascribing to women a fixed nature or a set of unalterable, inherent characteristics. The writing of the French critics principally involved – Julia Kristeva, Hélène Cixous and Luce Irigaray (see Moi, *Sexual/Textual Politics*) – nevertheless encouraged others to explore the differences between women from varying countries, races and classes or castes (see hooks, *Ain't I a Woman* and *Feminist Theory*). But it is in the context of the late 1970s that the original production of Caryl Churchill's *Cloud Nine* obviously needs to be set in order to understand its powerful, contemporary political message. Churchill's introduction to *Cloud Nine* (first performed at Dartington College of Arts, 14 February 1979) emphasises that it emerged from workshopping ideas about 'sexual politics' with the Joint Stock Theatre Company which drew upon their personal 'attitudes and experiences' to explore 'stereotypes and role reversals' (iv). Consequently, *Cloud Nine* uses the theatrical device of cross-casting to undermine both naturalistic stage conventions and cultural stereotypes relating to sex, sexuality and race. By this means, Churchill aims to highlight the distinction between 'sex' as one's physical, anatomical or biological 'nature' and the prevailing expectations of 'feminine' or 'masculine' gendered behaviour. Accordingly, in the first act Betty is played by a male actor and her son Edward is played by a female actor, while, in the second act Lin's daughter Cathy is played by a male actor. Such instances of cross-casting were initially hailed for their 'gender-bending' possibilities and have been viewed as anticipating Butler's theory of gender as performance (see Amoko 'Casting Aside Colonial Occupation'). For example, the male actor playing Betty in Act One is described within Victorian expectations of 'feminine' behaviour: s/he is her husband Clive's 'little dove' (Churchill 3), 'a brave girl' who, Clive reassures himself, has not suffered from 'fainting' or 'hysteria' (4) as s/he has spent her time reading poetry and playing the piano. So attuned is Betty to her husband's needs that his blister becomes experienced as 'My poor dear foot' (3). Here, as with the actors playing Edward (the son who likes playing with dolls) and Cathy (the daughter who is obsessed with guns), the intention is to reveal the distinction between biological 'sex' and gendered performance. Partly because of these practices, early discussions of *Cloud Nine* generally take it for granted that Churchill successfully challenged normative, 1970s assumptions about gender roles and sexual identity.

Some more recent discussions have been more sceptical, with James M. Harding in particular arguing that the very techniques Churchill employs to critique gender stereotypes function as a means of excluding and marginalising homoerotic desires. Harding insightfully draws attention to crucial moments in which the 'textual subversions of heterosexual discourse clash with their enactments on stage' (261). As one instance, he cites the way in which the textually transgressive lesbian kiss between Betty and Ellen becomes, in performance, a heterosexual expression of desire. From this and other examples, Harding argues that *Cloud Nine* reveals 'a performative strategy that renders gay men and lesbians acceptable by desexualising them' (262). Laying bare the structure of *Cloud Nine* (as in Figure 21.1 below) helps to clarify the connection between textual character and actor and, ultimately, reinforces Harding's critique of the play's subordination of homoerotic desires. In Figure 21.1, Victoria is in italics because the stage directions indicate that she is represented by a doll rather than an actor.

For example, this figure reveals the potential irony that in having Clive's wife played by a man, the very structure of the patriarchal household is undermined as the 'ideal' 'heterosexual' couple is performed by two men. Arguably, therefore, homosexuality is central to the play; however, although Clive and Betty have had progeny and must, therefore, at some point have had sexual relations, there is nothing textually to indicate an erotic charge between them. Consequently, this pairing becomes another example of making homosexuality 'acceptable' by desexualising it.

This dovetails with another issue highlighted in the diagrammatic structure

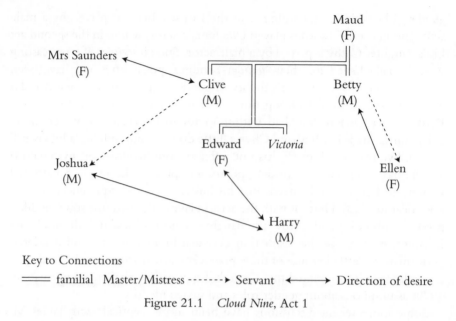

Figure 21.1   *Cloud Nine*, Act 1

of the play; that is, that for the most part, desire and sexuality exist outside of the nuclear family. Significantly, only Harry and Mrs Saunders have tangential relations to that unit. As such they are 'outsiders' who represent a potential threat to the established household. That threat is specifically manifested in their illicit sexualities. Harry's dalliances with Betty, pederastic desire for Edward and fucking of Joshua all threaten Clive's position as patriarch. Clive's revulsion at Harry's revelation of his homosexuality is only mitigated by his sense of relief that this must mean that Betty really has not been unfaithful to him. This revelation is further repressed by Clive's forcing Harry (a gay man) to enter into the economy of compulsory heterosexuality by marring Ellen (a lesbian); hence, their 'aberrant' erotic desires are translated into a heterosexual union through their onstage performance between a male and a female actor (Harding 268).

Although Mrs Saunders' desire for Clive is not clear ('I don't like you at all' (Churchill 16)), her enjoyment of the sensation of sexual arousal makes their relationship erotically charged. While Clive's desire for Mrs Saunders empha-sises a sexual double standard, Mrs Saunders' desire for him positions her as an adulteress and, therefore, outside the parameters of 'acceptable' Victorian female sexuality. Mrs Saunders' relationship with Clive is hetero-erotic both in terms of character and performer; however, it is worth pausing to consider the effects of the dramatic convention of doubling in this instance. Churchill asserts that 'the doubling of Mrs Saunders and Ellen is not intended to make a

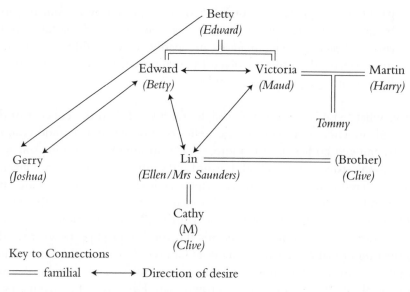

Key to Connections

===== familial   ◄─────► Direction of desire

Figure 21.2   *Cloud Nine*, Act 2

point so much as for sheer fun' (vi). In this, it seems, Churchill is oblivious to the fact that both these characters are associated with *illicit* forms of female sexuality: the former, as a widow, enjoying the sexual delights of a married man; the latter as the 'invisible' (v) lesbian. The significance of this connection is further reinforced by the doubling of the original performance at least, insofar as the same actor who plays these two characters in Act One, also doubles as 'Lin', the 'out' Lesbian, in Act Two. In fact, in Act Two the relationship between sex and gender is primarily challenged by the re-allocation of roles through doubling in which the same actor plays a different role including a different sex-role. (See Figure 21.2, in which italics within brackets are used to indicate the pairing of doubled roles as allocated in the original performance at Dartington College; italics are also used for Tommy because he never appears on stage.)

Set in 1979 London, in what Churchill describes as 'the changing sexuality of our own time' (v), the second act ostensibly places women and female desire centre stage. The displacement of patriarchal authority is arguably epitomised by the decision to make the actor who played Clive in Act One take the role of Lin's daughter Cathy in Act Two. However, all the other characters are now played by actors of a consonant sex; thus, there is an associated slippage into naturalism. Indeed, Churchill states that 'Betty is now played by a woman, as she gradually becomes real to herself' (v). And the justification for Cathy's cross-casting is

> partly as a *simple* reversal of Edward being played by a woman, partly
> because of the *size and presence of a man onstage seemed appropriate to the*
> *emotional force of young children,* and partly, as with Edward, to show
> more clearly the issues involved in learning what is considered correct
> behaviour for a girl' (v; my emphasis)

But in what sense is any reversal 'simple' for a start? Also the concept of the
'size and presence of a man onstage' relies on normative assumptions about
sexed/gendered bodies. Furthermore, what is missing from this explanation?
Whereas the cross-casting of both Edward and Cathy is intended to foreground
how gendered behaviour is imposed upon children of either sex, Churchill
also states that Edward 'is played by a woman . . . partly [because of] the stage
convention of having boys played by women (Peter Pan, radio plays, etc)'
(iv). Edward's cross-casting has a specific theatrical history; yet nowhere in the
explanation of Cathy's cross-casting does Churchill mention the Renaissance
theatrical convention of boys enacting female roles. This may be because
Cathy is played not by a boy but a grown man. However, the asymmetry of
these cross-castings is significant. Harding compares Betty's cross-casting with
Edward's, arguing that while the former encourages audiences to question
why Betty is played by a man, there is already an answer to why Edward is
played by a woman 'in the arsenal of stereotypes that reinforce the continued
dominance of heterosexual discourse: Edward is played by a woman because
he is homosexual' (Harding 265). Consequently, he argues that 'this cross-
casting suggests that beneath the socialization, there is something effeminate
or feminine at the core of Edward's being' (265). By analogy, as the actor
who plays Cathy also plays Lin's dead soldier brother it would seem that there
is something intrinsically 'masculine' at the 'core' of Cathy's being: the girl
child who loves playing with guns doubles as the grown man whose death has
been caused by violence in Northern Ireland. Here Harding, like Churchill,
erases the historical theatrical convention of male actors playing female roles.
In *Cloud Nine* cross-casting is character specific: what difference to our sense
of the relationship between sex, gender and performance might it make to
consider a situation in which *all* characters were played by men?

TWELFTH NIGHT

In a modern context, any use of such cross-casting exists in opposition to the
normative assumptions of naturalism. In a Renaissance context, however,
cross-casting was itself the norm. While *Shakespeare in Love* ultimately suggests
that what the Elizabethans wanted was naturalism, the scant evidence we have
for audience responses to all-male staging suggests that for most people this

convention was unremarkable. Indeed, for the Elizabethans it would seem that it was 'naturalism' which was surprising. Having been to the theatre in Venice, Thomas Coryat notes that 'I saw a woman act, a thing that I never saw before' and registers his impression that 'They performed it . . . with as good a grace, as ever I saw any masculine Actor' (qtd in Greenblatt et al. at 1761). That said, Gina Bloom's 2007 study of references to the boy player in Renaissance drama, particularly with regard to the 'cracked voice' (40), argues compellingly that 'the precarious voice, as a function of the unstable body, problematizes gender and erotic categories' (65). The propensity for the convention of the boy player to embody the problematic relationship between sex, gender and performance is absolutely crucial to the plot of *Twelfth Night*.

This point is epitomised in Act Two Scene Two. After visiting Olivia on behalf of Orsino, Malvolio chases after the cross-dressed Viola/Cesario and gives her/him a ring s/he supposedly left with his mistress. In a soliloquy musing on the significance of this event, Viola/Cesario concludes:

> How will this fadge [turn out]? My master loves her dearly,
> And I, poor monster, fond as much on him,
> And she mistaken, seems to dote on me.
> What will become of this? As I am a man,
> My state is desperate for my master's love.
> As I am a woman, now alas the day.
> What thriftless sighs shall poor Olivia breathe!
> O time, thou must untangle this, not I.
> It is too hard a knot for me t'untie.
>
> (II, ii, 32–40)

Viola/Cesario's speech specifically highlights the complexities of this perform-ance: as 'a man' through cross-dressing, s/he is unable to attain 'her' desire as s/he is excluded from her 'master's love;' but as 'a woman' in character, s/he is also the object of what s/he terms Olivia's 'mistaken' desire. In either case, Viola/Cesario's reaction to her/his position is structured by a 'norma-tive' model of hetero-eroticism; co-extensively, the excluded or 'mistaken' desire that s/he identifies is predicated upon the repression of any homoerotic impulses. However, despite the fact that the play appears to end in the tradi-tional comic manner, with the central characters all being married off to each other, the play as a whole, and, most importantly, its conclusion, is far less restricting than this apparent resolution would suggest.

Despite the fact that many company lists included only the principal actors and provided little or no information about 'hirelings or about the number of boys who played female roles and other parts' (Ringler 113), William A.

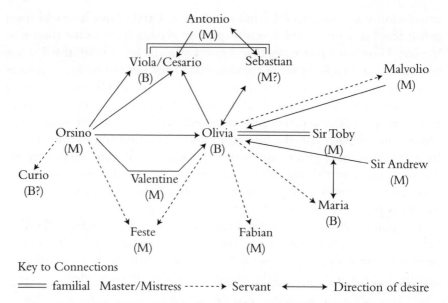

Figure 21.3   Characters in *Twelfth Night*, showing relationships and cast assignment

Ringler, Jr established that Shakespeare's early plays were primarily acted by companies of up to sixteen actors (usually comprising of twelve adults and four boys), with actors doubling roles where necessary. He also provided a broad methodology for establishing the assignation of roles. Having considered the principal actors, and the entrances and exits of the more minor characters, Ringler stated that 'boys should be assigned women's and children's parts, and they can also play pages and mute attendants such as soldiers or servants' (120). Taking Ringler's propositions literally, then, a Renaissance production of *Twelfth Night* can be figuratively represented as shown in Figure 21.3. As the sheer number of different connections and arrows of desire between character and actor in Figure 21.3 makes clear, the relationship between sex, gender and performance in *Twelfth Night* is dizzyingly complicated. Here I can only note that, using this method of role assignment, two pairings stand out as unusual in relation to the conjunction of character and player: that is, Viola and Olivia, and Antonio and Sebastian. Whereas all the relationships which are textually designated as hetero–erotic are played by a combination of a 'man' and a 'boy' player, these two potentially homoerotic pairings are played, respectively, by two boys and two men. Thus it appears that the 'difference' of these two pairings is signified both textually and performatively.

How might these 'differences' be significant? Studies of homoeroticism have suggested that the most common model for such relationships is that they involve a man and a boy or, more occasionally, two men (see Bray, *Homosexuality in Renaissance England*). If this is correct, it would seem that the (ostensibly) hetero-erotic couplings at the conclusion of the play (Olivia and Sebastian, Maria and Sir Toby and (less conclusively) Orsino and Viola) embody two forms of 'normative' erotic practice. While Antonio and Sebastian's relationship is portrayed by a less common man–man bond there is no indication that their relationship is textually denigrated. But where does this leave Viola and Olivia? With reference to these hypotheses, it would seem that *Twelfth Night* doubly disavows a specifically female homoerotic desire: on a textual level, the potential for this kind of desire is repudiated and, on a performance level, the enactment of this 'mistaken' desire by two boy actors reinforces its exceptional and transgressive status.

However, this does not do justice to the complex entanglements figured above. Apart from the Antonio/Sebastian relationship, all of the central relationships involve some degree of mediation: for example, Orsino never directly woos Olivia but uses an intermediary (Valentine, Viola/Cesario). Arguably even Antonio and Sebastian's relationship could be said to be mediated, given the confusion of the twins. Furthermore, the conclusion of the play is far from a simple resolution of complex desires: Antonio is still on stage and Sebastian's address to him does not suggest that in response to the marriage he is no longer homoerotically attracted by Antonio; through Sebastian and Olivia's marriage, and with the impending marriage of Orsino and Viola, Olivia positions herself as both Orsino's and Viola's sister; and the interconnections between the two households do not suggest a severing of existing desires. While Sebastian echoes Viola's remark that Olivia's desire for her was 'mistaken' (V, i, 257) and alludes to 'nature's' role in drawing men and women together, he concludes with this speech, 'Nor are you therein, by my life, deceiv'd: / You are betroth'd both to a maid and man' (260–1). Given the way in which the play establishes similarities between the two twins, this suggests that the kind of man Olivia desires in Sebastian is one with 'feminine' characteristics. And, finally, of course, there is the much commented on fact that Viola is still dressed as Cesario at the end of the play and that Orsino articulates a desire for 'her/him' which is not easily definable as hetero-erotic.

Returning to Figure 21.3, I would like now to draw attention to the question mark next to the casting of Sebastian as required by Ringler's theory. Renaissance audiences seem to have accepted boys playing women's roles, but would they also have accepted a 'boy' and a 'man' as twins? In 1927, with the aid of the extant cast list for the performers of *The Seven Deadly Sins* (1592) and the records of the membership of the companies who are known to have acted Shakespeare's plays, Thomas W. Baldwin attempted to reconstruct

possible cast lists. What difference might his suggestions make to our perception of how *Twelfth Night* might have been performed? In accordance with the
structuring principles of the acting companies (that is, the hypothesised 'career'
path from apprentice boy player to adult actor and sharer), Baldwin postulates
a full cast list for a performance of *Twelfth Night* in 1600. Cross-referencing
his allocation of the central characters' roles with the biographical information
on these actors in David J. Kathman's *Biographical Index of English Drama Before
1660* reveals some potentially surprising results:

Orsino	Richard Burbage (1568–1619, c.32/33 yrs old)
Viola	'Ned'(acting 1590) /Shakespeare (1564–1616, c.36 yrs old)
Sebastian	William Slye (1573?–1608, c.27 years old)

Antonio	Henry Cundell/Condell (1576–1627, c.24 years old)
Olivia	Samuel Gilburne (acting 1605, age unknown)
Maria	Samuel Crosse (1568?–?, c.32 years old)
Malvolio	Augustine Phillips (d. 1605, acting in 1593)

Baldwin allocates 'boys' parts to players who are (potentially) the same age as
(or older than) the 'men'. Though the details he offers are highly conjectural,
they do suggest a number of interesting possibilities: firstly, that the supposedly rigid dichotomy between boy player/female character and male actor/
male character does not hold up; secondly, that the age of a player tells us
nothing about their physical appearance; and thirdly, that 'voice' is not necessarily a signifier of 'femininity' on the Renaissance stage. While this does
not amount to conclusive evidence, it does indicate that extant cast lists do
not always tally with the 'rules' expounded by Ringler. And, intriguingly,
if Sebastian was also played by a 'boy', the apparent disavowal of lesbian-
ism becomes performatively permitted at the play's conclusion through the
onstage union of two boy players.

Quite how a Renaissance audience would have responded to such a
performance is, of course, untraceable. And, unlike in Churchill's case,
we cannot be confident of Shakespeare's intentions. However, ironically
perhaps, these points suggest that *Shakespeare in Love* is more accurate in its
depiction of the all-male stage than my opening references to it indicated:
in the rehearsals and performance of *Romeo and Juliet* within the film, Juliet's
mother, Juliet and the nurse are played by different kinds of men/boys.
Similar decisions informed the all-male performance of *Twelfth Night* at the
new Globe Theatre on London's South Bank in 2003. James C. Bulman
argues convincingly that 'no other modern *Twelfth Night* has so explicitly
questioned the play's heterosexual affirmations or so pervasively queered the

audience' (584). Indeed, Bulman's reading explicitly suggests that this particular production embodied precisely the kind of performance Judith Butler seeks: 'a theatrical cross-dressing which undermines the essential nature of gender identity and the biological determinism of sexual desire' (Bulman 584).

NEXT STEPS

Barker, Deborah and Ivo Kamps, eds. *Shakespeare and Gender: A History*. London: Verso, 1995.

Butler, Judith. *Gender Trouble: Feminism and the Subversion of Identity*. New York and London: Routledge, 1990.

Moi, Toril. *What is a Woman? And Other Essays*. Oxford: Oxford University Press, 1999.

Works Cited

Details appear below of all works from which quotations are taken. There are separate sections for poems, narratives and plays as well as for background and critical material. Most of the poetry quoted can be found in the *Norton* and in other anthologies, but standard editions are suggested below to allow readers to extend their interest in the authors concerned. Where references are made to the various *Norton* anthologies, these are abbreviated as follows:

Norton Anthology of English Literature 1:
The Norton Anthology of English Literature, 8th edn, Volume 1. General Editor, Stephen Greenblatt. New York and London: W. W. Norton & Company, 2006.

Norton Anthology of English Literature 2:
The Norton Anthology of English Literature, 8th edn, Volume 2. General Editor, Stephen Greenblatt. New York and London: W. W. Norton & Company, 2006.

Norton Anthology of Theory and Criticism:
The Norton Anthology of Theory and Criticism. General Editor, Vincent B. Leitch. New York and London: W. W. Norton & Company, 2001.

Poems
Anonymous. 'A wayle whit as whalles bon'. In *Middle English Lyrics*. Eds Maxwell S. Luria and Richard L. Hoffmann. New York: W. W. Norton & Company, 1974.
Anonymous. 'Now goth sonne under wod'. In *Medieval English Lyrics*. Ed. R. T. Davies. London: Faber, 1963.

Anonymous. 'Sir Patrick Spens'. In *The Oxford Book of English Verse*. Ed. Christopher Ricks. Oxford: Oxford University Press, 1999.

Anonymous. 'Thomas the Rhymer'. In *Scottish Ballads*. Ed. Emily Lyle. Edinburgh: Canongate Classics, 1994.

Auden, W. H. 'William Blake'. In *Academic Graffiti*. London: Faber and Faber, 1972.

Beatles, The. 'Lucy in the Sky with Diamonds'. In *Complete Beatles Lyrics*. London: Omnibus Press, 1982.

Bishop, Elizabeth. 'Rain Towards Morning' and 'The Monument'. In *Complete Poems*. London: Chatto and Windus, 1991.

Blair, Robert. *The Grave*. London: M. Fenner, 1743.

Blake, William. 'A Poison Tree'. In *The Complete Poems*. London: Penguin, 2004.

Brathwaite, Edward Kamau. 'Wings of a Dove'. In *Hinterland: Caribbean Poetry from the West Indies & Britain*. Ed. E. A. Markham. Newcastle upon Tyne: Bloodaxe, 1984.

Burns, Robert. 'A Red, Red Rose', 'Holy Willie's Prayer', 'Open the Door to Me Oh', 'To a Louse'. In *Poems and Songs*. Oxford: Oxford University Press, 1969.

Chaucer, Geoffrey. *The Canterbury Tales, The Parliament of Fowls*. In *The Riverside Chaucer*. Ed. Larry D. Benson. Oxford: Oxford University Press, 1988.

Dabydeen, David. 'Slave Song', 'Song of the Creole Gang Women'. In *Slave Song*. Australia: Dangaroo Press, 1984.

Dickinson, Emily. '"Hope" is the thing with feathers'. In *The Complete Poems*. London: Faber, 1975.

Doolittle, Hilda (H. D.). 'Oread'. In *Collected Poems 1912–1944*. New York: New Directions, 1986.

Duffy, Carol Ann. *New Selected Poems*. London: Picador, 2004.

Eliot, T. S. 'Burnt Norton', from *Four Quartets*. In *Collected Poems 1909–1962*. London: Faber and Faber, 1963.

Flint, F. S., 'Houses'. In *Imagist Poetry*. Ed. Peter Jones. London: Penguin, 1972.

Ginsberg, Allen. 'America'. In *Collected Poems 1947–1997*. London: Penguin, 2009.

Gray, Thomas. 'Elegy Written in a Country Church Yard'. In *Selected Poems of Thomas Gray, Charles Churchill and William Cowper*. London: Penguin, 1998.

Harrison, Tony. 'Marked with D.', 'Them & [uz] I, II'. In *Collected Poems*. London: Penguin, 2007.

Hopkins, Gerard Manley. 'Pied Beauty', 'The Starlight Night'. In *Gerard Manley Hopkins: The Major Works*. Oxford: Oxford University Press, 2002.

Howard, Henry, Earl of Surrey. 'Wyatt resteth here. . .'. In *Poems*. Oxford: Clarendon Press, 1964.

Johnson, Linton Kwesi. 'Di Great Insohreckshan'. In *Tings an Times: Selected Poems*. Newcastle upon Tyne: Bloodaxe, 1991.

Keats, John. 'Lines on the Mermaid Tavern', 'Ode on a Grecian Urn', 'To Autumn'. *The Complete Poems*, 3rd edn. London: Penguin, 1988.

Larkin, Philip. 'This Be the Verse'. In *Collected Poems*. London: Penguin, 2003.

Marvell, Andrew. 'To His Coy Mistress'. In *The Complete Poems*. London: Penguin, 2005.

Morgan, Edwin. 'Gangs', from *Sonnets from Scotland*, 'Glasgow Sonnets', 'Siesta of a Hungarian Snake'. In *Collected Poems*. Manchester: Carcanet, 1990.

Morgan, Edwin. 'Forcryinoutloud!' In *Collected Translations*. Manchester: Carcanet, 1996.

Nichols, Grace. 'Epilogue'. In *I Is A Long Memoried Woman*. London: Karnak House, 1993.

Petrarch. 'Love and I, as full of wonder' (Sonnet 160). In *Petrarch's Lyric Poems. The Rime Sparse and Other Lyrics*. Cambridge: Harvard University Press, 1976.

Pope, Alexander. 'Windsor Forest'. In *The Major Works*. Oxford: Oxford University Press, 2006.

Pound, Ezra. 'Ts'ai Chi'h'. In *Poems and Translations*. New York: The Library of America, 2003.

Shakespeare, William. 'When I do count the clock that tells the time', 'Shall I compare thee to a summer's day?', 'That time of year thou mayst in me behold', 'My mistress' eyes are nothing like the sun' (Sonnets 12, 18, 73, 130). In *The Sonnets and A Lover's Complaint*. London: Penguin, 1986.

Shelley, Percy. 'Ozymandias', 'Song of Apollo'. In *The Major Works*. Eds Zachary Leader and Michael O'Neill. Oxford: Oxford University Press, 2003.

Sidney, Philip. 'Queen Virtue's court, which some call Stella's face', from *Astrophil and Stella*. In *The Major Works*. Oxford: Oxford University Press, 2002.

Smith, Stevie. 'Le Désert de l'Amour'. *Selected Poems*. London: Penguin, 1978.

Tennyson, Alfred Lord. 'In Memoriam'. In *Selected Poems*. London: Penguin, 2007.

Whitman, Walt. 'Song of Myself'. In *The Complete Poems*, rev. edn. London: Penguin, 2004.

Wordsworth, William, 'A slumber did my spirit seal', 'Surprised by joy – impatient as the Wind'. In *The Major Works*. Oxford: Oxford University Press, 2000.

Wyatt, Sir Thomas. 'Lux, my fair falcon, and your fellows all', 'Mine Own John Poins, since ye delight to know', 'They flee from me that sometime did me seek'. In *The Complete Poems*. London: Penguin, 1978.

Narratives

Carver, Raymond. 'Cathedral'. In *The Norton Anthology of American Literature*, 5th edn, Volume 2. Ed. Nina Baym. New York and London: W. W. Norton & Company, 1998. 2197–208.

Conrad, Joseph. 'Heart of Darkness'. In *Norton Anthology of English Literature 2*. 1891–1947.

Dickens, Charles. *Great Expectations*. Harmondsworth: Penguin, 1971.

Dickens, Charles. *Hard Times*. Harmondsworth: Penguin, 1970.

Joyce, James. 'Araby'. In *Norton Anthology of English Literature 2*. 2168–72.

Joyce, James. 'The Dead'. In *Norton Anthology of English Literature 2*. 2172–99.

Lawrence, D. H. 'The Horse Dealer's Daughter'. In *Norton Anthology of English Literature 2*. 2258–73.

Lessing, Doris. 'To Room Nineteen'. In *Norton Anthology of English Literature 2*. 2544–65.

Nabokov, Vladimir. *Lolita*. London: Penguin Classics, 2000.

Pynchon, Thomas. 'Entropy'. In *The Norton Anthology of American Literature*, 5th edn, Volume 2. Ed. Nina Baym. New York and London: W. W. Norton & Company, 1998. 2180–90.

Stevenson, Robert Louis. 'The Strange Case of Dr Jekyll and Mr Hyde'. In *Norton Anthology of English Literature 2*. 1645–85.

Woolf, Virginia. 'The Legacy'. In *The Norton Anthology of English Literature*, 7th edn. Eds M. H. Abrams and Stephen Greenblatt. New York; London: W. W. Norton, 2000. Vol. 2, 2226–30.

Woolf, Virginia. *Mrs Dalloway*. London: Vintage, 2004.

Plays

Beckett, Samuel. *Endgame*. In *Norton Anthology of English Literature 2*. 2394–420.

Churchill, Caryl. *Cloud Nine*. London: Nick Hern, 2007.

Ethelwold, St. *Visitatio Sepulchri*. In *The Drama of the Medieval Church*, Volume 1. Ed. Karl Young. Oxford: Clarendon Press, 1933. 249–50.

Everyman. In *Norton Anthology of English Literature 1*. 463–84.

Hare, David. *The Permanent Way*, 2nd edn. London: Faber and Faber, 2007.

Norman, Marc and Tom Stoppard. *Shakespeare in Love* (screenplay). London: Faber and Faber, 1999.

Shakespeare, William. *King Lear*. In *Norton Anthology of English Literature 1*. 1143–223.

Shakespeare, William. *Twelfth Night*. In *Norton Anthology of English Literature 1*. 1079–139.

Udall, Nicholas. *Roister Doister*. In *Three Sixteenth-Century Comedies*. Ed. Charles W. Whitworth. London: New Mermaids, 1984. 89–211.

Wilde, Oscar. *The Importance of Being Earnest*. In *Norton Anthology of English Literature 2*. 1699–740.

Yeats, W. B. *The Resurrection*. In *The Variorum Edition of the Plays of W. B. Yeats*. Ed. Russell K. Alspach. London and New York: Macmillan, 1966. 900–36.

Background and Critical

Adams, Stephen. *Poetic Designs: An Introduction to Meters, Verse Forms and Figures of Speech*. Peterborough, ON: Broadview Press, 1977.

Adorno, Theodor. *Aesthetic Theory*. Trans. Robert Hullot-Kentor. London: Athlone Press, 1997.

Amoko, A. 'Casting Aside Colonial Occupation: Intersections of Race, Sex, and Gender in *Cloud Nine* and *Cloud Nine* Criticism'. *Modern Drama* 42 (1999): 45–58.

Aristotle. *Poetics*. In *Norton Anthology of Theory and Criticism*. 90–117.

Armstrong, Isobel. *Victorian Poetry: Poetry, Poetics and Politics*. London: Routledge, 1993.

Attridge, Derek. *Poetic Rhythm: An Introduction*. Cambridge: Cambridge University Press, 1995.

Augustine. *Confessions*. Harmondsworth: Penguin, 1961.

Bakhtin, Mikhail. *The Dialogic Imagination*. Austin: University of Texas Press, 1981.

Bakhtin, Mikhail. *Rabelais and his World*. Trans. Hélène Iswolsky. Cambridge, MA: MIT Press, 1984.

Baldwin, T. W. *The Organisation and Personnel of the Shakespearean Companies*. Princeton: Princeton University Press, 1927.

Benjamin, Walter. 'The Storyteller'. Trans. Harry Zohn. In *Illuminations*. Ed. Hannah Arendt. New York: Schocken Books, 1968. 83–109.

Bloom, Gina. *Voice in Motion: Staging Gender, Shaping Sound in Early Modern England*. Philadelphia: University of Pennsylvania Press, 2007.

Boswell, James. *Life of Johnson*. Oxford: Oxford University Press, 1980.

Brathwaite, Edward Kamau. *History of the Voice: The Development of Nation Language in Anglophone Caribbean Poetry*. London: New Beacon Books, 1984.

Bray, Alan. *Homosexuality in Renaissance England*, 2nd edn. New York: Columbia University Press, 1995.

Brecht, Bertolt. *Brecht on Theatre: The Development of an Aesthetic*. Ed. John Willett. London: Methuen, 1964.

Bulman, J. C. 'Queering the Audience: All-Male Casts in Recent Productions of Shakespeare'. In *A Companion to Shakespeare and Performance*. Eds Barbara Hodgdon and W. B. Worthen. Oxford: Blackwell, 2005. 564–87.

Butler, Judith. *Gender Trouble: Feminism and the Subversion of Identity*. New York and London: Routledge, 1990.

Butler, Judith. *Bodies that Matter: On the Discursive Limits of 'Sex'*. New York and London: Routledge, 1993.

Camus, Albert. *The Myth of Sisyphus*. Trans. Justin O'Brien. Harmondsworth: Penguin, 1975.

Carper, Thomas and Derek Attridge. *Meter and Meaning: An Introduction to Rhythm in Poetry*. Oxford: Routledge, 2003.

Carson, Christie and Jackie Bratton, eds. *The Cambridge King Lear, CD-ROM Text and Performance Archive*. Cambridge: Cambridge University Press, 2000.

Carson, Christie and Farah Karim-Cooper. *Shakespeare's Globe*. Cambridge: Cambridge University Press, 2008.

Cocteau, Jean. *Modern French Plays: An Anthology from Jarry to Ionesco*. London: Faber and Faber, 1964.

Coleridge, Samuel Taylor. *Biographia Literaria.* Ed. George Watson. London: J. M. Dent, 1975.

Cook, Jon, ed. *Poetry in Theory: An Anthology.* Oxford: Blackwell, 2004.

Craig, Edward Gordon. *On the Art of the Theatre.* London: Heinemann, 1911.

Culler, Jonathan. *Structuralist Poetics: Structuralism, Linguistics, and the Study of Literature.* London: Routledge, 1975.

Dabydeen, David. *Slave Song.* Australia: Dangaroo Press, 1984.

de Man, Paul. 'Autobiography as De-Facement'. In *The Rhetoric of Romanticism.* New York: Columbia University Press, 1984. 67–81.

Dollimore, Jonathan. *Radical Tragedy: Religion, Ideology and Power in the Drama of Shakespeare and his Contemporaries.* Brighton: Harvester Wheatsheaf, 1989.

Dryden, John. *An Essay of Dramatick Poesie.* In *The Works of John Dryden: Vol. 17. Prose 1668–1691.* Ed. Samuel Holt Monk. Berkeley: University of California Press, 1971. 3–81.

Durgnat, Raymond. *A Long Hard Look at 'Psycho'.* London: BFI Publishing, 2002.

Eagleton, Terry. *Heathcliff and the Great Hunger: Studies in Irish Culture.* London: Verso, 1995.

Eagleton, Terry. *How to Read a Poem.* Oxford: Blackwell, 2006.

Eagleton, Terry. 'Political Beckett?' *New Left Review* 40 (2006): 67–74.

Emerson, Ralph Waldo. *Nature and Selected Essays.* London: Penguin, 2003.

Erasmus, Desiderius. *The Correspondence of Erasmus,* 2 vols. Eds R. A. B. Mynors and D. F. S. Thomson. Toronto: University of Toronto Press, 1975.

Ferber, Michael. *A Dictionary of Literary Symbols.* Cambridge: Cambridge University Press, 1999.

Ferguson, Margaret, Mary Jo Salter and Jon Stallworthy, eds. *The Norton Anthology of Poetry,* 5th edn. New York: W. W. Norton & Company, 2005.

Fish, Simon. *A Supplicacyon for the Beggers.* Antwerp: Johannes Grapheus, 1529.

Forster, E. M. *Aspects of the Novel.* Harmondsworth: Penguin, 1971.

Frost, Robert. *The Collected Prose of Robert Frost.* Cambridge, MA: The Belknap Press of Harvard University Press, 2007.

Frye, Northrop. *Anatomy of Criticism: Four Essays.* New York: Atheneum, 1966.

Furniss, Tom and Michael Bath. *Reading Poetry: An Introduction,* 2nd edn. Harlow: Pearson, 2007.

Fussell, Paul. *Poetic Meter and Poetic Form,* rev. edn. New York: McGraw-Hill, 1979.

Gaskell, Elizabeth. *The Life of Charlotte Brontë.* London: Everyman, 1992.

Gilbert, Stuart and Richard Ellmann, eds. *The Letters of James Joyce,* 3 vols. New York: Viking, 1957–66.

Greenblatt, Stephen, Walter Cohen, Jean E. Howard and Katharine Eisaman Maus, eds. *The Norton Shakespeare.* New York and London: W. W. Norton & Company, 1997.

Harding, J. M. 'Cloud Cover: (Re)Dressing Desire and Comfortable Subversions in Caryl Churchill's *Cloud Nine*'. *PMLA* 113 (1998): 258–72.

Hawkes, Terence. *Metaphor*. London: Methuen, 1972.

Hemingway, Ernest. *Green Hills of Africa*. New York: Scribners, 1935.

Hobsbaum, Philip. *Metre, Rhythm and Verse Form*. London: Routledge, 1995.

Holmes, Richard. *Footsteps: Adventures of a Romantic Biographer*. London: Hodder and Stoughton, 1985.

hooks, bell. *Ain't I a Woman: Black Women and Feminism*. London: Pluto, 1982.

hooks, bell. *Feminist Theory from Margin to Center*. Boston, MA: South End Press, 1984.

Horace. 'On the Art of Poetry'. *Classical Literary Criticism*. Ed. and trans. T. S. Dorsch. London: Penguin, 1965.

Hughes, Glenn. *Imagism and the Imagists: A Study in Modern Poetry*. London: Bowes & Bowes, 1960.

James, Henry. 'The Art of Fiction'. In *Norton Anthology of Theory and Criticism*. 855–69.

Johnson, Samuel. *Samuel Johnson on Shakespeare*. Ed. W. K. Winsatt, Jr. New York: Hill and Wang, 1960.

Jones, Daniel. 'Introduction'. *An English Pronouncing Dictionary*, 12th edn. London: Everyman, 1964.

Kathman, David J. *Biographical Index of English Drama Before 1660*, accessed 18 November 2009. http://www.shakespeareauthorship.com/bd/.

Keats, John. *Selected Letters*. Oxford: Oxford University Press, 2002.

King, Pamela M. 'Morality Plays'. In *The Cambridge Companion to Medieval English Theatre*. Ed. Richard Beadle. Cambridge: Cambridge University Press, 1994. 240–64.

Knowlson, James. *Damned to Fame: The Life of Samuel Beckett*. London: Bloomsbury, 1996.

Koch, Kenneth. *Making Your Own Days: The Pleasures of Reading and Writing Poetry*. New York: Touchstone, 1999.

Kundera, Milan. 'The Day Panurge No Longer Makes People Laugh'. In *Testaments Betrayed*. London: Faber, 1995. 1–32.

Lee, Hermione. *Virginia Woolf*. London: Chatto and Windus, 1996.

Leech, Clifford. *Tragedy: The Critical Idiom*. London: Methuen, 1969.

Leggatt, Alexander. *English Stage Comedy 1490–1990*. London: Routledge, 1998.

Lejeune, Philippe. *On Autobiography*. Ed. Paul John Eakin; trans. Katherine Leary. Minneapolis: University of Minnesota Press, 1989.

Lewis, C. Day. *The Poetic Image*. London: Jonathan Cape, 1947.

Lohafer, Susan, and Jo Ellyn Clarey, eds. *Short Story Theory at a Crossroads*. Baton Rouge: Louisiana State University Press, 1989.

Loy, Mina. 'Modern Poetry'. *The Lost Lunar Baedeker: Poems of Mina Loy*. Manchester: Carcanet, 1997.

Lyle, Emily, ed. *Scottish Ballads*. Edinburgh: Canongate Classics, 1994.

Markham, E. A., ed. *Hinterland: Caribbean Poetry from the West Indies and Britain*. Newcastle upon Tyne: Bloodaxe, 1989.

May, Charles Edward. *The Short Story: The Reality of Artifice*. New York: Twayne, 1995.

Mey, Jacob L. *When Voices Clash: A Study in Literary Pragmatics*. Berlin and New York: Mouton de Gruyter, 2000.

Milton, John. *Complete Shorter Poems*, 2nd edn. Ed. John Carey. London: Longman, 2007.

Moi, Toril. *Sexual/Textual Politics: Feminist Literary Theory*. London: Methuen, 1985.

Moi, Toril. *What is a Woman? And Other Essays*. Oxford: Oxford University Press, 1999.

Morris, Pam, ed. *The Bakhtin Reader: Selected Writings of Bakhtin, Medveded, Voloshinov*. London: Edward Arnold, 1994.

Norbrook, David. *Poetry and Politics in the English Renaissance*, rev. edn. Oxford: Oxford University Press, 2002.

O'Connor, Frank. *The Lonely Voice: A Study of the Short Story*. London: Macmillan, 1963.

Oppenheim, Lois. 'Interview with JoAnne Akalaitis'. In *Directing Beckett: Interviews with and Essays by Twenty-two Prominent Directors of Samuel Beckett's Work*, Michigan: Michigan University Press, 1997. 135–41.

Paterson, Don. 'The Lyric Principle, Part 1: The Sense of Sound'. *Poetry Review*, 97. 2 (Summer 2007): 56–72.

Paterson, Don. 'The Lyric Principle, Part 2: The Sound of Sense'. *Poetry Review* 97. 3 (Autumn 2007): 54–70.

Paulin, Tom. *The Faber Book of Vernacular Verse*. London: Faber and Faber, 1990.

Paulin, Tom. *The Secret Life of Poems: A Poetry Primer*. London: Faber and Faber, 2008.

Pavis, Patrice. *Dictionary of the Theatre*. Toronto: Toronto University Press, 1999.

Poe, Edgar Allan. 'Review of Nathaniel Hawthorne's *Twice-Told Tales*'. In *Modernism: An Anthology of Sources and Documents*. Eds Vassiliki Kolocotroni, Jane Goldman and Olga Taxidou. Edinburgh: Edinburgh University Press, 1998. 93–4.

Pound, Ezra. *Literary Essays of Ezra Pound*. New York: New Directions, 1968.

Preminger, Alex and T. V. F. Brogan, eds. *The New Princeton Encyclopedia of Poetry and Poetics*. New Jersey: Princeton University Press, 1993.

Puttenham, George. 'The Arte of English Poesie'. *English Literary Criticism: The Renaissance*. Ed. O. B. Harrison. London: Peter Owen, 1967.

Rich, A. 'Compulsory Heterosexuality and Lesbian Experience'. *Signs* 5 (1980): 631–60.

Ringler, W. A. 'The Number of Actors in Shakespeare's Early Plays'. In *The Seventeenth-Century Stage: A Collection of Critical Essays*. Ed. G. E. Bentley. Chicago and London: University of Chicago Press, 1967. 110–34.

Rousseau, Jean-Jacques. *The Confessions*. Trans. J. M. Cohen. Harmondsworth: Penguin, 1953.

Ryan, Lawrence V. 'Doctrine and Dramatic Structure in *Everyman*'. *Speculum*, 32 (1957): 722–35.

Schofield, Martin. *The Cambridge Introduction to the American Short Story*. Cambridge: Cambridge University Press, 2006.

Shaw, George Bernard. *Pen Portraits and Reviews*. London: Constable, 1949.

Shelley, Percy. 'A Defence of Poetry'. *The Major Works*. Ed. Zachary Leader and Michael O'Neill. Oxford: Oxford University Press, 2003.

Shklovsky, Victor. 'Art as Technique'. *Modern Literary Theory: A Reader*, 2nd edn. Eds Philip Rice and Patricia Waugh. London: Edward Arnold, 1992.

Sidney, Philip, Sir. 'The Defence of Poesy' (1595). *The Major Works*. Oxford: Oxford University Press, 2008.

Steiner, George. *The Death of Tragedy*. Oxford: Oxford University Press, 1980.

Stevens, Wallace. 'The Noble Rider and the Sound of Words'. In *Poetry in Theory: An Anthology 1900–2000*. Ed. Jon Cook. Oxford: Blackwell, 2004.

Strand, Mark and Eavan Boland. *The Making of a Poem: A Norton Anthology of Poetic Forms*. New York: W. W. Norton & Company, 2000.

Truffaut, François. *Hitchcock: The Definitive Study of Alfred Hitchcock*, rev. edn. London: Simon and Schuster, 1984.

Twain, Mark. *The Adventures of Huckleberry Finn*, rev edn. London: Penguin, 2003.

Valéry, Paul, *The Art of Poetry*. Trans. Denise Folliot. New York: Vintage, 1961.

Vives, Juan Luis. *De ratione dicendi*. Ed. Jose Manuel Rodriguez Peregrina, Granada: Universidad de Granada, 2000.

Whitman, Walt. *The Complete Poems*, rev. edn. London: Penguin, 2004.

Wimsatt, W. K. *The Idea of Comedy: Essays in Prose and Verse: Ben Jonson to George Meredith*. Englewood Cliffs, NJ: Prentice Hall, 1969.

Wolosky, Shira. *The Art of Poetry*. New York: Oxford University Press, 2001.

Woolf, Virginia. *Moments of Being: Autobiographical Writings*. London: Pimlico, 2002.

Woolf, Virginia. 'Modern Fiction'. In *Norton Anthology of English Literature 2*. 2087–92.

Wordsworth, William. *The Prose Works of William Wordsworth*, 3 vols. Eds. W. J. B. Owen and Jane Worthington Smyser. Oxford: Clarendon Press, 1974.

Wordsworth, William. *The Major Works*. Oxford: Oxford University Press, 2000.

Wordsworth, William. 'Preface' to *Lyrical Ballads* (1802). In *Norton Anthology of Theory and Criticism*. 648–68

Wordsworth, William and Dorothy Wordsworth. *The Letters of William and Dorothy Wordsworth: Vol. 1, The Early Years 1787–1805*. Ed. Ernest de Selincourt. Oxford: Clarendon Press, 1967.

Yeats, W. B. *Essays and Introductions*. London: Macmillan, 1961.

Notes on Contributors

All the contributors teach or have recently taught in the English Literature section of Edinburgh University's School of Literatures, Languages and Cultures.

Dermot Cavanagh's teaching and research interests are in the field of early modern literature. He is the author of *Language and Politics in the Sixteenth-Century History Play* (2003) and co-editor of *Shakespeare's Histories and Counter-Histories* (2006).

Rajorshi Chakraborti teaches modern literature and creative writing. His first novel, *Or the Day Seizes You*, was short-listed for the Hutch Crossword Book Award, 2006, the best-known prize for English-language writing in India. His second novel, *Derangements*, was published in India in August 2008, and a third, *Balloonists*, in 2010.

Sarah M. Dunnigan teaches medieval and Renaissance literature, Scottish literature and traditional literature, and has published widely in all these areas and on Robert Burns. She is currently writing a book about Scottish fairy tales, *Enchanting Scotland. Fairies, Fairy Tales, and the National Imagination*, and is co-editor of the *Scottish Literary Review*.

Penny Fielding teaches eighteenth- and nineteenth-century British literature. Her publications include *Writing and Orality: Nationality, Culture and Nineteenth-Century Scottish Fiction* (1996) and *Scotland and the Fictions of Geography: North Britain 1760–1820* (2008). She is the editor of *The Edinburgh*

Companion to Robert Louis Stevenson and the forthcoming Edinburgh Edition of the works of Robert Louis Stevenson.

Alan Gillis teaches creative writing and modern and contemporary poetry. His first book of poetry, *Somebody, Somewhere* (2004) won the Rupert and Eithne Strong Award. His second, *Hawks and Doves* (2007) was a Poetry Book Society Recommendation and shortlisted for the T. S. Eliot Prize. As a critic, he is author of *Irish Poetry of the 1930s* (2005) and is currently co-editing *The Oxford Handbook of Modern Irish Poetry*.

Keith Hughes teaches and researches US, African-American and Scottish Literature and the Black Atlantic. Recent publications include 'Walter Mosley and the Black Atlantic' in the collection *Finding a Way Home* (2008). He is currently writing a guide to African-American writing to be published in 2011.

Robert Irvine teaches and researches in the field of eighteenth- and nineteenth-century writing, particularly writing from Scotland. He is the author of *Enlightenment and Romance: Gender and Agency in Smollett and Scott* (2000) and *Jane Austen* (2005) and is currently working on a study of liberalism, imperialism and adventure fiction.

Aaron Kelly teaches modern and contemporary literature, particularly Scottish and Irish. He is author of *The Thriller and Northern Ireland since 1969* (2005), *Irvine Welsh* (2005), *Twentieth-Century Irish Literature* (2008) and *James Kelman: Politics and Aesthetics* (2009). He has also co-edited *Critical Ireland* (2001) and *Cities of Belfast* (2003).

Michelle Keown specialises in postcolonial literature and theory, particularly that of the Pacific region. She has published widely on Maori and Pacific writing and is the author of *Postcolonial Pacific Writing: Representations of the Body* (2005) and *Pacific Islands Writing: The Postcolonial Literatures of Aotearoa/ New Zealand and Oceania* (2007). She co-edited *Comparing Postcolonial Diasporas* (2009) and a special issue of the *Journal of New Zealand Literature* (2003).

James Loxley specialises in early modern literature and aspects of literary and cultural theory. Publications include *Royalism and Poetry in the English Civil Wars* (1997), *Ben Jonson* (2002) and *Performativity* (2007), as well as articles on authors including Marvell, Milton and Hobbes. With Greg Walker, he is currently editing *The Oxford Anthology of Renaissance Literature*.

Simon Malpas teaches and researches Romantic and modern literature, drama and contemporary literary theory. Publications include *The Postmodern* (2005), *Jean-François Lyotard* (2003), *Postmodern Debates* (2001) and, as co-editor, *The Routledge Companion to Critical Theory* (2006) and *The New Aestheticism* (2003).

Laura Marcus teaches modern and contemporary literature and has published widely in the fields of nineteenth- and twentieth-century literature and culture, modernism and auto/biography, including *Auto/biographical Discourses: Theory, Criticism, Practice* (1994), *Virginia Woolf* (1997/2004), *The Tenth Muse: Writing about Cinema in the Modernist Period* (2007) and, as co-editor, *The Cambridge History of Twentieth-Century English Literature* (2005).

Kenneth Millard teaches in a range of areas including US and Victorian literature, with particular research interests in contemporary American fiction. His publications include *Contemporary American Fiction* (2000) and *Coming of Age in Contemporary American Fiction* (2007), and he is currently writing a book on the fiction of the contemporary American West.

Colin Nicholson teaches eighteenth-century and modern literature and has published widely in the areas of Scottish, Canadian, English and postcolonial literature, including *Writing and the Rise of Finance* (1994) and edited collections of essays on Margaret Laurence, Margaret Atwood and Iain Crichton Smith. His study *Edwin Morgan: Inventions of Modernity* was published in 2002, and he is co-editor of the *Edinburgh Companion to Contemporary Scottish Poetry* (2009).

David Salter's teaching and research interest are in the later Middle Ages, focusing particularly on romance and the literature of traditional religion. He is the author of *Holy and Noble Beasts: Encounters with Animals in Medieval Literature* (2001), and is currently completing *St Francis and Cultural Memory: Catholicism and the English National Imagination*.

Roger Savage is an Honorary Fellow in English Literature who taught at Edinburgh University for three decades, during which he was also involved in a range of theatrical projects. He has published essays on Renaissance court entertainments, Shakespearean adaptations, the links between ancient Greek theatre and European opera, the history of opera production, libretto-making, national theatres and radio drama.

Lee Spinks teaches and researches US, modern and contemporary literature and is the author of *Friedrich Nietzsche* (2003), *James Joyce: A Critical Guide*

(2009) and *Michael Ondaatje* (2009) along with numerous critical articles upon American literature, postcolonial literature and postmodern culture and theory.

Randall Stevenson teaches and researches twentieth-century literature and drama. Recent publications include *Modernist Fiction* (1998), *The Oxford English Literary History: vol.12, 1960–2000* (2004) and, as co-editor, *Twentieth-Century Scottish Drama* (2000) and *The Edinburgh Companion to Twentieth-Century Literatures in English* (2006). He is General Editor of the forthcoming *Edinburgh History of Twentieth-Century Literature in Britain*.

Olga Taxidou teaches theatre history and performance theory and researches in the areas of modernist performance and theories of tragedy. Her publications include *The Mask: A Periodical Performance by Edward Gordon Craig* (1998), *Tragedy, Modernity and Mourning* (2004), *Modernism and Performance: Jarry to Brecht* (2007) and, as co-editor, *Modernism: An Anthology of Sources and Documents* (1998) and *Post-War Cinema and Modernity: A Film Reader* (2001).

Alex Thomson teaches and researches in Scottish literature and in modern critical and cultural theory. His publications include *Deconstruction and Democracy* (2005) and *Adorno: A Guide for the Perplexed* (2006), along with a range of essays on Scottish literary history. He is co-editor of the series *Taking on the Political* and plans to edit a volume of Stevenson's essays in the new Edinburgh Edition of the Works of Robert Louis Stevenson.

Suzanne Trill's teaching and research focus on sixteenth- and seventeenth-century women's writing, including devotional and self-writing. She has published widely in these areas, including *Lay by Your Needles Ladies, Take the Pen: Writing Women in England, 1500–1700* (1997), *Voicing Women: Gender and Sexuality in Writing, 1500–1700* (1998) and, most recently, *Lady Anne Halkett: Selected Self-Writings* (2007).

Greg Walker teaches and researches the history, literature and drama of the late- medieval and Renaissance periods. Recent books include *Medieval Drama: An Anthology* (2000) and *Writing Under Tyranny: English Literature and the Henrician Reformation* (2005). He is co-editor of *The Oxford Handbook to Medieval Literature in English* (2010).

Jonathan Wild teaches Victorian literature. He is the author of *The Rise of the Office Clerk in Literary Culture, 1880–1939* (2006) and of articles on topics including George Gissing, Jerome K. Jerome and *John o'London's Weekly*. He is a member of the editorial team working on Thomas Carlyle's letters and is completing a study of the Edwardian period for the *Edinburgh History of Twentieth-Century Literature in Britain*.

Index

In the listings below, **bold type** indicates a page or pages on which definitions or discussion of terms can best be found.